Discourse Analysis

D   t ·alysis: The Questions Discourse Analysts Ask and How They Answer Th   .e first introductory text organized around the kinds of questions d   r analysts ask and how they are systematically addressed by analysts   empirical persuasions, thereby cultivating a principled under-   e interdisciplinary field of discourse analysis. The text pro- n   ·t. is, integration, and a multidimensional understanding of the c   that preoccupy discourse analysts. (1) How is discourse struc- ture   How are social actions accomplished in discourse? (3) How are ide u   egotiated in discourse? (4) How are ideologies constructed in dis   ie answer to each question is illustrated with transcripts and an   f tual discourse as exemplified in key studies in the field. With a rar   ther features such as boxed definitions, study questions, and ana- lyt   this guide to the complex world of discourse is an ideal resource for c   on discourse analysis.

Ha sı hang Waring is Associate Professor of Linguistics and Educa- tio   hers College, Columbia University, USA. She is founder of The Lar   and Social Interaction Working Group (LANSI).

Discourse Analysis

The Questions Discourse Analysts
Ask and How They Answer Them

Hansun Zhang Waring

Routledge
Taylor & Francis Group

NEW YORK AND LONDON

First published 2018
by Routledge
711 Third Avenue, New York, NY 10017

and by Routledge
2 Park Square, Milton Park, Abingdon, Oxon, OX14 4RN

Routledge is an imprint of the Taylor & Francis Group, an informa business

Library of Congress Cataloging-in-Publication Data
Names: Waring, Hansun Zhang, author.
Title: Discourse analysis : the questions discourse analysts ask and how they
    answer them / Hansun Zhang Waring.
Description: New York, NY : Routledge, [2017] | Includes bibliographical
    references and index.
Identifiers: LCCN 2017004147 | ISBN 9781138657434 (hardback) |
    ISBN 9781138657441 (pbk.) | ISBN 9781317219668 (epub) |
    ISBN 9781317219651 (mobipocket/kindle)
Subjects: LCSH: Discourse analysis—Study and teaching.
Classification: LCC P302 .W37 2017 | DDC 401/.41—dc23LC record
    available at https://lccn.loc.gov/2017004147

ISBN: 978-1-138-65743-4 (hbk)
ISBN: 978-1-138-65744-1 (pbk)
ISBN: 978-1-315-62134-0 (ebk)

Typeset in Bembo
by Apex CoVantage, LLC

For Michael and Zoe

Contents

Figures

Tables

Preface and Acknowledgments

I "grew up" in an era of approach-based introductions to discourse analysis. I owe a tremendous debt to every other author who has written a text on discourse analysis for having taught me not only the foundations of the field but also what it means to be teaching a subject as complex as discourse analysis. This book is written out of, not discontent, but a desire to become part of the endeavor that has shaped and inspired me in the first place.

Having advised master and doctoral students on their discourse-related projects over the past 12 years and repeatedly answered questions of whether a particular method is correctly applied, I became interested in finding a way to get my students to develop another kind of concern—that of whether a question is adequately answered. Much of the materials in this book come from my own experiment with teaching Discourse Analysis in a way different from how I learned it. Instead of introducing my students to the various approaches to discourse analysis, I organize the syllabus by four broad questions discourse analysts ask and the various ways in which these questions may be answered. By juxtaposing different approaches *vis-à-vis* a particular question as such, I wish to cultivate an appreciation for the unique lens each approach brings to the task and for the kaleidoscopic vantage points as a basis for creativity rather than constraints. As such, this book offers one way of contextualizing and celebrating the breathtaking diversity of discourse analysis. I hope the reader will find this particular way somewhat appealing and consider it worthwhile to join our experiment.

As a trained conversation analyst, I face the obvious challenge of curbing my own bias in my attempt to present a picture of the field as evenhandedly as possible. That means not portraying conversation analysis as inherently superior and not depicting discourse as only limited to what can be captured on audio or video. On both accounts, my efforts have been earnest and painstaking—although not always to my own satisfaction. The reader will be the ultimate judge of to what extent I have succeeded in this undertaking.

For over a year, I worked on the manuscript in complete solitude as I watched my prose become tedious and my voice grow impatient. Eventually, it was the sounds of my fellow analysts that breathed life back into what began to feel like a lifeless project. As always, I thank members of *The*

Language and Social Interaction Working Group (LANSI) Nancy Boblett, Catherine Box, Lauren Carpenter, Sarah Creider, Drew Fagan, Allie King, Hoi-Yee (Carol) Lo, Elizabeth Reddington, Nadja Tadic, Junko Takahashi, Santoi Wagner, and Jean Wong for helpful comments on various chapters of the manuscript. I am also grateful to Frederick Erickson, Cynthia Gordon, John Hellermann, Jonathan Potter, and Angela Reyes for their generosity and visions that have in various ways shaped the content, the structure, and the tone of this final version, while I alone am responsible for its remaining flaws.

Elizabeth Reddington, who never fails to deliver with the elegance and precision of a Swiss watch, worked overtime during the 2016 holiday week to get my reference lists in shape. Di Yu responded to every single one of my requests for materials with ninja-like agility in lightning speed—regardless of the time of the day. I would never have completed this manuscript on time without the competent assistance of Elizabeth and Di, who I have no doubt will in no time write books of their own. Last, but not least, to the two anonymous reviewers of the initial book proposal as well as Kathrene Binag at Routledge, thank you.

New Year's Eve 2016
New York City

Part I
Introduction

1 Overview of Discourse Analysis

Introduction

As an applied linguist who does discourse analytic work, I introduce myself sometimes as an applied linguist and sometimes as a discourse analyst. Like many of my colleagues across the globe, we are discourse analysts in linguistics, applied linguistics, education, sociology, anthropology, psychology, gender studies, culture studies, communication studies, English language and literature, and other disciplines. We are housed in a vastly diverse array of academic programs or departments, most of which don't have "discourse analysis" in their titles. As the British linguist Michael Stubbs (1983) wrote more than 30 years ago:

> No one is in the position to write a comprehensive account of discourse analysis. The subject is at once too vast, and too lacking in focus and consensus. . . . Anything at all that is written on discourse analysis is partial and controversial.
>
> (p. 12)

Decades later, the vastness and disparity remain but have in some ways been cast in a more positive light. In their second edition of the *Handbook of Discourse Analysis*, Schiffrin, Tannen, and Hamilton (2015) wrote:

> Our own experiences in the field have led us to the conviction that the vastness and diversity of discourse analysis is a strength rather than a weakness. Far from its being a liability to be lamented because of the lack of a single coherent theory, we find the theoretical and methodological diversity of discourse analysis to be an asset.
>
> (p. 5)

Aim of the Book

Appreciating the vastness and diversity of discourse analysis is one thing, and attempting to introduce that vastness and diversity to beginning students of discourse is quite another. In this book, I make this attempt by organizing such vastness and diversity around the kinds of questions discourse analysts ask and how they answer them. By placing the questions that drive discourse analysts at the center stage, I hope to provide a spine that brings together what may otherwise appear to be a disparate set of facts about discourse, thereby alleviating the difficulty students often have in efficiently developing and articulating a coherent understanding of the subject. Considering how each broad question is systematically approached by analysts of different empirical persuasions also affords the possibilities for synthesis, integration, and a multidimensional understanding of the core issues that preoccupy discourse analysts. As such, it sidesteps the potential pitfall of a method-driven orientation that may at times constrain rather than inspire. Without considering the question each method is addressed to, for example, discussions on its strengths and weaknesses are ultimately unproductive. As students of discourse are sometimes observed to grapple with "Am I using the method correctly?" or "Is X allowed in this method?" rather than "Am I answering the question adequately?", this book is written in part to set the priorities straight.

Origins of Discourse Analysis

Before we proceed, one clarification is in order. In this book, I use discourse analysis as a general label that encompasses various approaches to discourse such as conversation analysis, interactional sociolinguistics, and critical discourse analysis (e.g., Cameron, 2001; Schiffrin, 1994). It is important to acknowledge, however, that the term "discourse analysis" is sometimes reserved for more specific traditions or approaches. In sociology and social psychology, for example, discourse analysis originated in the sociology of scientific knowledge associated with the work of Nigel Gilbert and Michael Mulkay (Wooffitt, 2005). By collecting various kinds of qualitative data including recorded interviews, Gilbert and Mulkay (1984) were trying to discover the processes through which scientists resolve a scientific dispute. Although they set out to provide a coherent account of how scientific knowledge was produced, what they found was the variability in accounts. There is, in other words, no such thing as "what really happened." They proposed, as a result, discourse analysis as a method to study the nature of that variability. This method of discourse analysis was later crystallized in Potter and Wetherell's (1987) classic volume *Discourse and Social Psychology* (also see *discursive psychology* in Edwards & Potter, 1992).

In linguistics, the enterprise of discourse came about as an attempt by linguists to go beyond the sentence level in the study of language. The belief was that just as sentences were built from identifiable elements and rules, so should be discourse. Scholars would take this search for structures beyond the sentence level in several directions: some discovered structures and rules for stories and narratives (Kintsch & Dijk, 1978; Labov & Waletzky, 1967), some proposed mapping rules and sequencing rules for conversation (Labov & Fanshel, 1977), and some identified IRF (initiation-response-feedback) as a distinct feature of classroom discourse (Sinclair & Coulthard, 1975). As the terms used to characterize language at or below the sentence level are no longer adequate for describing discourse, some have turned to concepts such as topic, "staging," information structure and the like, and efforts were made to understand the nature of reference and other cohesive ties in building text coherence (Brown & Yule, 1983; Halliday & Hasan, 1976). Because of the preoccupation with units and rules, linguistically oriented discourse analysis is often tied to the practice of imposing predetermined categories onto natural or even invented data, and in this regard, stands in stark contrast with other approaches such as conversation analysis, which features "unmotivated looking" into naturally occurring talk (Psathas, 1995). Levinson (1983), for example, made the distinction between conversation analysis and discourse analysis.

Returning to our consideration of discourse analysis as a superordinate category then, in this chapter, I provide a preview of the four broad questions that preoccupy discourse analysts—questions that provide some much-needed but ever-elusive coherence to the field. I also offer an initial sampling of how these four broad questions may be answered through the analysis of discourse. The goal is to pique the reader's interest in matters of discourse and to stage a road map for the kinds of expeditions we will embark on for the rest of the book. The chapter ends with a discussion on the question of why discourse analysts do the work they do or what real-world impact the work of discourse analysis can have. But first, a book on discourse analysis cannot begin without tackling two seemingly straightforward questions: (1) What is discourse, and (2) what is discourse analysis?

Discourse and Discourse Analysis

Task 1: Poll 10 people with the question, "What is discourse?" Compile your answers and report to the class. Try to reach some consensus regarding your definition of discourse. On the basis of this definition, consider whether the following are examples of discourse. Check "yes" or "no." Explain your choices.

1. _____ political speech
2. _____ gossip
3. _____ lecture
4. _____ group discussion
5. _____ music
6. _____ lyrics.

Here are some answers gathered from a casual poll in a university administrative office:

- communication or dialog between two people
- conversation between two or more people with an emphasis on content not relationships
- one's means of communication
- ((sigh))
- back-and-forth of conversation
- speech
- a fancy word for *talking*
- talking things over
- the act of conversation
- talking or a conversation that has a beginning and an end.

Some recurring words are *talking, conversation,* and *communication.* Our vernacular understanding of discourse seems to revolve around social interaction. Would an academic definition of discourse be any different?

Defining Discourse

One can approach the question by considering the sorts of things discourse analysts study. A cursory survey of the recent issues of major discourse journals such as *Text & Talk, Discourse Studies, Discourse Processes, Journal of Pragmatics,* and *Research on Language and Social Interaction* yields a rich assortment of interests including humor, reported speech, intercultural impoliteness, disaffiliation in Japanese interaction, discourse of resistance to racism, conversational style on Twitter, deception in computer-mediated communication, turn-taking in the skating pool, topical themes in research articles, plagiarism policies in Australian universities, and negotiating knowledge bases in pedagogical discourse. Like the responses gathered from the casual poll at a university office, the list here roughly points to an understanding of discourse as actual instances of language use in the real world as opposed to language as an abstract system, which would accommodate invented instances of language such as *Colorless green ideas sleep furiously* (Chomsky, 1957). The study of language as an abstract system, for example, is documented in *Language,* the flagship journal of the Linguistic Society of America, where topics such as case alternation, polarity particle, and patterns of contrast in phonological change are dealt with in great depth. As wide a chasm as there appears to be between (theoretical) linguistics and discourse analysis nowadays, there was a time when the study of discourse was simply the study of linguistics. In reflecting upon her foray into the field of discourse analysis, Deborah Tannen recalls an era devoid of any journals with "discourse" in their titles, where she did not think of what she was doing as anything but linguistics, and in searching for a label for the different kind of linguistics she was studying, she came to redefine her work as neither linguistics, nor sociolinguistics, but "discourse analysis" (Schiffrin et al., 2015, p. 3).

Beyond the commonality of highlighting language use in the real world between the vernacular and the academic lists, the information from the discourse journals also gives us a sense of what specific aspects of *talking, conversation,* and *communication* constitute objects of scientific investigations for discourse analysts. In other words, from the scholarly journals, we are afforded greater specificity in understanding what constitutes discourse. In the spirit of further pursuing such specificity, I make three additional observations in attempting a more comprehensive answer to the question of *what is discourse?* First, discourse is clearly not limited to face-to-face interaction but instead includes text and talk delivered through a variety of technologies (e.g., pen, phone, computer) and platforms (e.g., Facebook, Twitter, online learning management systems). Second, discourse is not limited to language but includes manifold semiotic resources such as gaze, gestures, body movements, artifacts, and the material setting. Indeed, topics such as gesture, multimodality, and embodied action are featured in the second edition of *Handbook of Discourse Analysis* (Tannen, Hamilton, & Schiffrin, 2015) and constitute the theme of the groundbreaking volume *Embodied Interaction: Language and Body in the Material World* (Streeck, Goodwin, & LeBaron, 2011; also see Nevile, 2015). This "language and beyond" notion of discourse provides a perfect segue into our third, related point that specifies what constitutes discourse. An influential dichotomy in the field of discourse analysis is that between the little "d" discourse and the Big "D" discourse (Gee, 2011).

The little **"d" discourse** refers to "any instance of language-in-use" (spoken or written) (Gee, 2011, p. 205), and the **Big "D" discourses** "ways of combining and integrating language, actions, interactions, ways of thinking, believing, valuing, and using various symbols, tools, and objects to enact a particular sort of socially recognizable identity" (Gee, 2011, p. 201).

In other words, Gee's Big "D" refers to a full ensemble of resources one employs to enact a particular identity; notably, it goes beyond language and multimodal resources to include one's beliefs and values, much of which, as I suspect, may be located in the actual use of language and multimodal resources. Being a first-time mom, for example, is more than the language one speaks. The Big D of a first-time mom includes not only her use of vocabulary such as *diapers, naps,* and *snacks* but also the nursery rhymes she learns, the Internet sites she visits, the section of the wood floor she learns to walk on in order not to wake up the baby, and much more. The Big D of a first-time mom is an entire way of comporting, behaving, and living, through close observations of which, we also become privy to what she thinks, believes, and values.

So where do all these specifications leave us? Are we in a better place to define what discourse is? I believe we are. Considering how the word *discourse* has been used in all its incarnations both vernacularly and academically, in this book, we define discourse as follows.

Discourse refers to the actual use of language along with other multi-modal resources (e.g., facial expression, gazes, gesture, body movements, artifacts, and the material settings) to accomplish actions, negotiate identities, and construct ideologies.

Task 2: On the basis of the definition of discourse we have discussed so far, decide whether the following are examples of discourse:

1. Political speech
2. Gossip
3. Lecture
4. Group discussion
5. Music
6. Newspaper article
7. Stop sign
8. Photograph
9. Painting
10. Book cover.

Defining Discourse Analysis

Once we have figured out what discourse is, the definition of discourse analysis cannot be more obvious, or so it seems. If discourse is the actual use of language along with other multimodal resources to accomplish actions, negotiate identities, and construct ideologies, discourse analysis must be the analysis of such actual use. But what is analysis? You are probably familiar with terms such as political analysis or psychoanalysis. If you are a linguistics or applied linguistics major, you have perhaps already done grammar analysis, phonetics analysis, sociolinguistic analysis, or interlanguage analysis. In the popular U.S. TV show *CSI Miami*, crime scene investigators conduct forensic analyses of a wide range of evidence in order to solve a criminal case.

Task 3: What kinds of analyses have you done? What is involved in those analyses?

In doing analyses, you look closely, you make observations, you ask questions, you pull things apart, you make connections, you uncover meanings, you conduct evaluations, or you identify problems and devise solutions. To various extents, we do all these things to discourse when we engage in discourse analysis. In an e-mail exchange I was carbon copied on, one writes, "Btw—Seeing as I'm the 'to' in your message, no need to emphasize my name again (inferring impatience) at the end of your sentence." The writer of the message is assigning the meaning of impatience to the mention of her name, arguing that such mention is otherwise unnecessary given her clearly marked recipient status. In her own way, she is doing a form of discourse analysis in this very e-mail message! In an academic tenure review, the committee members engage in repeated close readings of the candidate's dossier: They observe patterns, point to the presence or absence of particular indicators, and note items of greater or lesser values. They participate in a collective discourse analysis of the candidate's CV, statement, publications, teaching evaluations, and letters from external reviewers. In the United States, each time after the president has addressed the nation in a televised speech, a panel of pundits would analyze that speech on multiple television stations immediately thereafter. They would comment on what is highlighted, what is omitted, what they are hearing for the first time, what effects the president's remarks would have on various political contingencies, and so on. They too are engaging in a form of discourse analysis.

> **Discourse analysis** refers to the close reading of *actual use of language along with other multimodal resources* for the purpose of dissecting its structures and devising its meanings.

Task 4: What informal discourse analyses have you done at home, at work, or in any other social situations? What were your findings?

Questions and Analyses

In this section, I provide an initial sampling of what the work of doing discourse analysis looks like, that is, what doing *close reading* means in actual discourse analytic work, and I do so by presenting examples of discourse analysis in response to four broad questions discourse analysts ask: (1) how is discourse structured (e.g., what are the components of X?), and how does such structuring contribute to meaning making? (2) how are social actions (e.g., build rapport, manage conflict, balance work and play) accomplished in discourse, (3) how are identities (e.g., survivor, concerned parent, novice teacher) negotiated in discourse, and (4) how are ideologies (e.g., heteronormativity, gender discrimination, racial ideologies) constructed in discourse? It is important to register from the outset that these questions are not mutually exclusive but jointly elaborative. Understanding the structure of X can be the basis for understanding the work involved in accomplishing actions, negotiating identities, and constructing ideologies. It may also be argued that by performing a particular social action, one is inevitably engaged in some sort of identity work or even perhaps signaling a particular ideology. Regardless of such interwoven links, however, individual discourse analysts would typically choose to foreground one aspect of discourse over another in the presentation of their work, as evidenced, for example, in the title of the work, the research questions asked, and the contributions highlighted. For a useful discussion on what doing discourse analysis entails, see Antaki, Billig, Edwards, and Potter (2003).

How Is Discourse Structured?

The issue of discourse and structure will be addressed in greater detail in Chapters 2–3. As will be shown, discourse analysts have gone to great lengths to detail the structure of narrative, conversation, classroom discourse, various genres of text, and so on. The structure of a summary, for example, may be of interest to many. From second grade on and throughout graduate school, we are asked to summarize stories, articles, studies, books, speeches, arguments, and so on. Summary appears to be such a simple and straightforward genre, and yet young children are often at loss as to where to begin, and even graduate students can hand in summaries of a research article that miss key elements of that article. How do you teach someone to write a summary? A helpful answer may be found in Li and Hoey's (2014) analysis of strategies of writing summaries based on 80 hard news texts and summaries written by information retrieval experts. The authors addressed the question of how summaries are structured by identifying how summaries are assembled in the first place—via the strategies of deletion, substitution, and abstraction. **Deletion** involves omitting trivial and unimportant information and is found to be the first and easiest strategy to acquire in learning to do summaries. **Selection** is the next stage in the developmental sequence of summary writing and entails selecting a part of the original text as important to be repacked through nominalization, paraphrase, and the replication of linkages that do or do not occur in the original texts. **Abstraction** is the highest-level strategy and the most difficult to acquire because it requires one to combine several partial acts or events into an overall macroact or macroevent.

Li and Hoey made it very clear that a prerequisite of implementing the three summary strategies of deletion, substitution, and abstraction is a solid understanding of how the original text is structured. In order to make decisions on what to delete and what to select, for example, one needs to begin with a clear understanding of how the different parts of the texts relate to each other, and where such relationships are often signaled by linguistic devices such as subordinators, conjuncts, lexical repetitions, and parallelism. Propositions stated in the independent clauses in the leads of the original news stories, for example, are more likely to be considered core information to be included by summary writers. In the case of abstraction, for example, the original texts present a series of instances in support of a common theme without explicitly stating such a theme, and the equal status among the instances is signaled by their parallel structure created through repetition.

Task 5: Consider the following text taken from Li and Hoey (2014, p. 100). All the sentences are numbered for easy reference. Identify the relationships among the propositions in this text and any parallel instances that illustrate a common theme, and identify the common theme.

BEIJING—(1) A new circular by Fujian's provincial education department on Tuesday has targeted academic plagiarism by college teachers, amid increasing worries over the practice. (2) College teachers in Fujian may also be dismissed if they spread misinformation against the country's laws and regulations to mislead students, the circular said. (3) An increasing number of teachers in universities in China are turning to the Internet or other academics' research to advance their own careers. (4) Shen Yang, a professor at Wuhan University who released a research paper in 2009, said the country lacks an effective thesis supervision system and the convenience brought by the Internet drives the booming ghostwriting market. (5) His study shows there were more than 1.1 million full-time teachers in universities and colleges across the country in 2007. (6) They had to publish more than half a million theses within two years in nearly 1,800 important periodicals to keep their positions. (7) Other banned practices include teachers abusing their power for personal benefit and teachers acting fraudulently on student enrolment, assessment and exams. (8) The circular also emphasized that teachers will lose out on promotion opportunities and pay rises if they are irresponsible in students' safety or induce students to participate in any "illegal or superstitious activities". (9) It said teachers were not allowed to use "physical punishment on students or insult them". (10) Violators will have any academic award and honor canceled, and will not be able to apply for new research projects for specified periods.

Here are the three one-sentence summaries of the previous text written by experienced summary writers in Li and Hoey (2014):

(1) Circular was published to punish errant teachers in Fujian.
(2) Fujian published new circular to punish misbehaving teachers.
(3) New circular published by Fujian aims to punish misbehaving teachers.

As can be seen, *punish* and *misbehaving* are used to capture the common themes embedded in multiple sentences in the original text.

Thus, analyzing the structure of discourse involves identifying the recognizable components of a particular piece of text or talk. Insofar as understanding the structure of X often provides an effective entry point into understanding its meaning, discourse analysis offers an important resource for discovering such structures in the first place.

How Are Social Actions Accomplished in Discourse?

Questions such as how to request, compliment, built rapport, or manage conflicts, as will be discussed in great depth in Chapters 4–5, are in many ways the central preoccupation of discourse analysts. Take line 04 in the following extract for example (Schegloff, 1988, pp. 119–120). What is it doing? (Key: brackets = simultaneous speech; equals sign = second utterance latched onto first without perceptible break; colon = sound stretch; CAPS = loud speech; hehehheh = laughter.)

(1) Ice cream sandwich

```
01                   ((door squeaks))
02   Sherri:         Hi Carol.=
03   Carol:          =[Hi::.   ]
04   Ruthie:          [CA:RO]L, HI::
05   Sherri:  →      You didn't get an ice cream sandwich,
06   Carol:          I kno:w, hh I decided that my body didn't need it.
07   Sherri:         Yes but ours di:d=
08                   =hh heh heh heh heh heh heh .hhih
```

Schegloff (1988) offers an elaborate account of how Sherri's turn in line 05 is produced and recognized as a complaint. He does so by looking at how the turn is composed and how it is responded to. For example, *You didn't get an ice cream sandwich* is a negative observation of a failure. And Carol responds to that negative observation with an account, which is one of the ways complaints are typically responded to. Aside from answering this question of how social actions are accomplished in a single conversational turn such as this, discourse analysts have also tackled questions based on larger collections such as how agreements or disagreements are done. Agreements, according to Pomerantz (1984, pp. 65–68), are done as an upgrade, the same, or a downgrade *vis-à-vis* the prior speaker's talk and done so without any delay, mitigation, or account, as shown in the following three examples:

(2) Upgrade

01	A:		It's a beautiful day out isn't it?
02	B:	→	Yeh it's just gorgeous . . .

(3) Same

01	A:		. . . She was a nice lady—I liked her.
02	B:	→	I liked her too.

(4) Downgrade

01	A:		That's beautiful.
02	B:	→	Isn't it pretty.

Task 6: Consider the following data taken from Pomerantz (1984, pp. 71, 75). In what ways are disagreements done differently from the agreements? (Key: number in parentheses = length of silence in seconds; italics = stress)

(1)

01	C:		. . . You've really both basically honestly gone
02			your own ways.
03	D:	→	Essentially, except we've had a good relationship
04			at home.

(2)

01	A:		. . . You sound very far a*way.*
02		→	(0.7)
03	B:	→	I *do?*
04	A:		Yeah.
05	B:		No *I*'m no:t,

As Pomerantz (1984) pointed out, disagreement generally features delay (e.g., silence, questions, reluctance markers, agreement preface), mitigation (e.g., *essentially*), and accounts (e.g., *except we've had a good relationship at home*).

How Are Identities Negotiated in Discourse?

Another central question for discourse analysts concerns the role discourse plays in identity negotiation—an issue to be discussed in greater detail in

Chapters 6–7. Identities such as upper-class British vs. Jewish New Yorkers, for example, can become visible in their diverging conversational styles (Tannen, 1984, p. 120). In the following dinner conversation, for example, Sally's telling of her airplane meal encounters incurs multiple interjections from her co-participants, which are intended as cooperative prompting. (Key: *acc* = spoken quickly; two dots = less than half a second pause; three dots = half a second pause; four dots = full second pause; brackets = simultaneous talk)

(5)   Bagel and cream cheese

01	Sally:	Oh I was amazed to see the uh .. the meal on the
02		airplane today.
03	Peter:	What was it?
04	Sally:	It was .. a bagel with cream cheese . . . .
05	David:	[What's this?
06	Peter:	[For lunch?
07	Sally:	At lunch, . . . a bagel with cream [cheese
08	Peter:	[That's .. that's
09		Air Canada, right? . . . um Pacific=
10	Deborah:	=A .. a bagel [and cream cheese?
11	Sally:	[It was United.
12		A bagel and cream cheese, . . .
13		*acc*
14		and a whole pile of <u>ham</u>.
15		[laughter]

As Tannen observed, when Sally ends with *bagel and cream cheese* in steady intonation and a pause in line 04, the others thought she was done. But Sally keeps going back to *a bagel and cream cheese* first in line 07 and then in line 12, the latter of which is done with accelerated speed, clearly indicating that the point of her story is yet to come. It turns out that her point is not that bagel and cream cheese were served as lunch but that these Jewish food items were served with the nonkosher ham (line 14)! During playback interviews where the participants listened to their own talk and made comments, Tannen (1984) found that the cooperative prompting offered by herself (Deborah) and Peter (Jewish New Yorkers) were considered obstructive by Sally (upper-class British) who "couldn't understand why Peter kept interrupting her story to question her about irrelevant details" (p. 121). In this case, the same linguistic conduct is intended as cooperative but interpreted as obstructive. Tannen attributed this style difference in part to geographic and ethnic differences (e.g., upper-class British vs. Jewish New Yorkers).

In a study on a family political identity, Gordon (2004) showed how a 4-year-old boy and his parents collaboratively create their shared identity as Democrats and supporters of Al Gore. They do so by, for example, using referring terms that create closeness to Gore and distance from Bush (Gordon, 2004, pp. 617–618). (Key: angle brackets = enclose descriptions of vocal noises; <*manner*>words> = angle brackets enclose descriptions of the manner in which an utterance is spoken; square brackets = enclose simultaneous talk.)

(6) We want Al

01	Jason:	So they—
02		And we're also voting for President at my school too.
03	Neil:	<*exaggerated surprise*> For President?>
04		[Or just ice cream?]
05	Jason:	[(They're) talking] about the President.
06	Neil:	<*louder*> Oh well you tell 'em you're votin' for **Al Gore.**>
07	Jason:	[Yea:h!]
08	Clara:	[Yea:h!]
09	Neil:	Not **that ['W' guy.]**
10	Clara:	[(That's the one.)]
11		Not **W**!
12	Neil:	Say no **W**.
13	Clara:	No [**W**!]
14	Neil:	[We] want **Al**.
15	Clara:	<*louder*> We want **Al**.>
16	Jason:	Who's Al?
17	Neil:	**Al Gore**.
18		He's a **cool guy** [that we–]
19	Clara:	[He's **Daddy's**] **friend**.
20	Neil:	That's right.
21		He's **my friend**.
22		He's gonna be President.
23	Clara:	We hope.
24	Neil:	We hope.
25	Clara:	He's **Jackie's friend** too.
26	Neil:	<*sniffs*>
27		That's right,
28		Jackie knows him.

As shown, the democratic nominee Al Gore is referred to affectionately as *AL* (line 15), *a cool guy* (line 18), *Daddy's friend* (line 19), *my friend* (line 21), and *Jackie's friend* (line 25)—the person the family wants to be president (line 22). Republican nominee George W. Bush, on the other hand, is dismissed as *That 'W' guy* (line 09) or just *W* (lines 11–13)—the guy that they as a family *say no* to (lines 11–13).

Task 7: Consider the following extract taken from Gordon (2004, p. 622), where Jason is watching TV with his mom. What discourse evidence is there to show how the family identity of Democrats is being constructed?

```
01   Clara:   That's the man that Daddy doesn't like.
02   Jason:   Who.
03            Where.
04   Clara:   That guy.
05            Bu- GW.
06            <coughs>
07   Jason:   (Is that the guy?)
08   Clara:   That's the one.
09   Jason:   Oh.. how come they're all clapping about him.
10   Clara:   Um,
11            I guess some people like him,
12            but- but I think–<sighs>
13            I think it's the hunters,
14            and the pe- the other people who don't know any better.
```

How Are Ideologies Constructed in Discourse?

Aside from performing actions and negotiating identities, discourse is also, as will be discussed in greater detail in Chapters 8–9, a crucial means through which ideologies are constructed. In his effort to elucidate how anti-immigration ideology is perpetuated in a 1989 article published in the British tabloid the *Sun*, Dijk (1996) called attention to the large banner headline **"Get Lost, Spongers!"**, the adjectives *bogus* and *phony* used to describe immigrant students and the colleges that admit them, and the popular rhetorical styles ("get lost," "spongers," etc.) engaged to legitimize what is assumed to be the popular resentment against immigration.

Task 8: Consider the note pasted on our office refrigerator years ago. Is there any particularly notable choice of language? If yes, how does the choice construct realities in a certain way? What ideology is manifested in the choice?

Please help keep this room clean!
No one's mother works here!
Montse works here, but it's not her job.
Jessie works here, but it's not her job.

. . . IT'S YOUR job to keep it clean!
~the Anti-Cockroach Coalition

One might note the use of "mother" in this message, wherein "mother" is constructed as the resident cleaning person. Consider the alternative: "No one's father works here!" Some would say it doesn't make sense, or it's not natural. The message reveals the writer's understanding of a world in which the job of cleaning belongs to the female parent. It naturalizes the view that mothers are there to clean after you, thereby making it unquestionable. It advances a particular ideology.

Clearly, there are many different ways of doing discourse analysis. In the previous illustrations, for example, the analysis of news summaries would be typically identified as a type of genre analysis, the study of agreement and disagreement is presented as one of conversation analysis, the exploration of family political identity is done within the interactional sociolinguistic approach and, finally, the scrutiny of anti-immigration ideology in newspaper papers is an example of critical discourse analysis. Crucially, however, it is important to register that genre analysis is not the only approach to addressing issues of discourse and structure, nor is conversation analysis the only approach to answering questions of discourse and social action, or interactional sociolinguistics the only approach to investigating discourse and identity. Even with issues of discourse and ideology, which are often considered a specialty for critical discourse analysis, these too can be dealt with from multiple perspectives.

Approaches and Transcriptions

As a matter of fact, not all scholars in discourse analysis would identify their work with a specific approach; some simply frame their studies as discourse analytic. Still, it might be useful to highlight some key features of a few approaches that are relatively distinct from each other and will make repeated appearances throughout the book (for a comprehensive treatment of approaches to (spoken) discourse, please consult the seminal texts of Cameron, 2001; Schiffrin, 1994).

With its origin in sociology and a commitment to "naturalistic inquiry" (Schegloff, 1997, p. 501), **conversation analysis (CA)** insists on using data collected from naturally occurring interaction as opposed to interviews, field notes, native intuitions, and experimental methodologies (Heritage, 1984, p. 236). Analysts work with audiorecordings or videorecordings along with the transcripts of these recordings, using transcription notations originally developed by Gail Jefferson to capture a full range of interactional details such as volume, pitch, pace, intonation, overlap, inbreath, smiley voice, the length of silence as well as nonverbal conduct. The goal of conversation analysis is to uncover the tacit methods and procedures of social interaction. Analysis begins with the meticulous inspection of single instances and is guided by the question "Why that now?" (Schegloff & Sacks, 1973), that is, why a particular bit of talk is produced in that particular format at that particular time: What is it accomplishing? It is in these minute details that evidence is located for how social actions such as requesting or complaining are accomplished by the participants themselves. This obsession with participant orientation or members' methods as made evident in their own conduct is what mainly distinguishes conversation analysis from other methods of qualitative research (for an extended discussion on conversation analysis as a methodology including how issues such as validity, reliability, and generalizability are dealt with, see Waring, 2016; also see Have, 2007 on how to do conversation analysis). Two approaches closely related to conversation analysis are discursive psychology (Edwards & Potter, 1992) and interactional linguistics (Couper-Kuhlen & Selting, 2001). In the case of discursive psychology, conversation analysis is drawn upon to respecify traditional matters of psychology such as memory and emotions. In the case of interactional linguistics, central issues of linguistics such as grammar and prosody are reconceptualized with the analytical tool of conversation analysis.

Interactional sociolinguistics (IS) is a qualitative, interpretive approach to the analysis of social interaction developed at the intersection of linguistics, anthropology, and sociology. Broadly speaking, it is concerned with how speakers signal and interpret meaning in everyday communicative practice with special attention to the taken-for-granted background assumptions recruited in the course of negotiating shared interpretations (Gumperz, 1999). Working with audiorecorded or videorecorded materials, interactional sociolinguists have produced illuminating accounts of phenomena such as miscommunication, stereotype, and discrimination as well as culture-specific discourse strategies, using a set of analytic concepts such as contextualization cues, frame, or intertextuality. In addition to transcripts of naturally occurring interaction, analysts sometimes also consult the participants' perspectives through (playback) interviews, where the participants are invited to comment on recordings of their own interaction (see Tannen, Kendall, & Gordon, 2007 for a collection of interactional sociolinguistics studies).

The attempt to link the micro and the macro in interactional sociolinguistics (Gordon, 2011) is also reflected in other ethnography-related discourse analytic approaches, such as ethnography of communication (Hymes, 1974), sociocultural linguistics (Bucholtz, 2011), linguistic anthropology (Goodwin, 2006; Wortham & Reyes, 2015), or **microethnography**— a term coined by Frederick Erickson to capture the kind of approach that combines participant observation with detailed analyses of audiovisual recordings that capture "key scenes in people's lives—often scenes in which people from different speech communities meet to do business that is important to them" (Erickson & Mohatt, 1982, p. 133). Microethnography, according to Erickson (2004), is most similar to John Gumperz's interactional sociolinguistics. Contemporary microethnographic studies, however, tend to employ conversation analysis as its core analytic method, often without consulting the participants' perspective through interviewing (Streeck & Mehus, 2005). Ethnography-related approaches to discourse analysis typically feature a wide range of data sources beyond audiorecordings or videorecordings of social interaction such as interviews, field notes, surveys, and various artifacts.

Finally, **critical discourse analysis (CDA)** is devoted to studying the relationships between language and power (Fairclough & Wodak, 1997; also see Chapter 8). Scholars in critical discourse analysis view language along with its meaning and use as inherently historical, political, and ideological. As such, their work centers on critically examining the processes through which power, dominance, discrimination, gender inequality, racism, and so on get signaled, legitimized, and naturalized through discourse, using various methods ranging from small-scale case study and ethnographic research to large-scale corpora analysis. For systematic accounts of how critical discourse analysis can be done, see Gee (2014a, 2014b) and Wodak and Meyer (2009).

The differences in approaches are in part observable in the different transcription conventions employed (e.g., Edwards & Lampert, 1993), which reflect to various degrees the researchers' theoretical assumptions (Ochs, 1979). Conversation analysts, for example, believe that no detail can be dismissed *a priori* because it is in these very details that tacit methods of social interaction are uncovered. As such, conversation analytic transcripts tend to be extremely detailed (Jefferson, 1983), and part of such detail entails, especially in first-generation conversation analysis studies (Lerner, 2004), the use of "eye dialect" where, for example, *to* is transcribed as *tih*, *was* as *wuz*, or *and* as *en*. Some scholars, on the other hand, believe that too much detail in a transcript can hinder readability and that "[a] more useful transcript is a more selective one" (Ochs, 1979). As will become evident, transcription conventions vary in the degrees of details documented as well as the symbols used to represent specific speech or nonspeech activities. Table 1.1 lists a set of baseline transcription symbols commonly used by discourse analysts across different approaches. Throughout the book, variations as well as additional notations specific to particular methodologies or individual scholars will be noted as they arise. Rather than standardizing the transcription conventions for this book, I have made an effort, to the extent feasible, to remain faithful to the notations employed by various scholars in their original studies for the exact purpose of exposing the reader to the different systems of documenting discourse. For a recent treatment of transcribing in social research, see Hepburn and Bolden (in press).

Task 9: Audiorecord or videorecord a two-party conversation. Transcribe 30 seconds of that recording using the notations listed in Table 1.1. Create any additional notations to capture any verbal or nonverbal features that cannot be captured by those notations.

Table 1.1 Transcription Notations

Symbol	Meaning
.	(period) falling intonation
?	(question mark) rising intonation
,	(comma) continuing intonation
-	(hyphen) abrupt cutoff
<u>word</u>	(underline) stress
:	(colon(s)) sound stretch
WORD	(all caps) loud speech
[ ]	(lined-up brackets) co-occurrence involving speech or nonspeech activities
=	(equals sign) latch between utterances without perceptible break or contiguous utterances of the same speaker
(.)	(period in parentheses) micropause
(word)	(parentheses) uncertain transcription or indecipherable speech
((*gazing*))	(double parentheses) nonspeech activity

Applications of Discourse Analysis

Why do discourse analysts do the work they do? Discourse analysis is done for various reasons, the most basic of which is to develop a better understanding of language use. As Cameron (2001) wrote, "When linguists and other social scientists analyse spoken discourse, their aim is to make explicit what normally gets taken for granted; it is also to show what talking accomplishes in people's lives and society at large" (p. 7). As with most academic disciplines, better understanding is the aim. Knowledge is the goal in and of itself. Some might say that's not a reason: that's just what discourse analysis is. But knowledge is power—it is useful, and it can make the world a better place.

In the illustrations offered earlier, for example, the knowledge of how summaries are structured makes it possible to teach that structure to students who are emerging writers, the knowledge of how agreements or disagreements are done in English can be usefully drawn upon to develop authentic language learning materials, the knowledge of how the same linguistic behaviors are interpreted differently by different social or ethnic groups can be leveraged to achieve greater harmony among these groups and, finally, the knowledge of how anti-immigration ideologies are perpetuated in media outlets can raise public awareness and rally public support for fighting against that ideology. As James Paul Gee (2005) so eloquently wrote,

When we sit back and reflect on what people have said and written—a luxury we have too little in life, but the basis of discourse analysis—we often discover better, deeper, and more humane interpretations. The small child whom the teacher assumed made no sense at sharing time looks a lot smarter after a little reflection, which can be helped along by recording the child for a later, more reflective listening. A person from a different race, class, or culture looks, on reflection, if the reflection is based on any knowledge, to have made both a better point and a better impression on second thought than on first.

(pp. xi–xii)

Some analysts are driven by real-world concerns from the outset. Critical discourse analysts may begin with the assumption that the world is an unjust place, and to unveil that injustice becomes their mission. Interactional socio-linguists have produced important work to salvage relationships and to elimi-nate misunderstandings. John Gumperz, for example, served as a consultant on BBC's *Crosstalk*—a television program designed to raise awareness of pos-sible causes of intercultural miscommunication in workplaces and of the role of language in stereotyping and discrimination. Conversation analytic work has become instrumental in improving doctor-patient communications, human-computer interactions (HCI), and even public speaking techniques. Max Atkinson, whose book *Lend Me Your Ears* is considered a bible for many politicians seeking the art of effective speaking, began as a conversation analyst investigating speaker-audience interaction. As Paddy Ashdown, the former leader of the British Liberal Democrats, wrote, "There was scarcely a single speech in my eleven years as leader of the Liberal Democrats that I made without benefiting from Max Atkinson's personal advice and help" (Atkinson Communications, 2013). More recently, the conversation ana-lyst Elizabeth Stokoe developed CARM (Conversation Analytic Role-Play Method)—a training program aimed at improving communication skills in any workplace or institutional encounter (www.carmtraining.org). In fact, as documented in a special issue of *Research on Language and Social Interaction* ("Conversation Analysis and Intervention," 2014), conversation analysts have been actively engaged in intervention work to improve aphasic conversations, enhance effectiveness in telephone help line services, promote more accurate diagnosis of seizure, influence policy changes concerning service delivery to government benefits claimants, and inform the design and development of a prototype communication system. Because of the work discourse analysts do, professional practices are enhanced, relationships are saved, and the world is becoming a less prejudiced place.

As an applied linguist with a particular interest in language learning and teaching, I do discourse analysis for two reasons, that is, to help solving two larger jigsaw puzzles: *what to teach* and *how to teach*. Insofar as the goal of lan-guage teaching is to help learners develop their communicative competence, findings of discourse analysis are integral to specifying the stuff that commu-nicative competence is made of. Becoming communicatively competent in a second language is more than learning its vocabulary, mastering its gram-mar, and appropriating its pronunciation. As Rintell and Mitchell (1989) wrote, "No 'error' of grammar can make a speaker seem so incompetent, so inappropriate, so foreign, as the kind of trouble a learner gets into when he or she doesn't understand or otherwise disregards a language's rules of use" (p. 248). Discourse markers such as *but, also, anyway*, and *actually* can present grave challenges for nonnative speakers, who often use the markers literally, overuse them, or misuse them. Tyler (1992) showed that part of the difficulties international teaching assistants (ITAs) have in getting themselves understood has to do with the use of discourse markers. According to Jung (2009), there is a subtle difference in the use of *but* in her data: nonnative speakers (NNS) of English use it to preface their disagreement (e.g., *but you're wrong*), whereas native speakers (NS) use it to preface a softening move (e.g., *It's not X, but lots of people make the same mistake*). The nonnative speakers come off as unduly abrupt and argumentative. These are subtle functions that cannot be easily explained by a native speaker of English, and they are not even immediately apparent to a researcher. It is up to discourse analysts to uncover them. Knowledge of how to use discourse markers appropriately is but one small indication of the kinds of materials that need to be worked into our language teaching curriculum. Wong and Waring (2010), for example, brought together a large body of conversation analytic findings on interactional practices, which are the foundational skills a language learner must master in order to become interactionally competent in a second language.

I do discourse analysis also with the question of *how to teach* in mind. I analyze classroom interaction, for example, to unveil how instructional practices can block or promote participation, and by extension, learning. I discovered that within certain contexts, the use of explicit positive assessments such as *very good* can deliver the news of "case closed"—no further discussion warranted. By not providing any interactional space for questioning, exploring, or simply lingering upon any specific pedagogical point at the time, explicit positive assessments (EPAs) can effectively remove the opportunities for voicing understanding problems or exploring alternative correct answers, that is, the opportunities of learning (Waring, 2008; Wong & Waring, 2009). A detailed look into classroom interaction can also reveal that tasks do not always unfold as planned. Mori (2002) showed, for example, that what was planned as a "discussion meeting" for learners of Japanese to have an opportunity to converse with native speakers turned into a structured interview, and part of the problem was that the learners were not equipped with the sequential resources to implement some of the required activities. Although they were largely successful with initiating actions such as asking the visitors about their fathers, they had difficulty fulfilling the task of telling the visitors about their own fathers, not knowing how to do that without being asked. Findings such as this force us to think twice about task designs in language teaching. Are we so narrowly focused on outlining the macroprocedures of task planning at the expense of the microinteractional resources necessary to bring about those steps? Discourse analytic work in education settings such as classrooms or tutoring settings play an important role in boosting the efficacy of the practices in those settings. It contributes to answering the question of *how to teach*.

Task 10: Given your understanding of discourse analysis so far, how can knowledge of discourse analysis benefit you in any way? Hypothetically, what would be your personal purpose for doing discourse analysis?

Overview of the Book

Parts II–V of this book are addressed in turn to Discourse and Structure, Discourse and Social Action, Discourse and Identity, and Discourse and Ideology. Each part contains a chapter on classics and one on empirical endeavors. Although the book is not organized around approaches to discourse, through the chapters on empirical endeavors, the reader will be introduced to the actual working of the various approaches in the context of answering the four overarching questions of discourse analysis. In the chapters on the classics, on the other hand, the reader will be exposed to the theoretical groundings and key analytical concepts of the various approaches. While a structural concept such as *adjacency pair* is introduced in the classics chapter in Discourse and Structure, it is an analytical tool deployed to answer questions beyond discourse and structure and therefore will inevitably make its appearance in other parts of the book. Cross-references will be made in the event of such cross-chapter reappearances of key analytical concepts. A final caveat to heed is that the division between "classics" and "empirical endeavors" is a somewhat arbitrary one, as most of the classics are themselves empirical studies. They are treated as classics in this book in part because they are well-known and widely cited early works and, more important, they were the trailblazing investigations that in many cases established the foundations for later inquiries and discoveries.

Key Points

- Discourse refers to the actual use of language along with other multimodal resources.
- Although the term "discourse analysis" sometimes takes on specific disciplinary meanings, it is used in this book as an overarching term to capture the various analytical endeavors to study the actual use of language along with other multimodal resources.
- Discourse analysts ask a set of core questions, each of which can be addressed with multiple approaches.
- The four overarching questions discourse analysts ask are: how is discourse structured, how are social actions accomplished, how are identities negotiated, and how are ideologies constructed?
- Approaches to discourse differ in their origins, goals, types of data, and methods of analyses.

- Transcription systems vary in the extent to which details are recorded and the types of symbols used to represent any speech or nonspeech activities.
- Discourse analysis is done to gain a better understanding of language use along with other multimodal resources, and out of that understanding, real-world problems may be solved.

References

Antaki, C., Billig, M., Edwards, D., & Potter, J. (2003). Discourse analysis means doing analysis: A critique of six analytic shortcomings. *Discourse Analysis Online, 1*(1). Retrieved from http://extra.shu.ac.uk/daol/articles/v1/n1/a1/antaki2002002.html

Atkinson Communications. (2013). [Client testimonials]. Retrieved from www.speaking. co.uk/Atkinson%20Comunications/books.public_html

Atkinson, M. (2004). *Lend me your ears: All you need to know about making speeches and presentations.* New York: Oxford University Press.

Brown, G., & Yule, G. (1983). *Discourse analysis.* Cambridge: Cambridge University Press.

Bucholtz, M. (2011). 'It's different for guys': Gendered narratives of racial conflict among white California youth. *Discourse & Society, 22*(4), 385–402.

Cameron, D. (2001). *Working with spoken discourse.* London: Sage.

Chomsky, N. (1957). *Syntactic structures.* Berlin: Mouton de Gruyter.

Conversation analysis and intervention. (2014). *Research on Language and Social Interaction, 47*(3), 201–329.

Couper-Kuhlen, E., & Selting, M. (2001). Introducing interactional linguistics. In M. Selting & E. Couper-Kuhlen (Eds.), *Studies in interactional linguistics* (pp. 1–22). Philadelphia, PA, and Amsterdam: John Benjamins Publishing.

Dijk, T. A. van (1996). Discourse, power and access. In C. R. Caldas-Coulthard & M. Coulthard (Eds.), *Texts and practices: Readings in critical discourse analysis* (pp. 84–104). London: Routledge.

Edwards, D., & Potter, J. (1992). *Discursive psychology.* London: Sage.

Edwards, J. A., & Lampert, M. D. (Eds.). (1993). *Talking data: Transcription and coding in discourse research.* Hillsdale, NJ: Lawrence Erlbaum Associates.

Erickson, F. (2004). *Talk and social theory.* Malden, MA: Polity Press.

Erickson, F., & Mohatt, G. (1982). Cultural organization of participation structures in two classrooms of Indian students. In G. Spindler (Ed.), *Doing the ethnography of schooling: Educational anthropology in action* (pp. 132–174). New York: Holt, Rinehart, and Winston.

Fairclough, N., & Wodak, R. (1997). Critical discourse analysis. In T. van Dijk (Ed.), *Discourse studies: A multidisciplinary introduction* (Vol. 2) (pp. 258–284). London: Sage.

Gee, J. P. (2005). *An introduction to discourse analysis: Theory and method* (2nd ed.). London and New York: Routledge.

Gee, J. P. (2011). *An introduction to discourse analysis: Theory and method* (3rd ed.). London and New York: Routledge.

Gee, J. P. (2014a). *An introduction to discourse analysis: Theory and method* (4th ed.). London and New York: Routledge.

Gee, J. P. (2014b). *How to do discourse analysis: A tool kit* (2nd ed.). New York: Routledge.

Gilbert, G. N., & Mulkay, M. (1984). *Opening Pandora's box: A sociological analysis of scientists' discourse.* Cambridge: Cambridge University Press.

Goodwin, M. H. (2006). The hidden life of girls: Games of stance, status, and exclusion. Oxford: Blackwell.

Gordon, C. (2004). 'Al Gore's our guy': Linguistically constructing a family political identity. *Discourse & Society, 15*(5), 607–631.

Gordon, C. (2011). Gumperz and interactional sociolinguistics. In R. Wodak, B. Johnstone, & P. E. Kerswill (Eds.), *The Sage handbook of sociolinguistics* (pp. 67–84). London: Sage.

Gumperz, J. J. (1999). On interactional sociolinguistic method. In S. Sarangi & C. Roberts (Eds.), *Talk, work, and institutional order* (pp. 453–471). New York: Mouton de Gruyter.

Halliday, M. A. K., & Hasan, R. (1976). *Cohesion in English.* London: Longman.

Have, P. ten (2007). *Doing conversation analysis* (2nd ed.). Thousand Oaks, CA: Sage.

Hepburn, A., & Bolden, G. (in press). *Transcribing for social research.* London: Sage.

Heritage, J. (1984). *Garfinkel and ethnomethodology.* Oxford: Basil Blackwell.

Hymes, D. (1974). *Foundations in sociolinguistics: An ethnographic approach.* Philadelphia, PA: University of Pennsylvania Press.

Jefferson, G. (1983). Notes on some orderliness of overlap onset. *Tilburg Papers in Language and Literature, 28*, 1–28.

Jung, J.-Y. (2009). Discourse markers in contrast: But, actually and well in native-nonnative English conversations between friends (Doctoral dissertation). Retrieved from ProQuest Dissertations and Theses Global. (Accession No. 3368401).

Kintsch, W., & Dijk, T. A. van (1978). Toward a model of text comprehension and production. *Psychological Review, 85*(5), 363–394.

Labov, W., & Fanshel, D. (1977). *Therapeutic discourse: Psychotherapy as conversation.* New York: Academic Press.

Labov, W., & Waletzky, J. (1967). Narrative analysis: Oral versions of personal experience. In J. Helm (Ed.), *Proceedings of the 1966 annual spring meeting of the American Ethnological Society* (pp. 12–44). Seattle and London: University of Washington Press.

Lerner, G. (Ed.). (2004). *Conversation analysis: Studies from the first generation.* Philadelphia, PA, and Amsterdam: John Benjamins Publishing.

Levinson, S. C. (1983). *Pragmatics.* Cambridge: Cambridge University Press.

Li, Y. K., & Hoey, M. (2014). Strategies of writing summaries for hard news texts: A text analysis approach. *Discourse Studies, 16*(1), 89–105.

Mori, J. (2002). Task design, plan, and development of talk-in-interaction: An analysis of a small group activity in a Japanese language classroom. *Applied Linguistics, 23*(3), 323–247.

Nevile, M. (2015). The embodied turn in research on language and social interaction. *Research on Language and Social Interaction, 48*(2), 121–151.

Ochs, E. (1979). Transcription as theory. In E. Ochs & B. Schieffelen (Eds.), *Developmental pragmatics* (pp. 43–71). New York: Academic Press.

Pomerantz, A. (1984). Agreeing and disagreeing with assessments: Some features of preferred/dispreferred turn shapes. In J. M. Atkinson & J. Heritage (Eds.), *Structures of social action: Studies in conversation analysis* (pp. 57–101). New York: Cambridge University Press.

Potter, J., & Wetherell, M. (1987). *Discourse and social psychology: Beyond attitudes and behavior.* London: Sage.

Psathas, G. (1995). *Conversation analysis: The study of talk-in-interaction.* Thousand Oaks, CA: Sage.

Rintell, E., & Mitchell, C. J. (1989). Studying requests and apologies: An inquiry into method. In S. Blum-Kulka, J. House, & G. Kasper (Eds.), *Cross-cultural pragmatics* (pp. 248–272). Norwood, NJ: Ablex.

Schegloff, E. A. (1988). Goffman and the analysis of conversation. In P. Drew & A. Wootton (Eds.), *Ervin Goffman: Exploring the interaction order* (pp. 89–135). Boston, MA: Northeastern University Press.

Schegloff, E. A. (1997). Practices and actions: Boundary cases of other-initiated repair. *Discourse Processes, 23,* 499–545.

Schegloff, E. A., & Sacks, H. (1973). Opening up closings. *Semiotica, 8,* 289–327.

Schiffrin, D. (1994). *Approaches to discourse.* Cambridge, MA: Blackwell.

Schiffrin, D., Tannen, D., & Hamilton, H. (2015). Introduction to the first edition. In D. Tannen, H. Hamilton, & D. Schiffrin (Eds.), *The handbook of discourse analysis* (2nd ed.) (pp. 1–7). Malden, MA: Wiley Blackwell.

Sinclair, J. M., & Coulthard, M. (1975). *Towards an analysis of discourse: The English used by teachers and pupils.* London: Oxford University Press.

Streeck, J., Goodwin, C., & LeBaron, C. (2011). *Embodied interaction: Language and body in the material world.* New York: Cambridge University Press.

Streeck, J., & Mehus, S. (2005). Microethnography: The study of practices. In K. L. Fitch & R. E. Sanders (Eds.), *Handbook of language and social interaction* (pp. 381–404). Mahwah, NJ: Lawrence Erlbaum Associates.

Stubbs, M. (1983). Discourse analysis: The sociolinguistic analysis of natural language. Chicago: The University of Chicago Press.

Tannen, D. (1984). *Conversational style: Analyzing talk among friends.* New York: Oxford University Press.

Tannen, D., Hamilton, H. E., & Schiffrin, D. (Eds.). (2015). *The handbook of discourse analysis* (2nd ed.). Malden, MA: Wiley Blackwell.

Tannen, D., Kendall, S., & Gordon, C. (Eds.). (2007). *Family talk: Discourse and identity in four American families.* Oxford: Oxford University Press.

Tyler, A. (1992). Discourse structure and the perception of incoherence in international teaching assistants' spoken discourse. *TESOL Quarterly, 26,* 713–729.

Waring, H. Z. (2008). Using explicit positive assessment in the language classroom: IRF, feedback, and learning opportunities. *The Modern Language Journal, 92*(4), 577–594.

Waring, H. Z. (2016). Theorizing pedagogical interaction: Insights from conversation analysis. New York: Routledge.

Wodak, R., & Meyer, M. (Eds.). (2009). *Methods of critical discourse analysis* (2nd ed.). London: Sage.

Wong, J., & Waring, H. Z. (2009). 'Very good' as a teacher response. *ELT Journal, 63*(3), 195–203.

Wong, J., & Waring, H. Z. (2010). *Conversation analysis and second language pedagogy.* New York: Routledge.

Wooffitt, R. (2005). *Conversation analysis and discourse analysis: A comparative and critical introduction.* London: Sage.

Wortham, S., & Reyes, A. (2015). *Discourse analysis beyond the speech event.* New York and London: Routledge.

Part II
Discourse and Structure

2 Classics in Discourse and Structure

Introduction

Almost all kinds of analyses involve deconstructing and categorizing of some sort, and the most obvious level at which such deconstruction and categorization can be done is structure, which concerns the compositions or distributions of some discursive entity (e.g., talk, text, noverbal conduct): how is it assembled, what are its subunits, and how do those subunits hang together? One may wonder, for example: What are the different parts of a story? How is conversation structured to enable participants' understanding of each other? What are the components of a text that make it recognizable as a text? Is there a difference between the gaze duration of a speaker and a recipient? What types of hand gestures are there?

Discourse analysts have made illuminating discoveries about the structure of text, talk, and nonverbal conduct. Given that structure is primarily a linguistic concern, it is not surprising that much of the work on discourse and structure come from linguists of various backgrounds—theoretical, social, or critical. Conversation analysts have also contributed some of the most influential work on the sequential aspects of discourse structure. In this chapter, I introduce some classics in the study of discourse and structure and have chosen to define "classics" as early works that are widely cited or continue to have an impact on current research practices. Given the vastness of the area, my treatment of the subject is necessarily selective. In particular, we consider seminal works addressed to the structure of narrative, the structure of conversation, the structure of classroom discourse, the structure of text, and the structure of nonverbal conduct, thus moving from talk, to text and, finally, to conduct beyond talk and text. As will be shown, the question of how discourse is structured is inevitably related to the question of how such structure contributes to meaning making.

Structure of Talk

In this section, we consider some classics in illuminating the structure of spoken discourse and, in particular, the structures of narrative, conversation, and classroom interaction.

Narrative (Labov)

Labov and Waletzky (1967) (L&W) made one of the earliest attempts at describing the structure of discourse and, in particular, the structure of narratives. Their work on narratives was a by-product of a larger sociolingustic study on New York City English in the 1960s (Labov, 1997). In their quest to find a solution to the Observer's Paradox—observe how speakers talk when they are not being observed, Labov and his colleagues discovered that "the elicitation of narratives of personal experience proved to be the most effective" and became particularly interested in the "compelling power" of the kinds of narratives that "produce in the audience a profound concentration of attention that creates uninterrupted silence and immobility, an effect that continues long after the ending is reached" (Labov, 1997, p. 396). It is the structure of these particular narratives that became their object of inquiry.

Observer's Paradox refers to the paradox that systematic observation of how people talk in their natural state is obtainable only when they are not being observed.

In the L&W framework, narrative is informally defined as a method of recapitulating past experience. A more technical definition, however, includes concepts such as sequence of clauses and temporal junctures.

Narrative is a method of recapitulating past experience by matching a verbal sequence of clauses that contains at least one temporal juncture to the sequence of events which actually occurred.

Temporal juncture refers to the juncture that separates two clauses temporally ordered with respect to each other, where the order of the two clauses cannot be changed without changing the actual events.

In the example *I took a step forward, and I fell*, there is a temporal juncture between *I took a step* and *I fell*. Switching the order of these two clauses would change the representation of the events.

Labov and Waletzky's (1967) search for a formal structure of narratives yields the following components: orientation, complication, evaluation, resolution, and coda (see Table 2.1).

According to L&W, the simplest kind of narrative can be a single line of complication; other minimal narratives can have complication + resolution (e.g., *He hit me hard and I hit him back*); more complex narratives told by

Table 2.1 Narrative Components

Component	Function
Orientation	Scene setting: who, when, what, where?
Complication	Main event: then what happened?
Evaluation	Point of the story: so what?
Resolution	Outcome of the story: what finally happened?
Coda	Connection to the present time: *no more problems.*

speakers with greater verbal ability tend to have the full range of components (p. 41). In addition, some of these components must occur in a specific order: Resolution must follow, not precede, Complication. Orientation and Evaluation, on the other hand, have greater freedom in their placement in the overall structure. Table 2.2 shows a narrative taken from Labov and Waletzky (1967, p. 18), in which we see an illustration of how the structure of narrative may be analyzed.

Importantly, what distinguishes a narrative from a pointless story, according to L&W, is the component of evaluation. As the key to advancing the point of the narrative, evaluation can be done in different ways (Labov, 1972): external evaluation (e.g., *It was the strangest feeling.*), embedding of evaluation (e.g., *So I say, "Well I just gotta fight this girl."*), evaluative action (e.g., *And everybody heaved a sigh of relief*), and evaluation by suspension of the action. In the following e-mail to me with the subject heading "the strangest thing . . ." from Santoi Wagner (1/23/09 12:57 a.m.), for example, we see evaluation in the subject heading and various other places in the narrative.

(1)   Evaluation in narrative

> . . . just happened while I was working late on the dissertation. Poppy came up to our room at 12.30am and said she needed to go to the bathroom (she doesn't like to go on her own at night). So, I helped her and was expecting to have to (a) coax/cajole/threaten her to go back to her room, (b) go with her to her room, (c) lie down with her in her bed, (d) get really grumpy while she tossed and turned and generally fidgeted, and (e) fall asleep myself and wake up at 4am to go back to my room. BUT, as I was washing my hands, she looked at me, said "Goodnight mummy", waved, and left. I was SHOCKED. She even closed the door to her room (she NEVER closes her door as she is scared of monsters). I really thought something was wrong so I went down and stood outside her door for a few minutes. I admit, it crossed my mind that aliens had taken my Poppy and replaced her with a well-behaved version. So, no noise from her (it's now 12.54)—she must be asleep. Elvis won't believe me when I tell him tomorrow (he slept through it all). This e-mail is evidence that I didn't dream it!!!

As we can see, evaluation is embedded in Santoi's report of what she was expecting—all to the contrary of what actually happened, as signaled by the

Table 2.2 Sample Narrative Structure Analysis

Orientation	a	well, one (I think) was with a girl.
	b	Like I was a kid, you know,
	c	And she was the baddest girl, the baddest girl in the neighborhood.
	d	If you didn't bring her candy to school, she would punch you in the mouth.
	e	And you had to kiss her when she'd tell you.
	f	This girl was only about 12 years old, man,
	g	but she was a killer.
	h	She didn't take no junk;
	i	She whupped all her brothers.
	j	And I came to school one day
	k	and I didn't have no money
	l	My ma wouldn't give me no money.
	m	And I played hookies one day,
	n	(She) put something on me.[1]
	o	I played hookies, man,
	p	so I said, you know, I'm not gonna play hookies no more 'cause I don't wanna get a whupping.
Complication	q	So I go to school.
	r	and this girl says, "Where's the candy?"
	s	I said, "I don't have it."
	t	She says, powww!
Evaluation	u	So I says to myself, "There's gonna be times my mother won't give me money because (we're) a poor family.
	v	And I can't take this all, you know, every time she don't give me any money."
	w	So I say, "Well, I just gotta fight this girl.
	x	She gonna hafta whup me.
	y	I hope she don't whup me."
Resolution	z	And I hit the girl: powwww!
	aa	And I put something on it.
	bb	I win the fight.
Coda	cc	That was one of the most important.

Note: a–cc are labels for individual clauses

capitalized *BUT, SHOCKED,* and *NEVER.* The "strange" sense of the event is further intensified in remarks such as *I really thought something was wrong* and *It crossed my mind that aliens had taken my Poppy and replaced her with a well-behaved version.* Finally, it is solidified in her resolve to document it for her husband who would otherwise not believe her.

According to Labov (1997), the narrative framework is applicable to a wide variety of narratives including "oral memoirs, traditional folk tales, avant garde novels, therapeutic interviews and, most important, the banal narratives of every-day life" (p. 396). He continued,

> Narratives are privileged forms of discourse that play a central role in almost every conversation. Our efforts to define other speech events

with comparable precision have shown us that narrative is the prototype, perhaps the only example of a well formed speech event with a beginning, a middle, and an end.

(p. 396)

In sum, a narrative can be systematically analyzed in terms of its components and how these components relate to one another, and such analysis makes an important contribution to our understanding of how discourse is structured.

Task 1: Consider the following story told by an advanced ESL (English as a Second Language) student Jose (pseudonym) while sharing his travel experience in class: (1) analyze the narrative structure of Jose's story using Labov and Waletzky's (1967) framework (i.e., identify orientation, complication, evaluation, and resolution); (2) given your analysis, discuss the strengths and weaknesses (if any) of this framework in capturing what is going on when one tells a story; (3) evaluate Jose's storytelling competence. (Key: T = teacher; Ss = students; ↑ = raised pitch; ↓ = lowered pitch; $ = smiley voice; hhh = outbreath.)

```
01  Jose:  u::h yes. whe::n I was ↑here in the >United
02         States< after September ele- eleventh. I
03         entered by Chicago? in Decembe:r two::
04         thousand and one? u::h whe::n I::- the- the
05         immigration officer? started to:: ask me di-
06         different things? I ask he:r? that if she can
07         speak slowly? because I::- I couldn't
08         understand? she told me: oka::y? this is
09         United State? we ca:n't (.) speak slowly?
10         You have to understand English?
11  Ss:    hhhh
12  Jose:  so, I try to: understand? (.)
13         I (.) couldn't understand?
14  Ss:    hhh
15  Jose:  so she put me? in the seat? and told me?
16         you have to wait (.) one hour?
17         an' you:: will have an interview with our boss?
18  Ss:    ↓o::.h.
19  Jose:  I- I lost my connection fly? I was afraid?
20         it was $terrible.$
21  Ss:    ↓a:::h. hhh
22  Jose:  yes. Bad experience.
23  T:     °'kay so° that wasn't part of the plan.
```

Conversation (Sacks, Schegloff & Jefferson)

While narrative in the Labovian sense is more or less a monologic event with a beginning, a middle, and an end, the structure of conversation is an entirely different matter—one taken up by conversation analysts. As noted in Chapter 1, championed by sociologists Harvey Sacks, Emmanuel Schegloff, and Gail Jefferson, conversation analysis emerged as a radical approach to sociological inquiry in the 1960s with the aim of uncovering the tacit methods and procedures of social interaction through meticulous examinations of detailed transcripts of audiorecordings or videorecordings. Among its wealth of findings on the sequential structures of ordinary conversation (see Wong & Waring, 2010 for a comprehensive account), we focus on three of the most influential features that have been particularly productive in illuminating our understanding of the conversation structure: adjacency pair, preference, and turn-taking.

Adjacency Pair

Although conversation comprises a series of conversational turns contributed by different participants, the basic unit of conversation is not a turn, but an adjacency pair (AP).

Adjacency pair (AP) is a pair of two turns that are produced by different speakers and ordered as first pair-part (1pp) and second pair-part (2pp), where a particular first pair-part calls for a particular second pair-part.

Some examples of adjacency pairs are question-answer, greeting-greeting, and offer-acceptance/refusal. A question, for example, calls for an answer, and when that answer is not forthcoming or this structural requirement is not fulfilled, the question asker can engage in a variety of practices to pursue that answer, and various attributions such as avoidance or guilt may be directed to the recipient. Although the adjacency pair is a basic unit of conversation, not all conversations are adjacency pair–based; some are structured around larger units such as story or topic. It is also important to note that the pairs are not succeeding actions that invariably occur adjacently. A greeting is not always followed by a return greeting although that return greeting is expected. In other words, the adjacency pair organization is a normative framework, not an empirical generalization. It shapes the expectations, understandings, and actions of interactants. In the following example, when the expectation that summons is answered is not met, the child makes it known by pursuing that missing second pair-part in a louder voice in line 03. (Key: number in parentheses = length of silence in seconds.)

(2) Pursuing missing second pair-part

```
01   Child:      Mom?
02               (1.0)
```

03 Child: → MOM!
04 Mom: I'll be right there.

Conversation is not an aggregate of isolated adjacency pairs. Pairs can hang together in intricate ways. In particular, the base adjacency pair may be expanded upon with a pre-expansion, insert expansion, or post-expansion:

←Pre-expansion

A: First Pair-Part (1pp)

←Insert expansion

B: Second Pair-Part (2pp)

←Post-expansion

Pre-expansion is an adjacency pair that precedes the base adjacency pair. It is generally done to ensure the smooth sailing of the latter. In the following segment, for example, lines 01–02 constitute a pre-expansion designed to check the availability of B before the actual invitation is done in line 03.

(3) Pre-expansion

01 A: → What are you doing after class?
02 B: → Nothing.
03 A: Wanna go shopping?
04 B: Sure.

Insert expansion is an adjacency pair that comes in between a base adjacency pair. Some come after the base first pair-part to seek clarification (see segment (4); data from Schegloff & Lerner, 2004), and some come before the based second pair-part to ensure that the conditions for fulfilling the second pair-part are met. (see segment (5)).

(4) Post-first

01	Debbie:	What i̲s the d̲ea::l	Base 1pp
02	Shelley: →	Whadayou m̲ea::n.	insert 1pp
03	Debbie: →	yuh not gonna go:̲:?	insert 2pp
04		(0.2)	
05	Shelley:	well -hh now: my boss wants ((continues))	Base 2pp

(5) Pre-second

01	A:	What are you doing after class?	Base 1pp
02	B: →	Why?	insert 1pp
03	A: →	Just asking.	insert 2pp
04	B:	Nothing.	Base 2pp

In other words, although both post-first and pre-second occur between the first and second pair-parts of the base adjacency pair, they differ in the specific relationship to that base adjacency pair.

Post-expansion can be minimal or nonminimal. The minimal post-expansion, also referred to as sequencing-closing third, is the one additional turn beyond the second pair-part of the base adjacency pair designed not to project any within-sequence talk beyond itself. Line 03 is an example (Schegloff, 2007, p. 283).

(6) Minimal post-expansion

```
01   Ava:        Where's he goin.
02   Bee:        To Wa:shin'ton.
03   Ava:   →    Oh.
```

Non-minimal post-expansion is typically done when the second pair-part of the base adjacency pair is treated as unfinished, inadequate, or unsatisfactory in some way. In extract (7) (Schegloff, 2007, p. 270), Bee does not accept Ava's response in line 05 and initiates a post-expansion in line 06.

(7) Non-minimal post-expansion

```
01   Bee:        =((line omitted) Yih sound HA:PPY, hh
02   Ava:        I sound ha:ppy?
03   Bee:        Yeeuh.
04               (0.3)
05   Ava:        No:,
06   Bee:   →    Nno:?
07   Ava:   →    No.
```

Here, the expansion is nonminimal in the sense that it consists of a full adjacency pair instead of one single turn. In the next example, we see a series of nonminimal post-expansions as the bus driver in the *New York Times* story refuses to let a woman carry her dog onto the bus.

(8) Non-minimal postexpansion

```
01   Bus Driver:        You can't bring the dog on the bus.
02   Woman:             But I'm carrying him.
03   Bus Driver:   →    You can't bring the dog on the bus.
04   Woman:        →    But he always let me take the dog.
05   Bus Driver:   →    You can't bring the dog on the bus.
06   Woman:        →    I have a shopping bag with me. I'll
07                      put the dog in the bag.
08   Bus Driver:   →    You can't bring the dog on the bus.
```

((After a few minutes of exchanged glares, the woman ceremoniously carried the dog on the bus.))

In a tutoring session, Heidi the tutor pursues Lena the tutee's acceptance by redoing her original first pair-part with a non-minimal post-expansion.

(9) Non-minimal postexpansion

01	Heidi:	You might need to rephrase the questions.
02	Lena:	I don't know, it took us a year and a half to
03		come up with these questions.
04	Heidi: →	Okay, for now maybe just reorganize a bit.
05	Lena: →	Okay I can do that.

Preference

Another important structural feature of conversation is preference. It is important to know that the technical notion of preference in conversation analysis is not a psychological concept referring to one's personal desires or wishes. The dispreferredness in a refusal has nothing to do with the personal preference of the one who refuses (i.e., the person might be dying not to go to the party.).

Preference is an organization in which the alternatives that fit in a certain slot in talk (e.g., second pair-parts in an adjacency pair) are treated as nonequivalent. Some are "preferred"; others are "dispreferred." Preferred actions are the "seen but unnoticed." They are the "natural," "normal" actions. Their absence is noticeable. The absence of the preferred response is basis for inferring the presence of the dispreferred response.

After an invitation, for example, acceptance is preferred, and the absence of acceptance is a basis for inferring the presence of rejection even if there is no explicit rejection. The preference organization has a number of features. First, preferred actions are invited. As in "You've seen this, haven't you?," first pair-parts can be designed to prefer or invite certain seconds (Sacks, 1987), and the tag question invites a *yes* answer. Second, preferred actions promote the course of action of the first pair-part; dispreferred actions impede the course of action of the first pair-part. In an advising sequence, advice is given to be accepted, so the acceptance of advice is preferred over its rejection. Or in a more mundane situation, the best way to end a disagreement is to say *Yes, you're right*. Third, preferred actions are produced in the preferred format without any delay, mitigation, or accounts, and dispreferred actions are produced in the dispreferred format *with* those features. In the following example, for instance, Priya's acceptance of Liam's advice is done quickly with brevity. (Key: ↑ = raised pitch.)

(10) Preferred response in preferred format

01	Liam:		Okay be↑fore I lose this, go through all of
02			those. Periods. Double space.
03	Priya:	→	Oh yeah I will.
04	Liam:		Okay.

By contrast, Lena's resistance of Heidi's advice in the next example is pro-duced with delay (the silence in line 03; *I'll think about it* in line 05), mitiga-tion (laughter in line 05), and an account (*cuz that . . .* in lines 05, 07, and 09–10). (Key: number in parentheses = length of silence in second.)

(11) Dispreferred response in dispreferred format

01	Heidi:		((lines omitted)) Yeah you need to re(.)phrase the
02			questions.
03		→	(0.8)
04			if that's what you (.) wanna do.
05	Lena:	→	I'll think about it. [((laughs)) cuz that-
06	Heidi:		[If- yeah yeah
07	Lena:		You don't know what it- [took (.) for us [to get to
08	Heidi:		[Yeah [I kno:w.
09	Lena:		=these three questions. u- u- you know. Over a
10			year of going back and [forth of different things.
11	Heidi:		[O- O- O-
12			Okay.

Fourth, preferred actions such as acceptance or agreement minimize the threats to "face," maintain social solidarity, and avoid conflicts (Heritage, 1984, p. 265, 1989, pp. 26–27).

Preferred format is the format in which preferred actions are typi-cally delivered—without any delay, mitigation, or accounts; **dispre-ferred format** is the format in which dispreferred actions are typically produced—with delay, mitigation, or accounts.

Preference applies to both first and second pair-parts. For example, in medi-cal encounters, patient-initiated questions tend to be dispreferred. In other words, they are not normal occurrences, and when they do show up, they tend to be produced with delay, mitigation, or accounts. Furthermore, some dis-preferred responses are given in the preferred format, and preferred responses given in the dispreferred format. This happens when one gives a quick and brief "No" to an invitation or hedges on an acceptance. By manipulating the preference structure in these particular ways, the speaker can project an impression of being either uncooperative or extra nice. Finally, what is preferred or dispreferred varies from occasion to occasion. After self-deprecation, disagreement, not agreement, is preferred. In oral proficiency interviews, however, self-deprecation is not responded to with disagreement (Lazaraton, 1997).

Task 2: Consider the beginning of a phone conversation between Debbie and Shelley (Schegloff & Lerner, 2004). Identify all the relevant sequence types (e.g., base sequence and pre-, insert- or post-expansion). Is Shelley's response to Debbie's question in line 06 preferred or dispreferred? What format is the response delivered in—preferred or dispreferred? (Key: number in parentheses = lengths of silence in seconds; > < = quickened pace; < = jump start.)

```
01                ring
02                (5.0)
03   Shelley:     district attorneys office,
04   Debbie:      Shelley:?
05   Shelley:     Debbie?=
06   Debbie:      =what is tha dea::l.
07   Shelley:     whadayou mean.
08   Debbie:      yuh not gonna go::?
09                (0.2)
10   Shelley:     well -hh now: my boss wants me to go: an: uhm finish
11                this >stupid< trial thing,u[hm
12   Debbie:                                [<its not causeuh:m (0.5) Mark's
13                not going.
14   Shelley:     no- well that wuz initially and then I'm like no:
15                I'll just go and then uhm yaknow this- this tow
16                bandit (·) thing that I have, that were doing, [he    w]a:nts
17   Debbie:                                                    [mmhm]
18   Shelley:     ((continues))
```

Turn-Taking

Aside from adjacency pair and preference, another way of appreciating the structure of conversation is by looking at how conversation turns are built and how one person's turn follow that of another's. According to Sacks, Schegloff, and Jefferson (1974), the basic unit of a conversational turn is the turn constructional unit (TCU).

Turn constructional unit (TCU) is the basic unit out of which conversational turns are built. These units can be lexical, phrasal, clausal or sentential. At the end of the end each TCU is the possible completion point (PCP) or transition-relevance place (TRP) where transition to next speaker becomes relevant.

In the following extract (Schegloff & Lerner, 2004), Debbie calls her friend Shelley at the district attorney's office. In line 03, Shelley answers the phone with *district attorney's office*, which is a noun phrase that constitutes a phrasal TCU. (Key: number in parentheses = length of silence in seconds; ↑ = raised pitch.)

(12) TCU

01			((ring))	
02			(5.0)	
03	Shelley:	→	district attorney's office.	phrasal TCU
04	Debbie:	→	Shelley:,	lexical TCU
05	Shelley:		Debbie,=	
06	Debbie:	→	↑what is the dea::l.	sentential TCU
07	Shelley:		what do you ↑mean.	

Each TCU is a possibly complete turn. At the end of each TCU is its possible completion point, where speaker transition becomes relevant:

(1) At a transition-relevance place, a set of rules apply in quick succession:

   a. Current-selects-next.
   b. If not (a), next speaker self-selects.
   c. If not (b), current speaker continues.

(2) Rules 1(a)–1(c) reapplies at each next transition-relevance place.

If the current speaker wants to select the next speaker, she or he is under tremendous pressure to do so before anyone self-selects. By the same token, if anyone wants to self-select, she or he is under tremendous pressure to start early in case the current speaker continues. In fact, self-selectors monitor the unfolding turn very closely and orient to its *possible* (e.g., a point one can predict completion), not actual, completion.

Task 3: Consider the following dinner table conversation with 9-year-old Cindy and her parents (Schegloff & Lerner, 2004). How does each speaker come to have the turn? (Note that the question is not: what does each speaker do with his or her turn?) (1) Did the prior speaker select him or her? If so, how? (i.e., what specific practice is used to do the selection?) (2) Did she or he self-select? If so, how? (3) Did the preceding current speaker continue? If so, how? (Key: number in parentheses = length of silence in seconds.)

```
01  Dad:     So Ci:n (0.2) tell me about your day.
02           (0.5)
03  Cindy:   Uh::.h
04  Dad:     What did you learn.
05           (1.0)
06  Dad:     [O:::H yeah (we) went to the- we went to uh: (.)
07  Cindy:   [Uh:m-
08           Claim Jumper.
09  Dad:     Claim Jum[per today.
10  Mom:              [(uh huh)
11               May I have a roll [please,
12  Cindy:                         [For uh field trip.=
13  Dad:     =Sure.
14           An' may I have thuh- butter please.
15  Mom:     Yes.
16           (0.5)
17  Cindy:   Went to Claim Jumper for (our)/(uh) fie:ld trip.
18  Dad:     Yea:h, an'- an'- tell me about it.
```

As can be seen, there is an elegant systematicity to how conversational turns are built and distributed. The structure of turn-taking revolves around the basic unit of a TCU and the speaker transition opportunities it provides for near or at its end. Proceeding one TCU at a time as such, we can appreciate the reality of conversational turn-taking that is entirely unpredictable when it comes to who gets to speak next, and yet, the machinery that engenders this unpredictability is remarkably systematic at the same time.

Classroom Interaction (Sinclair & Coulthard; Lemke)

So far, we have considered the structures of personal narratives and conversations, which are distinctly different from the structures of institutional interactions such as courtroom hearings, grant proposal review meetings, or office hour appointments. In what follows, we introduce some earlier works on classroom interaction and, more specifically, the notions of IRF and activity types.

Initiation-Response-Feedback/Evaluation (IRF/IRE)

Aside from interest in the structure of mostly mundane talk, earlier discourse analytic work also illuminated the structure of certain institutional discourse. Around the same time sociolinguists were examining narrative structures and conversation analysts conversation structures, a group of British linguists known as the Birmingham School (e.g., Coulthard & Brazil, 1981; Sinclair & Coulthard, 1975) were investigating the structure of classroom discourse and produced one of the most influential findings on classroom discourse—the IRF structure (initiation-response-feedback) (also see IRE(valuation) in Mehan, 1979 and "triadic dialog" in Lemke, 1990).

IRF is a sequential structure of classroom that begins with teacher initiation (I), followed by student response (R), and ends with teacher feedback (F).

In the Birmingham framework, initiation (I), response (R), and feedback (F) are the three moves that make up an exchange—a bundle of turns that hang together. In the following segment (Sinclair & Coulthard, 1975, p. 21), for example, lines 01–04 amount to an exchange, which consists of teacher initiation (I) (line 01), student response (R) (line 03), and teacher feedback (F) (line 04).

(13) IRF

```
01   T:   Can you tell me why do you eat all that food?
02        Yes.
03   S:   To keep you strong.
04   T:   To keep you strong. Yes. To keep you strong.
05        Why do you want to be strong.
```

As in the case of lines 04–05, a single turn can contain more than one move (e.g., feedback and initiation). A move can then be further broken down into acts. Think of acts as the "morphemes" (i.e., smallest unit of meaning) of classroom discourse, and there are a total of 17 acts, according to Sinclair and Coulthard (1975, pp. 40–44), in classroom discourse (see Table 2.3).

The following initiating move contains multiple acts including marker, metastatement, directive, informative, and elicitation (Sinclair & Coulthard, 1975, p. 23).

(14) Move with multiple acts

```
01   T:   Now (marker) I'm going to show you a word (meta statement)
02        and I want you-anyone who can-to tell me if they can tell me
```

03	what the word says (directive). Now it's a bit difficult. It's
04	upside down for some of you isn't it? (informative) anyone
05	think they know what it says (elicitation)?

Put otherwise, the various types of acts are assembled to formulate moves, which are then organized to bring off exchanges (see Table 2.4). As can be seen, not all exchanges are made up of the IRF sequence (e.g., boundary exchange).

As shown, the main exchange types are directing, eliciting, and informing, and there is also the boundary exchange which functions as the hinge that connects the various main exchanges. Table 2.5 specifies the moves within each major exchange (Sinclair & Coulthard, 1975, pp. 56–57).

Table 2.3 Types of Acts

Metainteractive	Interactive	Turn-Taking
• Marker (*now, right, now, good, well*) in falling intonation followed by pause) • Metastatement (*We'll talk about holidays.*) • Loop (*pardon, what did you say?*)	• Informative • Directive • Elicitation • Starter (*What about this?*) • Accept • Acknowledge • React • Reply • Comment • Evaluate	• Cue (*Hands up*) • Bid (hands raised) • Nomination (*Joan*)
	Aside (*Where did I put my chalk?*)	

Table 2.4 Exchanges, Moves, and Acts

EXCHANGES	Directing, Eliciting, and Informing			Boundary	
⬆️ MOVES	Initiation	Response	Feedback	Frame	Focus
⬆️ ACTS	Informative Directive Elicitation Cue Nomination	Acknowledge React Reply *Bid*	Accept Evaluate Comment	Marker	Metastatement

Table 2.5 Major Exchange Types

Directing	Eliciting	Informing
I: Elicit	I: Directive	I: Inform
R: Reply	R: React	R: Acknowledge
F: Accept	Acknowledge	
Evaluate	F: Accept	
Comment	Evaluate	
	Comment	

Task 4: Consider the following segment taken from an adult ESL class: (1) analyze the structure of this interaction using the linguistic approach developed by the Birmingham School (i.e., identify acts, moves, and exchanges); (2) given your analysis, discuss the strengths and weaknesses (if any) of this approach in helping us understand classroom interaction. (Key: number in parentheses = length of silence in seconds; >t <=faster speech; ° ° =quiet speech.)

01 T: Okay.
02   (1.0)
03   Next part.
04   (0.2)
05   Enrico Caruso:: (.) is ((looks up))

((five lines omitted where a student responds, and the teacher accepts that response))

11 T: >Mark would you< do: the AMERICAN Dream?
12 Mark: °Okay.° u:::m American drea:m is–
13 T: >everybody wait uh< wait are we listening?
14 Mark: >American dream< is a car which is 16 feet long.
15 T: which is sixty feet (.) lo:ng.
16 S: °yeah.°
17 Mark: °ah sixty feet.°
18 S: ( )?
19 Mark: Car.
20   (2.0)
21 T: Who has paparazzo.
22 Maria: Me. ((raises hand))

In their ambitious attempt to encapsulate the structure of an entire lesson, the Birmingham School also went beyond the level of exchange onto transaction and, finally, lesson (see Figure 2.1).

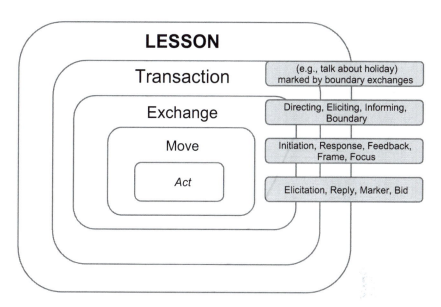

Figure 2.1 Lesson Structure

Activity Types

The structure of classroom discourse can also be described in terms of what Lemke (1990) called the unwritten rules of classroom discourse—a series of activity types: *Going Over the Do Now, Going Over Homework, Review, Teacher Narrative, Demonstration, Teacher Exposition, Triadic Dialog, External Text Dialog, Student-Questioning Dialog, Teacher-Student Duolog, Teacher-Student Debate, True Dialog, Cross-Discussion, Copying Notes, Media Presentation, Seatwork, Boardwork, Groupwork, Labwork, Teacher Summary,* and *Testing.* Some of the activity types are fairly self-explanatory, but four of them warrant some explication. *External text dialog* is a variation of *triadic dialog* (cf. IRF sequence), where a textbook item, for example, plays the role of initiation. *Teacher-student duolog* refers to sustained talk between the teacher and an individual student. *True dialog* occurs when the teacher asks a genuine, rather than a known-answer, question. *Cross-discussion* takes place among the students without any teacher intervention. *True dialog* and *cross-discussion,* as Lemke has observed, are rare in the science classroom. The success of a lesson hinges upon whether whatever activity type as planned by the teacher runs off smoothly as planned.

Task 5: Observe and record a class. On the basis of the data you gathered, offer an example of each of the following if possible: *triadic dialog (external text dialog), teacher-student duolog, true dialog, cross-discussion,* and *teacher-student debate.* If you don't have access to a classroom at the moment, see if you can think of examples based on what you have experienced as a student or instituted as a teacher.

In sum, classroom discourse constitutes a distinct form of talk as manifested in its hierarchical and sequential organizations, its turn-taking system, and its specific set of activity types.

Structure of Text

So far, we have been looking at how earlier discourse analytic work has made important discoveries of the structure of talk in both mundane and institutional settings, but discourse is not limited to talk, and interest in the structure of discourse must inevitably involve understanding the structure of text as well. Just as talk has its own structure, be it narrative, conversation, or classroom interaction, so does text. In this section, we consider three ways in which the structure of text may be examined—through macrostructure, Rhetorical Structure Theory, and cohesive devices.

Macrostructure (van Dijk)

A global understanding of text structure is best captured in Dijk's (1980) classic text on macrostructures.

> **Macrostructure** is a sequence of propositions that explicitly represent the global meaning of a text.

Macrostructures may be informally and intuitively thought of as theme, topic, upshot, or gist. They may be expressed by topical words or sentences, summaries, short paraphrases, and conclusions. The macrostructure of a text is obtained through applying to that text the four macrorules of deletion, selection, generalization, and construction. **Deletion** involves deleting information that is irrelevant for building a macroproposition of the text. In *The meeting went on forever. Outside it was snowing*, for example, the detail of the snowy weather is irrelevant to the topic of the first sentence and of the sequence given the definite article *the*. **Selection** is essentially the flip side of the same rule and involves selecting information relevant to the building of macroproposition of the text. **Generalization** refers to the process of abstracting from the details of the text to build a proposition that is more general. The sequence of *John was playing with his top. Mary was building a sand castle, and Sue was blowing soap bubbles,* for example, can lead to the generalization of *The children are playing.* **Construction** entails substituting local propositions with a macroproposition that denotes a more-or-less stereotypical sequence of events (e.g., frame or script). *I took a plane to New York,* for example, would be a macroproposition that subsumes all kinds of details such as getting the boarding pass, going through the security checkpoints, boarding the plane, and so forth.

Task 6: Consider the following segment taken from a crime story by James Hadley Chase, *Tiger by the Tail* (1966) (Dijk, 1980, p. 52). Identify the macrostructure of this text by applying the macrorules.

a. A tall slim blond in a white summer frock walking just ahead of him, caught Ken Holland's eye.
b. He studied her, watching her gentle undulations as she walked.
c. He quickly shifted his eyes.
d. He hadn't looked at a woman like this since he had first met Ann.
e. What's the matter with me? he asked himself.
f. I'm getting as bad as Parker.
g. He looked again at the blonde.
h. An evening out with her, he thought, would be sensational.
i. What the eye doesn't see, Parker was always saying, the heart doesn't grieve about.
j. That was true.
k. Ann would never know.
l. After all, other married men did it.
m. Why shouldn't he?
n. But when the girl crossed the road and he lost sight of her, he jerked his mind back with an effort to the letter he had received that morning from Ann.
o. She had been away now for five weeks, and she wrote to say that her mother was no better, and she had no idea when she was coming back.

Throughout this process, you may have deleted details such as *white summer frock,* generalized from *caught his eye, studied, watching,* and *shifted his eyes* to *looking at,* and constructed the macroproposition of a *guilty conscience* from *What's the matter with me? he asked himself.* and *I'm getting as bad as Parker.*

According to Dijk (1980), the macrostructure of this particular text consists of the following three macropropositions (p. 56):

a. KH (Ken Holland) is looking at a beautiful girl in the street
    [from (a), (b), (g), (h) by *generalization*].
b. He has a guilty conscience about that because he is married
    [from (c), (d), (e), (f) by *construction*].
c. He is frustrated because his wife is absent (for some weeks to see her ill mother)
    [from (n), (o), and the following fragment, by *construction*].

Analyzing the macrostructure of a text, in other words, allows one to identify its main topics or themes—the very basis for producing summaries of texts.

Rhetorical Structure Theory (Mann & Thompson)

Another descriptive framework designed to understand the organization of text is the **Rhetorical Structure Theory (RST)**, which "identifies hierarchic structure in text" and "describes the relations between text parts in functional terms" (Mann & Thompson, 1988, p. 243). In the earlier stages of developing Rhetorical Structure Theory, Mann and Thompson noticed that texts can generally be broken down into "pair of spans," and the relationship between the two members of each pair were mostly "asymmetric," rendering one span nucleus and the other span satellite, where the nucleus can stand alone (but not vice versa) and is more essential than the satellite (pp. 265–266). In the following text, for example, 1 is the nucleus and 2 the satellite (Mann & Thompson, 1988, p. 251).

(15) Nucleus and satellite

1. The program as published for calendar year 1980 really works.
2. In only a few minutes, I entered all the figures from my 1980 tax return and got a result which agreed with my hand calculation to the penny.

Units of text (i.e., clauses), according to the authors, can relate to other units in a variety of ways, which they describe as an open set of relations in functional terms such as Circumstance, Elaboration, Background, Evidence and Justify, Anthesis and Concession, Interpretation and Evaluation, and Restatement and Summary (Mann & Thompson, 1988, p. 250). In the previous text, for example, 2 is "in an Evidence relation with" 1 (Mann & Thompson, 1988, p. 260). Analyzing the rhetorical structure of a text, in other words, largely involves identifying these relations.

Cohesive Devices (Halliday & Hasan)

While macrostructure and Rhetorical Structure Theory offer us tools for obtaining the main topics and identifying the rhetorical relationships among various parts of a text, the structure of a text is also analyzable at a more local level. How do we recognize and produce a text in the first place? Would any string of sentences amount to a text? An important (although not the only) resource for creating textuality or "the feeling that something is a text, and not just a random collection of sentences" (McCarthy, 1991, p. 35) is the use of a set of cohesive devices (Halliday & Hasan, 1976).

> **Cohesive devices** are a set of lexical and grammatical items used to link various parts of a text together to create a sense of coherence. These include reference, substitution, ellipsis, conjunction, and lexical cohesion.

Think of cohesive devices as the glue that holds pieces of wood together to create, for example, a bookcase, except that they are holding sentences together to create a text or sense of textuality. **References** are items that cannot be interpreted in their own right but point to the surrounding text for their interpretation. The three types of references in English are personals (e.g., *she, my, theirs*), demonstratives (e.g., *this, those, here*), and comparatives (e.g., *same, more, fewer*). References may be pointing to preceding or ensuing text. The reference that points to preceding text is called **anaphoric** reference, and that pointing to following text **cataphoric** reference. In *He spoke. This is very strange*, for example, the anaphoric reference *This* points to be preceding text *He spoke*. On the other hand, *This* becomes a cataphoric reference in *This is very strange. He spoke*. The function of anaphoric reference appears to be efficiency, and that of cataphoric reference engaging the reader's attention.

A second type of cohesive device is **substitution**—the replacement of one item by another. There are three types of substitution: nominal (*one, ones, some*), verbal (*do*), and clausal (*so, not*). Nominal substitutions replace noun phrase, verbal substitutions verb phrases, and clausal substitutions clauses:

- Nominal: She'll eat the **grapes**—especially the seedless **ones**.
- Verbal: I'd be happy to **help**, but I can't **do** Mondays.
- Clausal: Do you think **we'll get the grant**? Hope **so**.

A third type of cohesive device is **ellipsis**—the omission of an item, and what gets omitted can be nominal, verbal, or clausal as well:

- Nominal: Nelly liked the green tiles; I preferred the blue **(tiles)**.
- Verbal: The children will carry the small boxes, the adults **(will carry)** the larger ones.
- Clausal: She said she would speak up as soon as she could **(speak up)**, and he has **(spoken up)**.

A fourth type of cohesive device is **conjunction**, which includes addictive conjunctions (e.g., *and, in addition*), adversative conjunctions (e.g., *but, however*), causal conjunctions (e.g., *because, consequently*), temporal conjunctions (e.g., *then, subsequently*).

The final type of cohesion is **lexical** (i.e., using a different lexical item to express the same meaning), which can be repetition, antonyms (a word that has the opposite meaning of a given word), metonyms (a word that denotes one thing but relates to a different thing: Washington D.C. for the United States government), and hyponyms (a word that is more specific than a given word).

In the following passage taken from C. S. Lewis's (1960) *The Four Loves*, we observe multiple instances of cohesive ties.

(16) Cohesive ties

"God is love," says St. John. When I first tried to write this book I thought that his maxim would provide me with a very plain highroad through the whole subject. I thought I should be able to say that human loves deserved to be called love at all just in so far as they resembled that LOVE which is God. The first distinction I made was therefore between what I called Gift-love and Need-love. The typical example of Gift-love would be that love which moves a man to work and plan and save for the future well-being of his family which he will die without sharing or seeing; of the second, that which sends a lonely or frightened child to its mother's arms.

(p. 11)

As can be seen, *his* in the second sentence is a reference pointing back to *St. John* in the first, and *his maxim* is a substitution for *God is love*. Towards the end of the paragraph, *of the second* is an elliptical version *of the second type of love*. Throughout the passage, we also notice examples of lexical cohesion in the repeated mention of *love*. Without such cohesive ties, the sense of textuality that permeates Lewis's writing would no doubt be compromised.

Task 7: Identify the cohesive devices in the following text taken from Charles Dickens's *A Tale of Two Cities*. Discuss how they contribute to a sense of textuality or, alternatively, how their absence may render the text "less textual."

It was the best of times, it was the worst of times, it was the age of wisdom, it was the age of foolishness, it was the epoch of belief, it was the epoch of incredulity, it was the season of Light, it was the season of Darkness, it was the spring of hope, it was the winter of despair, we had everything before us, we had nothing before us, we were all going direct to Heaven, we were all going direct the other way—in short, the period was so far like the present period, that some of its noisiest authorities insisted on its being received, for good or for evil, in the superlative degree of comparison only.

(p. 1)

In sum, the structure of text is analyzable by identifying its sequence of topics (macrostructure), the relationships among its various idea units (Rhetorical Structure Theory), and the various devices that enable its sense of connectedness (cohesive devices). For a recent discussion on cohesion and texture, see Martin (2015).

Structure of Nonverbal Conduct

As noted in Chapter 1, discourse is not limited to talk and text but encompasses such nonverbal conduct as gaze, gesture, and body movement as well. In this section, we briefly introduce some early work on the structural features of these nonverbal elements.

Gaze (Kendon)

In his seminal study on gaze direction, the experimental psychologist Kendon (1967) filmed conversations between undergraduate dyads at the University of Oxford who were asked to "get to know one another other" for half an hour. His meticulous documentation and analyses yield the following patterns of gaze:

Speaker Gaze

- Speaker gazes less than recipient.
- Speaker gazes less during silence or slower speech than during faster speech.
- Speaker tends to look away at the beginning of a long utterance and look up at listener as the end of the utterance approaches.

Recipient Gaze

- Recipient looks at speaker when producing an attention signal but looks away when producing an agreement signal.
- Recipient looks at speaker when asking a question.
- Recipient looks at speaker during laughter and positive exclamation but looks away during negative exclamation.

General Observations

- Mutual gazes tend to be short.
- One can look away at points of high emotion to perform a "cutoff" act.

Gesture (McNeal)

Three types of gestures have been documented in the literature: head movements, facial gestures, and hand gestures. Head movements may be vertical or lateral. Facial gestures, on the other hand, can take on descriptors such as "thinking face" or what Streeck and Hartge (1992) called [a] face in Ilokano storytelling. The most extensive descriptions have been devoted to hand gestures. According to McNeil (1992), there are six types hand gestures:

1. Iconic gestures: representation of action or object
2. Metaphoric gestures: representation of an abstraction
3. Beats: quick movements at meta-level of discourse
4. Cohesive gestures: tying together thematically related materials
5. Deictic gestures: pointing to real or abstract space
6. Butterworths: gestures that result from speech failure.

Body Movement (Goodwin)

As Schegloff (1998) noted, body movement includes a variety of large-scale movements (as compared with hand gestures, for example) that involve the arms, legs, upper and lower bodies, and so forth. Goodwin (2000) distinguished body movement from gesture, specifying that body movements are characterized by longer temporal duration than that of gestures. In addition, while gestures function as individual actions or components of multimodal actions, body movements build participation frameworks that frame a variety of actions. Body torque, for example, is one type of body movement that can be utilized to manage multiple courses of actions (see Chapter 5).

> **Body torque** is one type of body movement that refers to divergent orientations of the body sectors above and below the neck and waist respectively.

In sum, our understanding of the structure of nonverbal conduct begins with how such conduct is distributed (gaze), categorized (hand gestures), or documented in specific descriptive terms (body movement).

Key Points

- Earlier work on discourse and structure addressed narrative structure, conversation structure, classroom discourse structure, text structure, and the structure of nonverbal conduct.

- Narrative structure entails such key components as orientation, complication, evaluation, and resolution, with evaluation being the crucial ingredient that advances the point of the story.
- Adjacency pair as a basic unit of conversational sequence consists of a first pair-part that makes relevant the production of second pair-part (e.g., invite-accept).
- Preferred actions are the "expected" actions typically produced without any delay, mitigation, or accounts (e.g., acceptance); dispreferred actions are the "unexpected" actions typically produced with delay, mitigation, or accounts (e.g., rejection).
- Turn constructional unit is a basic unit of a conversational turn; the possible completion point of a turn constructional unit presents opportunities for speaker transition or a transition-relevance place.
- Classroom discourse structure features IRF/IRE and various activity types.
- Macrostructure, a sequence of macropropositions that represents the global meaning of a text, can be identified by applying the rules of deletion, selection, generalization, and construction.
- Rhetorical Structure Theory is a descriptive framework for identifying the functional relationships between clauses in a text.
- Cohesive devices are items that contribute to creating a sense of textuality and include reference, substitution, ellipses, conjunction, and lexical cohesion.
- Nonverbal conduct includes gaze, gesture, and body movement.
- Speaker and recipient gaze follow systematic patterns.
- Gestures may involve the head, the face, and the hand; there are six types of hand gestures.
- Body movements are larger scale movements that involve multiple parts of the body with longer temporal durations.

Note

1 To put something on someone means to "to hit him hard."

References

Coulthard, M., & Brazil, D. (1981). Exchange structure. In M. Coulthard & M. Montgomery (Eds.), *Studies in discourse analysis* (pp. 82–106). London: Routledge & Kegan Paul.

Dickens, C. (1999). *A tale of two cities* (J. Nord, Ed.). Mineola, NY: Dover Publications.

Dijk, T. A. van (1980). Macrostructures: An interdisciplinary study of global structures in discourse, interaction, and cognition. Hillsdale, NJ: Lawrence Erlbaum Associates.

Goodwin, C. (2000). Action and embodiment within situated human interaction. *Journal of Pragmatics, 32*, 1489–1522.

Halliday, M. A. K., & Hasan, R. (1976). *Cohesion in English*. London: Longman.

Heritage, J. (1984). *Garfinkel and ethnomethodology*. Oxford: Basil Blackwell.

Heritage, J. (1989). Current developments in conversation analysis. In D. Roger & P. Bull (Eds.), *Conversation: An interdisciplinary perspective* (pp. 21–47). Clevedon: Multilingual Matters.

Kendon, A. (1967). Some functions of gaze direction in social interaction. *Acta Psychological, 26,* 22–63.

Labov, W. (1972). *Language in the inner city.* Philadelphia, PA: University of Pennsylvania Press.

Labov, W. (1997). Some further steps in narrative analysis. *Journal of Narrative and Life History, 7,* 395–415. Mahwah: Lawrence Erlbaum Associates.

Labov, W., & Waletzky, J. (1967). Narrative analysis: Oral versions of personal experience. In J. Helm (Ed.), *Proceedings of the 1966 annual spring meeting of the American Ethnological Society* (pp. 12–44). Seattle and London: University of Washington Press.

Lazaraton, A. (1997). Preference organization in oral proficiency interviews: The case of language ability assessment. *Research on Language and Social Interaction, 30*(1), 53–72.

Lemke, J. L. (1990). *Talking science: Language, learning, and values.* Norwood, NJ: Ablex.

Lewis, C. S. (1960). *The four loves.* New York: Harcourt Brace.

McCarthy, M. (1991). *Discourse analysis for language teachers.* Cambridge: Cambridge University Press.

McNeil, D. (1992). *Hand and mind.* Chicago: University of Chicago Press.

Mann, W., & Thompson, S. (1988). Rhetorical structure theory: Toward a functional theory of text organization. *Text, 8*(3), 243–281.

Martin, J. R. (2015). Cohesion and texture. In D. Tannen, H. E. Hamilton, & D. Schiffrin (Eds.), *The handbook of discourse analysis* (2nd ed.) (pp. 61–81). Malden, MA: Wiley Blackwell.

Mehan, H. (1979). *Learning lessons: Social organization in the classroom.* Cambridge, MA: Harvard University Press.

Sacks, H. (1987). On the preferences for agreement and contiguity in sequences in conversation. In G. Button & J. R. E. Lee (Eds.), *Talk and social organization* (pp. 54–69). Clevedon: Multilingual Matters.

Sacks, H., Schegloff, E. A., & Jefferson, G. (1974). A simplest systematics for the organization of turn-taking for conversation. *Language, 50*(4), 696–735.

Schegloff, E. A. (1998). Body torque. *Social Research, 65*(3), 535–596.

Schegloff, E. A. (2007). *Sequence organization in interaction: A primer in conversation analysis* (Vol. 1). Cambridge: Cambridge University Press.

Schegloff, E. A., & Lerner, G. (2004). [Transcript data]. Conversation Analysis Advanced Study Institute, University of California, Los Angeles.

Sinclair, J. M., & Coulthard, M. (1975). *Towards an analysis of discourse: The English used by teachers and pupils.* London: Oxford University Press.

Streeck, J., & Hartge, U. (1992). Previews: Gestures at the transition place. In P. Auer & A. di Luzio (Eds.), *The contextualization of language* (pp. 135–158). Amsterdam: John Benjamins.

Wong, J., & Waring, H. Z. (2010). *Conversation analysis and second language pedagogy.* New York: Routledge.

3 Empirical Endeavors in Discourse and Structure

Introduction

In this chapter, we sample some empirical endeavors in the investigation of discourse and structure that answer such questions as (1) how grammar constitutes a key resource for structuring narratives and organizing interaction, (2) how different text types or genres are structured and how such structures may vary across communities and, finally, (3) how gaze and gesture are describable by their own structural properties.

Grammar

As Mithun (2015) wrote, "A full understanding of the discourse structures of a language depends on the recognition of the grammatical devices that signal them" (p. 12). In this section, we show how discourse analysts have illuminated how grammatical devices signal the structure of discourse and, more specifically, how tense variations contribute to the structuring of narratives and grammatical units to the organization of social interaction.

Tense Variation to Structure Narratives

Students of English as a Second Language ESL are often taught to tell stories in the past tense—a rule sometimes enforced by their teachers. It can come as a surprise to these learners that storytelling in English is often not done in the past tense. Consider the following story about the teller's stepfather finding a fly in his coffee and not paying for it (Schegloff & Lerner, 2004).

(1) Fly in coffee (modified from the original transcript)

> He's drinking a cup of coffee, and there's this fly on the bottom. He goes "JESUS CHRIST!" He stands up: "Oh my God. WAITRESS! WAITRESS!" His waitress comes over, and he says, "There's a fly. I'm not paying for none of this, right?" He didn't pay for any of it.

Note that in recounting the story, the teller uses not the past tense, but exclusively the simple present (or more precisely present tense in its simple aspect) in setting up and describing the scene. This present tense used in storytelling is referred to in the sociolinguistic literature as the historical present (HP).

Historical present (HP) refers to the present tense used to refer to past events—a common occurrence in storytelling.

The sociolinguist Nessa Wolfson (1978) conducted the first study on how HP is used in everyday conversational interaction—a usage she termed conversational historical present (CHP). Wolfson succinctly articulated the relationship between discourse and structure as such: "It is only through the study of language *use* that one may fully analyze the linguistic structure just as one must understand the linguistic structure in order to uncover the rules of its use" (p. 215). Essentially then, Wolfson is asking: what are the rules of use for the CHP?

To answer this question, Wolfson uses what she called an ethnographic approach to both the data collection and analysis. She sampled a range of speech situations collected over 150 taped and transcribed stories told in real-life everyday situations. On the basis of these data, she observed that CHP or, more precisely, the alternation between CHP and the past tense is a feature of a performed narrative.

Performed narrative refers to a narrative that contains a range of co-occurring dramatizing features such as direct speech, repetition, expressive sounds, and gestures along with the alternation between CHP and the past tense.

Notably, the common explanation that CHP is used to make past actions come alive fails to account for Wolfson's data. While background information and asides to the audience are always delivered in the past, the narrative events themselves are depicted in either CHP or the past tense, and it is the *switch* into either tense that is significant. Such switch serves to partition important events, give structure to the story, and focus audience attention to what the narrator sees as important events, yielding a dramatic theatrical effect analogous to that of the change of lighting on stage. In the following snippets from a story about how the narrator just bought a house for a very good price, for example, the switching of tenses partitions and dramatizes the narrative events (Wolfson, 1978, pp. 219–220).

(2)   Tense switch

    a.   So he **calls** me up the next day and I **told** my wife exactly what to say.

b. So he **picks** up the agreement—all of a sudden he **looked** at the agreement. He **says**, "Well," he **says**, . . . "This date was changed."

Wolfson's argument is in part based on the co-occurrence of CHP-past switch with other dramatizing devices such as direct speech and expressive gestures. She also uses descriptive statistics such as frequencies and percentages to establish the regularity of CHP use in performed stories as well as the relationship between the use of CHP and other variables, showing that CHP is used more when the story involves the interaction between two or more individuals; when the teller and recipient share background such as gender, age, ethnicity; and when the story is about events that have occurred very recently. In addition, she uses inferential statistics such as the chi-square to confirm the strength of her results. In the end, Wolfson reiterated that the ethnographic method she adopted is the only reliable approach for studying a phenomenon such as CHP in performed narratives.

While largely confirming Wolfson's findings, on the basis of an analysis of 73 personal-experience narratives, Schiffrin (1981) went further to show that the direction of the switch does in fact matter: it is only the switch from HP to past that partitions important events; the switch from past to HP, on the other hand, does evaluation. In yet another study on tense variations, Johnstone (1987) focused specifically on a puzzle unresolved in Wolfson (1978); namely, the unaccounted-for tense switch between dialog introducers such as *says* and *said.*

Task 1: In the following narrative taken from Johnstone (1987, p. 34), a young woman is telling the story of her encounter with a police officer who stopped her on the road. Pay attention to how the speech of the narrator and the police officer is introduced respectively. Write down any observations you have.

And then **I said** what's the problem here?
He says well ma'am . . . ah . . . you didn't stop for that stop sign back there
I mean I was mad
I said WHAT
and **he says** . . . he says
it's the In–
he just starts off rattling
it's the Indi– Indiana State Law you must come to a complete stop . . .
    before the stop sign da da da da
I said I did
I said there's a crosswalk there and the thing's before that
I said where were you sitting anyway [laugh]
he says I was right in that parking lot by the church

and that parking lot's right back here [indicating on table]
you can't even see the stop sign
I said I'm sorry
I said you didn't see me
he said it's the Indiana State Law da da da da da

One pattern you might have noticed from examining the previous tran-script is that throughout the story, the police officer's speech is introduced by the present tense form *says*, and the narrator's own speech by the past tense form *said*. In fact, Johnstone makes a similar observation on the basis of 13 first-person "authority" stories, where the narrator recounts interactions with an authority figure. As it turns out, the nonauthority's speech is always introduced in the past tense, and the authority's speech is introduced either in the HP or not introduced at all (ɸ), as in the following story that involves the narrator's interaction with an older neighbor (Johnstone, 1987, p. 40).

(3)   Tense and dialog introducer

Misses Czinski's got her house coat on
And down the lawn by then . . . you know
ɸ What's going on here Carol? [raised pitch]
I said it's okay
I said this . . . this guy says he saw something
And he can't even see it from where he's parked anyway [laughs]

The tense variation in dialog introducers, in other words, plays an interest-ing role in structuring the story to some extent and marking the status dif-ferentiations of the characters in the story. Overall, the grammatical feature of tense variation can be arranged to dramatize a story, highlight evaluation, and distinguish characters.

Grammatical Units to Organize Interaction

Aside from structuring narratives, grammar is also a key resource for organiz-ing interaction—a position eloquently argued for by interactional linguists (Couper-Kuhlen & Ford, 2004; Couper-Kuhlen & Selting, 1996; Ford & Thompson, 1996).

Interactional linguistics is an interdisciplinary field founded by a group of linguists who drew upon conversation analysis to respecify the traditional domains of linguistics, arguing that grammar can only be understood and analyzed in its natural habitat of social interaction.

The relationship between grammar and interaction is in part captured in Thompson and Couper-Kuhlen's (2005) cross-linguistic argument that the clause is a basic unit that participants in an interaction rely upon to discern what the other person is saying, whether she or he has finished saying that, and when to start talking. In building this argument, they offer a range of evidence from both English and Japanese, showing how participants rely on the clausal unit to manage when and how to begin talking, complete another's utterance, and extend one's own utterance. In both English and Japanese, for example, the next speaker can start talking precisely when the prior speaker's clause has come to a completion (Thompson & Couper-Kuhlen, 2005, pp. 491–492). (Key: (h) or .hh = inhalation; .. = short pause; (h) or (H) = inhalation; bold = English translation of Japanese data.)

(4a) Next-turn onset English

```
01   G:   .. (H) the only thing you can do is the best you can.
02        .. [right?        ]
03   D:      [but definitely].
```

(4b) Next-turn onset Japanese

```
01   H:   =hijooni:: (.) uitotta n desu kedo
          (I) really stood out
02        [watashi tte..hh e(h)e.hh
          as for me .hh e(h)e .hh
03   I:   [iya sonna koto nai n chau?
          No, that couldn't be, could it?
```

The clause is also a unit the participants orient to when they jointly complete each other's utterances. They either jointly complete a mono-clausal unit as shown in segment (5a) or supply a second clausal component of a multiclausal unit as shown in segment (5b) (Thompson & Couper-Kuhlen, 2005, pp. 493–494).

(5a) Joint utterance completion Japanese

```
01   H:        asoko o:: (0.2) teteteto orite[itta]ra shoomen ni:.=
               If you go down there, in front of you,
02   K:                                       [u:n]
                                              Uh huh.
03   K:        =u:n.
               Uh huh.
04   H:        denwa ga- ano mi[dori] no denwa ga:[:]
               Phones, uhm, green phones
05   K:   →                     [aru]              [a]ru aru
                                 are there.        are there, are there.
```

(5b) Joint utterance completion English

```
01   R:        if you don't put things on yer calendar
```

[preliminary component]
02   (.)
03   D: →   yer outta luck. [secondary component]

Finally, by monitoring the development and completion of clauses in real time, participants in both English and Japanese also find an anchor for extending their turns. They both time their extensions to fit the endings of clauses. Given that clauses are built differently in the two languages, turn extensions are done differently as well. In English, a typical increment or turn extension is an adverbial phrase tagged onto an already completed clause, which is a typical position of an adverbial phrase in a clause as shown in segment (6a). In Japanese, turn extensions come in the form of a noun phrase not made explicit in the just completed clause, as shown in segment (6b) (Thompson & Couper-Kuhlen, 2005, p. 496). (Key: number in parentheses = length of silence in seconds; @ = laughter.)

(6a) Turn extension English

01   Guy: W'why don'I: uh (0.6) I'll call uh (.)
02   Have you got(.) uh: Seacliffs phone number? h
03   (1.1)
04   →   by any chance?
05   (0.3)
06   Jon: Yeeah?

(6b) Turn extension Japanese

01   R: soshitara @ oo- asokoi ikanakatta – n da tte.
           I hear (she) didn't go (to) Au- there then
02   [oosutora]riai akichan
           Australia Aki
03   H: [doko e]?
           to where?

Thus, in answering the overarching question of how discourse is structured, discourse analysts have shown how grammatical resources such as tense variations and clausal units contribute to the structuring of narratives and the organization of interaction. Put otherwise, the discourse of narrative and interaction is structured in part by manipulating tense variations and monitoring clausal units. For further discussions on a wider range of ways in which grammar functions in discourse, and in interaction in particular, see Auer and Pfander (2011), Ford (1993), Ochs, Schegloff, and Thompson (1996), and Selting and Couper-Kuhlen (2001).

Genre

Aside from grammar, another major area in which to find the answer to how discourse is structured is the study of genre.

Genre refers to text types used to achieve certain communicative purposes in a way that is recognizable and acceptable for other members of a given discourse community (i.e., a group of people who have texts and practices in common) (Hyland, 2008; Swales, 1990).

According to Swales (1990), a **discourse community** has a broadly agreed upon set of common public goals with mechanisms of intercommunication among its members primarily to provide information and feedback. A discourse community features one or more genres (e.g., research logs or lab reports for a team of biologists) along with specific lexis, and the members of a discourse community are equipped with a threshold level of relevant knowledge and discoursal expertise. A related term is Community of Practice (CofP) (Wenger, 1998, p. 45).

Community of Practice (CofP) is a community created over time by a sustained pursuit of a shared enterprise.

A community of practice has three dimensions: (1) mutual engagement (regular interaction), (2) joint enterprise (shared goals), and (3) shared repertoire (ways of talking and doing; experiences, stories, tools, ways of addressing recurring problems) (Wenger, 1998, pp. 72–85). *The Language and Social Interaction Working Group (LANSI)* at Teachers College, Columbia University, for example, may be considered a discourse community or a community of practice with its public aim of forging dialogs among, and sharpening analytical skills for, scholars and students of language and social interaction. We share information and feedback with each other through our listserv, Facebook and Twitter accounts, monthly data sessions, and annual international conference. We share a certain level of expertise in matters of language and social interaction and speak a language that individuals outside the community may at times find foreign or even amusing. A text type or genre that is certainly recognizable to members of LANSI is discourse analytic studies that contain transcripts with varying degrees of details.

Task 2: Using the definition of genre, (1) list five examples of genre, and for each, identify its communicative purpose and discourse community; (2) discuss whether the following are examples of genre: personal statement, personal ad, résumé, lesson plan, and State of the Union address. Why or why not?

Now that we have developed an initial understanding of what genre is, the next question is: how can genre be analyzed?

Doing Genre Analysis

Genre analysis refers to the analysis of text types that involves identifying (1) the **moves** (e.g., 'thanking' move) within the text and/ or (2) features of language use (e.g., self-mention) of that text, where **a move is a "rhetorically distinct sub-purpose"** within a text (Hyland, 2008, p. 544).

To illustrate how genre analysis is done, we may begin with the example of Pho's (2008) examination of how research article abstracts are structured, where the author collected 30 abstracts from three major journals (two in applied linguistics and one in educational technology), all of which are related to the broad field of teaching and learning. On the basis of a close reading of the 30 abstracts, Pho (2008) identified the following five functional or rhetorical moves, of which (2)-(4) are obligatory (p. 235):

(1) Situating the research (STR)
    (e.g., *Several studies have been conducted related to . . .*)
(2) Presenting the research (PTR)
    (e.g., *This article reports on a study investigating . . .*)
(3) Describing the methodology (DTM)
    (e.g., *The sample consists of . . .*)
(4) Summarizing the findings (STF)
    (e.g., *Results indicate that . . .*)
(5) Discussing the research (DTR)
    (e.g., *We suggest that . . .*).

The author also specifies how each move is executed by describing its linguistic realizations and authorial stances. The rhetorical moves, for example, can be distinguished by what constitute their grammatical subjects. While reference to others' work (e.g., *Several studies have shown that . . .*) is typically found in STR (situating the research), reference to the writer's own work becomes prominent in the STF (summarizing the findings). She also found that across all three journals, DTM (describing the methodology) is always done in the past tense (e.g., *The sample consisted of . . .*) and DTR (discussing the research) always in the present (e.g., *Findings suggest that . . .*). In addition, the moves are distinguished by how the author's voice or stance (i.e., attitude or judgment toward X) is expressed. While PTR and DTM (presenting the research and describing the methodology) are devoid of authorial stance, the author's stance is shown in STR (situating the research) via adjectives and adverbs that emphasize the importance of the topic (e.g., *Language learning motivation plays an important role in. . . .*). Words of epistemic stance (e.g., *possibly*) are found in STF (summarizing the findings), and modals and semi-modals are used in DTR (discussing the research) as hedging or boosting devices.

In sum, understanding the genre of research article abstract entails knowing what the rhetorical components of an abstract are, what linguistic devices are engaged to realize these components, and how and where the author's voice or stance may be expressed. Such knowledge would facilitate the learning of how to write a research article abstract—a skill often assumed rather than explicitly taught to graduate students from both English-speaking and non-English-speaking countries who are training to become future researchers.

Task 3: Identify the rhetorical moves, linguistic realizations, and authorial stances in the following abstract from Reddington and Waring (2015) and consider how well they fit the findings of Pho (2008).

Humor scholars have made great strides in identifying markers of humor such as prosody and laughter as well as the various social functions of humor in both everyday talk and workplace communication. Less research has been devoted to understanding the mechanisms of humor or how humor is done in naturally occurring interaction. Based on videotaped data from adult English-as-a-second-language (ESL) classrooms, we describe a specific set of sequential resources for producing humor in the language classroom and do so within a conversation analytic framework. We also give some preliminary consideration to the applicability of the findings in other interactional contexts as well as to the question of whether participants are oriented towards moments of humor as opportunities for language learning.

Variations of Genre

Given that genre is a text type recognizable to a particular discourse community, it is not surprising that the same text type may vary in features across, for example, disciplines and cultures. Discourse analysts have done interesting work showing such variations.

Genre Across Academic Fields

Hyland (2008), for example, compared research articles in "soft" knowledge fields (humanities and social sciences) with those in hard sciences and found that approximately 75% of all the features that mark author visibility (e.g., self-mention, personal evaluation, and explicit interaction with readers) occur in soft knowledge fields. As Hyland pointed out, this might not be surprising, as hard science fields represent findings from the laboratory without recourse to rhetoric. However, as Hyland argued, what hard science engages is simply a different kind of rhetoric. He highlighted three features that distinguish research articles in soft fields such as applied linguistics and sociology from those in hard sciences such as biology and engineering. In soft fields, for example, writers use more hedges and boosters to make their argument (see hedge examples in 7a and 7b). In hard sciences, on the other hand, writers prefer the use of modal verbs over cognitive verbs to minimize the researcher's role in the investigative process given their greater reliance on methods and procedures and equipment rather than argument (see 7c) (Hyland, 2008, p. 551).

(7) Hedges vs. modals

   a.   We tentatively suggest that The Sun's minimalist style creates an impression of working-class language, or restricted code . . . (applied linguistics)
   b.   As far as I know, this account has gone unchallenged. (philosophy)
   c.   The deviations at high frequencies may have been caused by the noise measurements (electronic engineering)

In addition, writers in soft fields often rely more on citations to build their argument. A more interesting difference, however, lies in the types of verbs used to report others' work:

Among the higher frequency verbs, almost all instances of *say* and 80% of *think* occurred in philosophy and 70% of *use* in electronics. It turns out, in fact, that engineers *show*, philosophers *argue*, biologists *find* and applied linguists *suggest*.

(Hyland, 2008, p. 553)

While soft fields feature verbs that refer to the writing activities such as *discuss, hypothesize, suggest*, and *argue*, hard science writings are populated with verbs referring to real-world actions that direct attention to the research itself such as *observe, discover, show, analyze*, and *calculate*.

Finally, writers in soft fields rely more on self-mention to emphasize own contributions (see 8a and 8b); whereas hard science writing tends to minimize self-mention for the purpose of establishing objectivity (see 8c and 8d) (Hyland, 2008, p. 555).

(8) Self-mention

   a.   **I argue** that their treatment is superficial because, despite appearances, it relies solely on a sociological, as opposed to an ethical, orientation to develop a response.

(sociology)

b. I bring to bear on the problem my own experience. This experience contains ideas derived from reading I have done which might be relevant to my puzzlement as well as my personal contacts with teaching contexts.

(applied linguistics)

c. It was found that a larger stand-off height would give a smaller maximum shear strain when subjected to thermal fatigue . . .

(mechanical engineering)

d. The images demonstrate that the null point is once again well resolved and that diffusion is symmetric.

(mechanical engineering)

Task 4: Consider Hyland's (2008) findings on how research articles in soft fields and hard sciences differ in the use of hedges and boosters, citations, and self-mention. Are these findings useful? If so, how?

Genre Across Cultures

One text type that appears to vary across cultures is that of expository writing. Expository writing in English is believed to follow a linear structure. One of the earlier works on tackling such a structure was done by the linguist A. L. Becker. In his 1965 article on the analysis of expository paragraph structures, Becker called attention to two major patterns of structures: TRI (topic-restriction-illustration) and PS (problem-solution). The first pattern TRI has three functional slots representing three levels of generality, each of which may be filled in various ways:

* Topic: statement of topic
* Restriction: restatement or clarification
* Illustration: support for topic by exemplification.

In a paragraph in Chapter 2 of this book on narrative structures, for example, we find an instance of the TRI structure.

(9) TRI paragraph structure

(T) Unlike the structure of a narrative with a linear organization with its own beginning, middle, and end, the structure of conversation cannot be described in such linear terms. (R) Although conversation comprises a series of conversational turns contributed by different participants, the basic unit of conversation is not a turn, but an adjacency pair, which is a pair of two turns that are produced by different speakers and ordered as first pair-part (1pp) and second pair-part (2pp), where a particular first pair-part calls for a particular second pair-part. (I) Some examples of adjacency pairs are question-answer, greeting-greeting, and offer-acceptance/refusal. A question, for example, calls for an answer, and when that answer is not forthcoming or this structural requirement not fulfilled, the question asker can engage in a variety of practices to pursue that answer, and various attributions such as avoidance or guilt may be directed to the recipient.

As can be seen, the topic (T) of the structure of conversation is first clarified (R) with the specification of its basic unit of adjacency pair and then further exemplified (I) with examples of adjacency pairs.

The PS or problem-solution structure, on the other hand, has two functional slots:

- Problem (P): statement of a problem or an effect to be explained
- Solution (S): statement of solution or cause of the effect.

The following paragraph taken from a children's nonfiction book *Sun, Earth and Moon*, for example, exhibits the PS structure.

(10) PS paragraph structure

(P) Why do we have season? **(S)** The earth orbits, or goes around, the Sun once a year. The Sun is very hot. SO, the part that faces the sun and gets the most rays is lighter and warmer. That's the part that gets summer.

Here the problem (P) of why we have seasons is solved (S) with an explanation of how the earth orbits the sun. The S slot in the PS structure, as Becker noted, is very often fulfilled in turn by a TRI structure, and these two patterns of TRI and PS may vary by four types of operations: deletion, reordering, addition, and combination. The R(estriction) slot, for example, is sometimes deleted, especially in lower quality writing. The TRI pattern may also be reordered as IRT at the beginning or end of an essay to create a sense of closure for the paragraph. The T slot may also be repeated at the end of TRI to render the paragraph less open-ended especially when the discourse is long and complicated. Finally, paragraphs may be combined to yield a structure such as P-S1-S2, where P-S1 and P-S2 would be either contrastive or parallel.

Task 5: Consider the "Review of Colorado" written by 6-year-old Zoe. Analyze the paragraph structure of this piece using Becker's

(1965) framework and evaluate Zoe's competence as a writer on the basis of your analysis.

> Come on everybody, come down to Colorado where you can have excitement while you hang out! You should go to Colorado because you will have a fantastic time! First, Colorado is a great place to go for skiing. At Crested Butte, you get to ski down flat hills, steep hills, and hills that are not so steep, not so fat, but just right. In fact, you can do it with family and friends! Second, there is a yellow brick road. The yellow brick road is a very cool trail to ski on because it is flat and you don't have to go so fast. Third, you can do different things while skiing. You can wear a costume, listen to music, and you can even play a game called popcorn. I did the popcorn game, and it is when you do little jumps while skiing. If you want to have a blast, just go to Colorado! I am very sure that you will have an awesome time!

The TRI and PS structures characteristic of English expository paragraphs may not fit with the paragraph structures found in other languages. In a 1966 article on contrastive rhetoric addressed to teachers of English to speakers of other languages, Robert Kaplan sought to identify certain cross-cultural variations in paragraph structures based on 700 foreign student compositions. He found that paragraph development in Arabic, for example, involves a complex series of parallel constructions while that in Chinese and Korean features indirection. Kaplan also observed greater freedom for digression in French and Spanish. Connor (1996) offered a book-length treatment of contrastive rhetoric with a specific focus on second language writing.

In sum, as a specific form of discourse analysis, genre analysis has contributed to our understanding of the structures and features of a wide range of text types (e.g., Bhatia, 1993; Hyland, 2004), and such understanding has significantly enhanced our capacity to systematically teach the various genres (e.g., J. Flowerdew, 1993; L. Flowerdew, 2000).

Gaze and Gesture

Just as there is a structure to talk, there is also a structure to nonverbal conduct such as gaze direction and gesture trajectory.

Gaze

Goodwin (1980) proposed the following two rules with regard to speaker and recipient gaze:

Rule 1: Speaker should obtain recipient gaze during a turn-at-talk.
Rule 2: Recipient should be gazing at speaker when being gazed at.

In the following segment, for example, when the speaker does not yet have the recipient's gaze as he starts speaking, he restarts as in segment (11) and pauses as in segment (12) to obtain that gaze (Goodwin, 1980, pp. 281, 283). (Key: dashes in parentheses = 10th of a second of silence; dots = movement bringing gaze to speaker; X = beginning of gaze; solid line = recipient is gazing toward speaker.)

(11) Restart to obtain gaze

```
01   Chil:    She- she's reaching the p- she's at the
02   Helen:                         . . . . . .
03   Chil:    [point I'm reaching.
04   Helen:   [X_____
```

In line 01, note that Chil's first restart following *She-* fails to secure Helen's gaze. At his second restart after *p-*, however, Helen begins to bring her gaze to Chil. Chil then is able to produce his entire TCU (see Chapter 2) for Helen as the hearer. Goodwin has argued that speaker restart-recipient gaze works very much like the summon-answer sequence, where a summon is typically re-issued to obtain an answer after its initial failure.

Aside from the restart, pause is another way of securing recipient gaze, as shown in the next example. (Key: dash in parentheses = recipient gaze toward speaker during a pause, each dash representing a 10th of a second.)

(12) Pause to obtain gaze

```
01   Anne:    When you had that big uhm:,
              (- - - - - - - - - - - - [- ) tropical
02   Jere:    . . . . . . . . ...        [X_____
```

As shown, when Anne begins to speak, she does not have Jere's gaze. It is when she terminates her talk in the middle of her TCU and enters a pause that Jere begins to move his gaze toward her.

Clearly, then, there is a structural relationship between gaze and talk in social interaction, where the two are organized with reference to each other. The speakers would structure their ongoing turns to maximize the possibility of delivering those turns with the gaze of an audience, and the recipients are sensitive, and would respond, to phrasal breaks by bringing their gaze to the speakers.

Gesture

As with gaze, gestures can also be analyzed with regard to their structures. Schegloff (1984) offered one such elegant analysis by showing that a gesture unfolds in relation to the word that the gesture is representing (i.e., its lexical affiliate).

> **Lexical affiliate** refers to the word that the gesture is representing.

More specifically, the gesture begins before, and works as a pre to, its lexical affiliate, following a trajectory that starts with onset (o), reaches acme (a), proceeds to retract (r), and returns to home position (hm) (Sacks & Schegloff, 2002).

> **Home position** refers to the position where a gesture originated and often returns to.

Excerpt (13) is an example of how the iconic gesture of both fingers pointing to temples works as a pre to the lexical affiliate *think* (Schegloff, 1984, pp. 278–279) (Key: o = onset; a = acme; r = retract; . . . . = extension in time of previously marked action; .HHH = large inhalation; (h) = exhalation.)

(13) Iconic gesture as pre

```
                          o. . . . . . . . . . . ...
01   F:   Jus' like a cl(h)a:ssic story, =.HHH an'
          a. . . . . . . . . . . . . . . . . . . . . . . . . . . . .r
02        now when I go out to a job, yihknow an'
                          o. . . .a. . . . . . . . . . . . . .
03        .HHH before we run the cable ev'rybody
          . . . . . . . . . . . . . . . . . . . . . . . . . . . . . .
04        thinks, .hh "fuck the tru:ck."
```

As can be seen, the "thinking" gesture begins around the boundary of *story*, reaches acme at *now* and is retracted at the beginning of *yih know*. It starts again around the boundary of *cable* and reaches acme soon thereafter before the lexical affiliate *thinks* is uttered. The gesture's onset and acme precede its lexical affiliate.

In the next instance, we observe how the locational gesture of "a point out to right with right thumb" works as a pre to its lexical affiliate *off* (Schegloff, 1984, pp. 285–286).

(14) Locational gesture as pre

```
01   M:   and he tried it about four different times finally
02        Keegan rapped im in a good one in the
03        o. . . . . .          a. . . . .   r. . . . . . . . .hm
04        a:ss'n then the-b- DeWald wen o:ff.
```

Here, the gesture begins at the boundary immediately before the TCU that houses the lexical affiliate, and notably, its acme coincides with the major stress closest to the lexical affiliate—*Wald* in this case. This positioning of acme turns out to be "a general ordering principle for locational gestures" (Schegloff, 1984, p. 285). Thus, just as there is a fine-grained structural relationship between talk and recipient gaze, talk and speaker gesture are exquisitely organized with reference to each other as well.

Increasingly, discourse analysts have turned their attention to the analysis of nonverbal conduct (Nevile, 2015), and at least part of those endeavors are addressed specifically to its structural properties, such as the gesture of pointing in organizing turn-taking (Mondada, 2007) or the structures of engagement in children's activities (Lerner, Zimmerman, & Kidwell, 2011).

Approaches to Discourse and Structure

In this chapter, we have shown that the issue of discourse and structure has been addressed through questions such as how tense variation structures narratives, how the clausal unit organizes interactions, how different genres are structured within or across discourse communities, and how nonverbal conduct such as gaze and gestures follows a distinct set of its own structural rules and trajectories. As can be seen, analyzing the structure of discourse involves identifying the recognizable components of a particular span of text, talk, or nonverbal conduct. Insofar as understanding the structure of X often provides an effective entry point into understanding its meaning, discourse analysis is an effective tool for discovering such structures in the first place.

What has become clear to the reader, I hope, is that discourse analysis is a truly interdisciplinary field. The broader question of how discourse is structured (and its attending question of how such structure contributes to meaning making) is addressed by scholars of a wide variety of backgrounds including sociolinguistics (Wolfson), applied linguistics (Hyland), sociology (Schegloff), interactional linguistics (Thompson and Couper-Kuhlen), linguistic anthropology (Goodwin), and experimental psychology (Kendon in Chapter 2). Some employ distinct analytical methods such as conversation analysis, genre analysis, or sociolinguistic analysis. For some, their work is simply discourse analytic because they are engaged in the close reading of text, interaction, and nonverbal conduct. In some cases, the fittedness between the question and the method seems obvious. To understand the structure of text types, for example, the identification of rhetorical moves and linguistics devices seems to be the most reasonable and viable approach. In a similar vein, using descriptive statistics to establish the regularity of CHP in performed narratives is arguably the best option. In other cases, we also see possibilities of broadening the range of the methods in addressing a particular question. The experimental psychologist's approach to discovering gaze patterns in the laboratory (see Chapter 2), for example, may be complemented by the conversation analysts' or linguistic anthropologists' attempt to capture such patterns in the details of naturally occurring interaction. There is no doubt that questions surrounding discourse and structure go far beyond tense variation, clausal unit, text types, gaze, and gestures. Infinite possibilities lie ahead as we continue to explore discourse and structure with creative means that draw upon multiple methodological resources.

Despite the apparent heterogeneity, analysts of discourse and structure share the common interest of answering the question of how discourse is structured by examining actual instances of text and talk as well as nonverbal conduct. In reading a discourse analytic study on the structure of discourse then, it would be useful to ask the following questions:

a. What type of structure is under investigation (e.g., grammar, text type, structure of nonverbal conduct)?
b. What kinds of questions are being raised about this structure?
c. What kinds of data were collected to answer this question?
d. How exactly is the question being answered? What kinds of evidence and analytical reasoning are engaged?
e. Are the analyses convincing?

> Task 6: Read Fox and Thompson (2010) (see References) or any study on discourse and structure of interest to you and answer the previous questions.

Key Points

• Studies on discourse and structure have focused on grammar, genre, as well as gaze and gestures.
• The switch between (conversational) historical present and past tense in narratives plays an important role in partitioning events, staging evaluations, and differentiating characters.
• Clause is a key cross-linguistic resource for managing turn-taking and understanding co-participants' talk in interaction.
• Doing genre analysis involves identifying rhetorical moves and the linguistic features that implement each move.
• Features of a particular genre can vary across disciplines and cultures.
• Expository paragraph structures in English include two major types with some variations: topic-restriction-illustration and problem-solution.
• Speaker should obtain recipient gaze; recipient should be gazing at speaker when being gazed at.
• Gestures follow a specific trajectory from onset, acme, retract, to home position; they can work as iconic or locational pre's to their lexical affiliates.

References

Auer, P., & Pfander, S. (Eds.). (2011). *Constructions: Emerging and emergent.* Boston, MA: De Gruyter.

Becker, A. (1965). A tagmemic approach to paragraph analysis. *College Composition and Communication, 16*(5), 237–242.

Bhatia, V. K. (1993). *Analysing genre: Language use in professional settings.* New York: Routledge.

Connor, R. (1996). Contrastive rhetoric: Cross-cultural aspects of second-language writing. Cambridge: Cambridge University Press.

Couper-Kuhlen, E., & Ford, C. E. (2004). Conversation and phonetics: Essential connections. In E. Couper-Kuhlen & C. E. Ford (Eds.), *Sound patterns in interaction* (pp. 3–25). Amsterdam: Benjamins.

Couper-Kuhlen, E., & Selting, M. (1996). Towards an interactional perspective on prosody and a prosodic perspective on interaction. In E. Couper-Kuhlen & M. Selting (Eds.), *Prosody in conversation: Interactional studies* (pp. 11–56). Cambridge: Cambridge University Press.

Flowerdew, J. (1993). An educational, or process, approach to the teaching of professional genres. *ELT Journal, 47*(4), 305–316.

Flowerdew, L. (2000). Using a genre-based framework to teach organizational structure in academic writing. *ELT Journal, 54*(4), 369–378.

Ford, C. E. (1993). *Grammar in interaction: Adverbial clauses in American English conversations.* Cambridge: Cambridge University Press.

Ford, C. E., & Thompson, S. A. (1996). Interactional units in conversation. In E. Ochs, E. A. Schegloff, & S. Thompson (Eds.), *Interaction and grammar* (pp. 135–184). Cambridge: Cambridge University Press.

Fox, B. A., & Thompson, S. A. (2010). Responses to wh-questions in English conversation. *Research on Language and Social Interaction, 43*(2), 133–156.

Goodwin, C. (1980). Restarts, pauses, and the achievement of a state of mutual gaze at turn-beginnings. *Sociological Inquiry, 50*(3–4), 272–302.

Hyland, K. (2004). *Disciplinary discourses: Social interactions in academic writing.* Ann Arbor: The University of Michigan Press.

Hyland, K. (2008). Genre and academic writing in the disciplines. *Language Teaching, 41*(4), 543–562.

Johnstone, B. (1987). 'He says . . . so I said': Verb tense alternation and narrative depictions of authority in American English. *Linguistics, 25*(1), 33–52.

Kaplan, R. (1966). Cultural thought patterns in intercultural education. *Language Learning, 16*(1), 1–20.

Lerner, G., Zimmerman, D. H., & Kidwell, M. (2011). Formal structures of practical tasks: A resource for action in the social life of very young children. In J. Streeck, C. Goodwin, & C. LeBaron (Eds.), *Embodied interaction: Language and body in the material world* (pp. 44–58). Cambridge: Cambridge University Press.

Mithun, M. (2015). Discourse and grammar. In D. Tannen, H. E. Hamilton, & D. Schiffrin, (Eds.), *The handbook of discourse analysis* (2nd ed.) (pp. 11–41). Malden, MA: Wiley Blackwell.

Mondada, L. (2007). Multimodal resources for turn-taking: Pointing and the emergence of possible next speakers. *Discourse Studies, 9*(2), 194–225.

Nevile, M. (2015). The embodied turn in research on language and social interaction. *Research on Language and Social Interaction, 48*(2), 121–151.

Ochs, E., Schegloff, E. A., & Thompson, S. A. (Eds.). (1996). *Interaction and grammar.* Cambridge: Cambridge University Press.

Pho, P. D. (2008). Research article abstracts in applied linguistics and educational technology: A study of linguistic realizations of rhetorical structure and authorial stance. *Discourse Studies, 10*(2), 231–250.

Reddington, E., & Waring, H. Z. (2015). Understanding the sequential resources for doing humor in the language classroom. *HUMOR: International Journal of Humor Research, 28*(1), 1–23.

Sacks, H., & Schegloff, E. A. (2002). Home position. *Gesture, 2*(2), 133–146.

Schegloff, E. A. (1984). On some gestures' relation to talk. In M. Atkinson & J. Heritage (Eds.), *Structures of social action* (pp. 266–296). Cambridge: Cambridge University Press.

Schegloff, E. A., & Lerner, G. (2004). [Transcript data]. Conversation Analysis Advanced Study Institute, University of California, Los Angeles.

Schiffrin, D. (1981). Tense variation in narrative. *Language, 57*(1), 45–62.

Selting, M., & Couper-Kuhlen, E. (Eds.). (2001). *Studies in interactional linguistics.* Amsterdam: Benjamins Publishing.

Swales, J. (1990). Genre analysis: English in academic and research settings. Boston, MA: Cambridge University Press.

Thompson, S., & Couper-Kuhlen, E. (2005). The clause as a locus of grammar and interaction. *Discourse Studies, 7*(4–5), 481–506.

Wenger, E. (1998). *Communities of practice: Learning, meaning, and identity.* Cambridge: Cambridge University Press.

Wolfson, N. (1978). A feature of performed narrative: The conversational historical present. *Language in Society, 7*, 215–237.

Part III

Discourse and Social Action

4 Classics in Discourse and Social Action

Introduction

In the previous two chapters, we have shown how the broad question of discourse and structure has been tackled by discourse analysts from various fields of studies. We have considered both foundational writings that pioneered the investigation into how discourse is structured and exemplary empirical undertakings in that broad area. While analyzing the structure of discourse (be it narrative, ordinary conversation, classroom talk, or gesture) appears to be the natural first step toward understanding the nature of that discourse, for discourse analysts, perhaps the most prevailing question is what a particular spate of talk and text as well as nonverbal conduct does. What does it accomplish? In other words, what social action does it perform?

> **Social action** in discourse analysis refers to the business that gets done or the goal that gets accomplished in and through talk, text, and multimodal resources.

Social action then concerns what one is doing with that talk, text, or multimodal resource, where such doing may be intentional or unintentional. Examples of social actions are wide-ranging—from requesting, complaining, insinuating, and rejecting to giving instructions, getting a child to comply with a directive, and balancing multiple agendas in a professional context. The notion that discourse does things for us—that most of our daily and professional life gets done in and through discourse—seems obvious. In other words, perhaps for most of us, it is entirely unremarkable that discourse accomplishes social actions. What else would it do? But this understanding of discourse as deeply intertwined with social actions was not always a given. Language (or discourse) was believed to be a tool for representing the world: if it did anything, it did representing. It was not until the 1960s and 1970s that a group of philosophers of language (Austin, 1962; Grice, 1975; Searle, 1975; Wittgenstein, 1953/2009) made the revolutionary leap toward arguing that language does more than describing, stating, or asserting: we do not simply say things, we do things with words, and we can mean more than what we say. In addition, through contextualization cues (Gumperz, 1982) and framing (Bateson, 1972/2000), we signal to each other what it is that we are doing or what activity we are engaging in. These classics form the foundation of what has now become one of the dominant concerns for discourse analysts: How are social actions accomplished? It is to this foundation that we now turn. We begin with a discussion on how we can do things with words, as crystallized in Wittgenstein's language games and Austin and Searle's Speech Act Theory. We then consider how we can signal (nonliteral) meanings through Grice's implicatures, Gumperz's contextualization cues, and Bateson's frames (as further developed by Goffman and Tannen).

Doing Things With Words

Although the two never met, and Austin never acknowledged any influence from Wittgenstein, both philosophers of natural language were "concerned with the flaws in philosophical conceptions of language" at the time with particular regard to "its treatment of language as an abstract referential system," and "[b]oth emphasized the practical, active uses of language" (Potter, 2001, p. 43).

Language Games (Wittgenstein)

Ludwig Wittgenstein was one of the earliest philosophers of language who took issue with the idea that the function of language was to represent the world (see his commonality with Saussure in Harris, 1988). As Wittgenstein (1953/2009) wrote,

> We name things and then we can talk about them: can refer to them in talk."—As if what we did next were given with the mere act of naming. As if there were only one thing called "talking about a thing". Whereas in fact we do the most various things with our sentences. Think just of exclamations alone, with their completely different functions. *Water! Away! Ow! Help! Splendid! No!* Are you still inclined to call these words "names of objects"?
>
> (p. 16)

This challenge of the conventional view of language is repeatedly voiced in his classic *Philosophical Investigations*—a book published posthumously in 1953 that brings together a vast array of ideas developed during his time at Cambridge as a professor of philosophy.

For Wittgenstein (1953/2009), "the meaning of a word is its use in the language" (p. 25), and he offers a nice illustration using the example of naming a chess piece (p. 18). Showing someone the king in chess by saying "This is the king" simply points to the shape of the piece and says nothing about its use, and the shape of the piece here is analogous to the sound and shape of word. In other words, simply naming something does not give it meaning. Rather, "when investigating meaning, the philosophers must 'look and see' the variety of uses to which the word is put" (Biletzki & Matar, 2014).

Further, the functions of words are "as diverse as the functions" of the tools in a toolbox (Wittgenstein, 1953/2009, p. 9). It is to capture such diversity of use that Wittgenstein introduced the concept of "language game"— a concept that never gets clearly defined in *Philosophical Investigations* but "is made to work for a more fluid, more diversified, and more activity-oriented perspective on language" (Biletzki & Matar, 2014). As Wittgenstein (1953/2009) wrote, "The word 'language games' is used here to emphasize the fact that the *speaking* of language is part of an activity, or of a form of life," and he offered the following examples of language games (p. 15).

(1) Language games

    a. giving orders and acting on them
    b. describing an object by its appearance or by its measurements
    c. constructing an object from a description (a drawing)
    d. reporting an event
    e. speculating about the event
    f. forming and testing a hypothesis
    g. presenting the results of an experiment in tables and diagrams
    h. making up a story and reading one
    i. acting in a play
    j. singing rounds
    k. guessing riddles
    l. cracking a joke and telling one
    m. solving a problem in applied arithmetic
    n. translating from one language into another
    o. requesting, thanking, cursing, greeting, praying.

These language games are, according to Wittgenstein (1953/2009), "as much a part of our natural history as waking, eating, drinking, and playing" and are what distinguish us from animals (p. 16).

Speech Act Theory (Austin and Searle)

The idea that language does more than representing finds its full-blown articulation in the Speech Act Theory developed by two other philosophers of language: John Austin and John Searle, who were the creators of such analytical vocabulary as performatives, (in)felicities, and (indirect) speech acts. "The most striking difference" between Wittgenstein and Austin, according to Potter (2001), is in

their overall conception of language. Whereas Wittgenstein has language fragmented into a huge number of diverse language games that are likely to defy a precise overall characterization, Austin's aim was specifically to give an overall, systematic account of this active language.

(p. 43)

Performatives and Infelicities

In a series of lectures delivered at Harvard University in 1955, Austin (1962) took issue with the prevailing assumption at the time that a statement simply states or describes some state of affairs which must be either true or false. Instead, he called attention to utterances that do not describe or report anything, where the delivering of those utterances is part of doing an action and cannot be simply described as *saying something*:

(2) Performatives

    a. *I do* (in the course of a marriage ceremony).
    b. *I name this ship the* Queen Elizabeth.
    c. *I bequeath this watch to my brother* (as in a will).
    d. *I bet you 20 bucks that this course will be phenomenal.*

With these examples that by no means represent everyday occurrences, Austin made the powerful case that certain statements do not do describing or stating at all. Rather, they get things done. As he wrote, "In these examples it seems clear that to utter the sentences is not to describe my doing or state that I am doing it; it is to do it" (Austin, 1962, p. 6). Through the previous utterances, one pledges willingness to be married, christens a ship, bequeaths a watch and issues a bet, none of which is either true or false. Because they do things, Austin labeled these utterances performatives on the basis that by issuing an utterance as such, one is performing an action, not just saying something (pp. 6–7). He contrasted performatives with constatives that simply represent the world (e.g., *The cat is sitting on the mat.*), the representation of which may be judged to be true or false. Notably, Austin later in the same lecture series abandoned this distinction and considers all utterances performative. After all, describing is a form of doing as well, and *The cat is sitting on the mat* may be stated as a veiled attempt to get the cat off the mat. In any case, the notion of performative constituted the beginning of Speech Act Theory—a theoretical model for language use that, as will be shown later, presents certain difficulty in accounting for actual language use.

Speech acts are performatives or "actions performed via utterances" (Yule, 1996, p. 47).

(3) Examples of speech acts

Greeting:	*What's up?*
Request:	*Can you give me Chapter 4 by March 10?*
Complaint:	*I requested this list of changes four months ago, and none of them has been made.*
Invitation:	*Please join us this Saturday if you have time.*
Compliment:	*That was a great talk!*
Refusal:	*I'd normally say yes, but I'm still scrambling to honor my existing commitments.*

For Austin, the abstract notion of speech act may be conceived of as including three specific acts: locutionary, illocutionary, and perlocutionary. The **locutionary act** is the act of saying something, the **illocutionary act** is the act of doing something (e.g., informing, ordering, warning), and the **perlocutionary act** is the act of producing some consequential effects on the participants (e.g., convincing, deterring, surprising, misleading). It may be helpful to think of the locutionary act as uttering the words composing the utterance and conveying the (literal) meaning those words amount to, illocutionary act as making the point or indicating the force of those words, and perlocutionary act as the delivering of effect. Austin offered the example of someone saying *Shoot her*, where the locutionary act is *He said to me "Shoot her*," the illocutionary act is *He urged, advised, or ordered me to shoot her*, and the perlocutionary act is *He persuaded me to shoot her* or *He got me to shoot her.*

It is notable that speech acts cannot be subject to the criterion of being true or false. What seems relevant in the performance of speech acts, on the other hand, is whether a particular speech act is recognizable as intended and whether it is truly intended as such. If your intention is to make a promise, is what you just said recognizable as a promise and do you truly intend to deliver that promise? Or put simply, did your speech act work? How do we know if a speech act has gone wrong or become a failure? According to Austin, in order for a speech act to work, it needs to be "happy," or else it becomes infelicitous.

> **Infelicities** are situations in which speech acts fail to be recognized as intended or are not intended at all. There are two types of infelicities: (1) misfires and (2) abuses.

Misfires are incurred by the wrong procedures or inappropriate roles in performing a certain speech act. A basic procedure for performing the speech act of *bet*, for example, is that the betting must precede rather than follow the event in question. If a child says to a parent, *Bring me the milk right now, or I'm giving you a time-out*, for example, we can say the speech act of a threat fails because the child is not in the position to give her parents a time-out. **Abuses**, on the other hand, comprise cases of performing a speech act without the intention encoded in the utterances that convey that speech act, e.g., request without any real intention to request, complain without any real intention to complain, and compliment without any intention to compliment. In the case of *abuse*, one lies. Saying *I promise* without any intention of keeping that promise is an example of *abuse*. Even though it is said and heard as a promise, we can say the speech act of promise in this case is "unhappy"—has gone wrong and become a failure.

What does all this mean when it comes to analyzing actual interaction? To begin with, it means that as analysts we would be concerned about not just what words an utterance contains (locutionary act) but also what the speaker is trying to accomplish (illocutionary force) with that utterance and what the effect it might have on the listener (perlocutionary force). It also means that we would be concerned about whether that particular utterance is successful in bringing off its intended point. In other words, is the speech act a "happy" one? Are the correct procedures employed or appropriate roles involved, and does the speaker mean it?

Task 1: Before reading the rest of this section, consider the following brief exchange taken from a dinner table conversation between 3-year-old Zoe and her mom. What speech act does Mom perform in line 03? Is it a "happy" act? What insights or constraints does Austin's theory of infelicities present to the analysis of this interaction?

```
01  Zoe:         don't like this. ((moves a tiny piece of leaf from own to
02               Mom's plate))
03  Mom:   →     Do you know what it is?
04  Zoe:         What?
05  Mom:         I don't know. I'm asking you.
```

As you might have discovered, two possibilities may be entertained here. In line 03, Mom may be seeking information, doing a preannouncement, or giving a test. The question *Do you know what X is?* can certainly be recognized as doing inquiring, informing, or testing, and Mom is certainly in the position to be doing such inquiring, informing, or testing. And one might argue that Zoe is also in the position of (1) receiving the information Mom is about to deliver or (2) giving information on the piece of food she is rejecting either as an informer or as a test taker. In other words, in either case, there is no *misfire* to be observed here. The question is, is there *abuse*? Does Mom intend to inquire, inform, or test? Does she sincerely want to know the answer to her question, is she about to tell Zoe what it is, or is she simply testing to see if Zoe knows what it is? How do we find out? Well, we do find out in line 05 that she is truthfully seeking the information although Zoe in line 04 has treated her speech act as that of a preannouncement, that is, Mom is about to tell her what it is, and she gives the go-ahead in line 04.

What this example shows is that Austin's infelicities and, in this case, *abuses*, are indeed an important puzzle piece in understanding the speech act (or social action) Mom is performing in line 03. In the case of Speech Act Theory, action is understood entirely from the speaker's perspective and deeply entwined with the notion of intention—knowing whether the speaker sincerely intends to perform a particular speech act seems crucial. At the same time, how do we as analysts access that intention? Luckily in this particular example, the speaker makes clear her intention only two lines later. Without any explicit evidence of intention in the data, how do we decide whether the sincerity condition of a particular speech is met? Do we interview the speaker? The reader may be reminded at this juncture that Speech Act Theory is a theoretical model not originally designed as an analytical tool for naturally occurring interaction.

Taxonomy of Speech Acts and Felicity Conditions

John Searle (1976) further developed Austin's Speech Act Theory by proposing a taxonomy of speech acts (see Table 4.1).

Task 2: Consider Searle's taxonomy of speech acts. Do the five types of speech acts encompass everything we do with words in everyday and professional settings? Give examples to justify your answers.

Table 4.1 Taxonomy of Speech Acts

Type	*Definition*	*Example*
Representatives	speech acts that state what the speakers believe to be or not be the case	describe, claim, hypothesize, etc.
Commissives	speech acts that speakers use to commit themselves to some future action	promise, offer, threaten, etc.
Expressives	speech acts that state what the speakers feel	thank, congratulate, apologize, etc.
Declarations	speech acts that change the world via the speakers' utterance	"You're guilty" by a judge.
Directives	speech acts that speakers use to get someone else to do something	request, invite, advise, etc.

Note: Based on Searle (1976)

Recall that in Austin's framework, whether a speech act works is tested against the notion of infelicities. Speech acts can fail to be recognized or simply mislead if they fall under the category of either *misfire* (wrong procedures or roles) or *abuse* (absence of intention). Rather than working with infelicities, Searle (1969) specifies a series of felicity conditions that produce speech acts that can be recognized as intended (see Table 4.2).

Let's take the speech act of request as an example. If I say to a student, *Please turn in your next draft by the end of June,* how do we know it will actually be recognized as a request by the student? According to Searle's framework, here is how: the utterance satisfies the propositional content condition by referring to a future act (A) of the hearer (H); it satisfies the preparatory condition because the speaker (S) is in the position to issue such a request, S believes that H is capable of carrying out the act (A) of turning in the next draft, A has not yet been carried out, and it is not obvious that H will do A of his or her own accord; it satisfies the sincerity condition because S genuinely wants H to do A; it satisfies the essential condition as the utterance counts as an attempt by S to get H to do A given its imperative format conventionally associated with requesting. The felicity conditions for directives, in other words, can be specified as follows:

Propositional content condition: Future A of H.
Preparatory condition: (S believes) H is able to do A; H is able
                                   to do A; not obvious that H will do A
                                   of his own accord.
Sincerity condition: S wants H to do A.
Essential condition: Utterance counts as an attempt to get H
                                   to do A.

Task 3: Before reading on, consider to which category of speech act the following three belong (see Taxonomy of Speech Acts in Table 4.1): (1) assert, (2) advise, and (3) warn. Spell out their felicity conditions.

As you might have figured out, *assert* belongs to the category of representative, *advise* to the category of directives, and *warn* to the category of commissives. Their felicity conditions may be specified as follows (see Table 4.3).

Table 4.2 Felicity Conditions for Speech Acts

Condition	Definition
propositional content condition	reference or prediction specific to the act
preparatory condition	appropriate role, object, and setting; act not yet carried out
sincerity condition	sincere about the act one is performing
essential condition	utterance counting as an attempt to do the act

Note: Based on Searle (1969)

Table 4.3 Samples of Felicity Conditions

	Assert	Advise	Warn
Propositional content	Any proposition P	Future A of H	Future event or state E
Preparatory	S has evidence for truth of P; not obvious that H knows P.	S has reason to believe A will benefit H; not obvious H will normally do A.	S has reason to believe E will occur and harm H; not obvious that E will occur.
Sincerity	S believes P.	S believes A will benefit H.	S believes E is not in H's best interests.
Essential	Counts as undertaking to the effect that P represents an actual state of affairs	Counts as an undertaking to the effect that A is in H's best interest	Counts as an undertaking to the effect that E is not in H's best interests

One might notice that preparatory conditions appear to be concerned with the need and possibility for doing the speech act. Taken together, the set of conditions address both the text (propositional content and essential) and certain aspects of context (preparatory and sincerity) of a particular utterance. One might now ask: What is the point of doing this kind of analysis? Where does this get us? Here is one way to answer this question. It allows us to say, *No, that's not going to work as a request* or the like. Or, if we were to teach someone how to make requests in English, it might give us some grounding for saying this is why X does not work as a request or in order for X to work as a request, one would need these element*s*.

Task 4: Consider the following dinner table conversation between Zoe and her mom. What speech acts are being performed by the bolded utterances in lines 07, 08, 12, and 15? Use the felicity conditions to justify your answers. (Key: dash connecting the verbal and the nonverbal = co-occurrence of the two.)

03 Zoe: ((*playing board game*)) Mom. I <u>don't</u> know how to <u>fix</u> this.
04 Mom: which one.
05 Zoe: ((*points*))-this.
06 Mom: Wow. you <u>did</u> this <u>all</u> by your<u>se</u>:lf.
07 Zoe: **I'm almost done, but I broke this.**
08 Mom: **Wo::w. this is really cool.**
09 Zoe: ((*moves pieces*))
10 Mom: Wow. High five,
11 Zoe&Mom: ((*high-fiving*))

12	Mom:	Okay. **Put it away.** Ready for dinner?
13	Zoe:	Not yet.
14	Mom:	Time for dinner.
15	Zoe:	**Not yet.**
16	Mom:	Yet.
17	Zoe:	Not yet.
18	Mom:	Yet.
19	Zoe:	Not yet.
20	Mom:	Yet.

Zoe's utterance of *Not yet* in line 15, for example, would be a refusal—a type of commissive in Searle's taxonomy. It satisfies the propositional content condition of referring to a future act (not getting ready for dinner in this case) of S, the preparatory condition that Zoe is in the position of doing A and her commitment to A is not obvious to H, the sincerity condition of (presumably) Zoe genuinely not intending to get ready for dinner, and the essential condition of the simple negation of Mom's *Yet* counting as an attempt to refuse on Zoe's part.

Task 5: Consider the following utterances. What speech acts are being performed here? How do you know?

(1) Bus driver to passenger sitting down: *I will be needing that seat, lady. I will be needing that seat.*
(2) Announcement on airplane: *The captain has turned on the "fasten your seat belt" sign.*
(3) Three-year-old to Daddy: *My legs are tired.*
(4) Three-year-old to Mommy: *I have a sore throat.*

One difficulty you might have run into while doing the previous exercise is indeterminacy of the illocutionary force of the various utterances. The utterances look like expressives or even representatives. The problem is they are normally understood as neither expressives nor representatives but as directives. *I will be needing that seat* means *Please don't sit there; The captain has turned on the "fasten your seat belt" sign* means *Please fasten your seat belt; My legs are tired* means *Please pick me up; I have a sore throat* means *Please help me feel better.* All these utterances are directives carried out under the guise of other speech acts, which brings us to the notion of indirect speech acts (Searle, 1969, 1975).

Indirect Speech Acts

> **Indirect speech act** is an act performed via the performance of a different act by addressing the conditions of the primary act.

Take, for example, the direct and primary speech act of *Shut the door*. How do we perform the same act indirectly? Let us start with the felicity conditions of the primary act. The preparatory condition is that (S believes) H is able to shut the door, it's not obvious that H will shut the door of his own accord, and the door has not yet been shut. The sincerity condition is that S wants H to shut the door. One way to build indirect speech acts from *Shut the door* is to talk about these conditions:

(1) *Can you shut the door?*   Question hearer's ability
(2) *Would you shut the door?*   Question hearer's willingness
(3) *Did you shut the door?*   Question whether the act has been done
(4) *I want you to shut the door.*   Assert speaker's desire

What makes all these acts indirect is that one can always choose not to interpret them as directives by, for example, answering (1)–(2) with *Yes*, (3) with *No*, and (4) with *Okay* without actually shutting the door.

In sum, the concepts of *language game* and *speech act* along with their taxonomies and felicity conditions not only instigated a major shift in our thinking about the function of language—from labeling things to performing actions—but also provided us with an initial set of vocabulary for capturing the nature of those actions.

Signaling Meaning With Implicatures, Cues, and Frames

As alluded to earlier, the notion of indirect speech act alerts us to the possibility that meaning is not always transparent in the words we utter. In fact, as will be made evident in this section, we have a variety of means of signaling meaning not explicitly encoded in the language we produce—by generating implicatures (Grice), using contextualizing cues (Gumperz), and establishing frames (Bateson, Goffman, and Tannen).

Implicature (Grice)

The term implicature was coined by another philosopher of ordinary language, Paul Grice. Consider the following response to an inquiry about a mutual friend: *Oh quite well . . . he hasn't been to prison yet.* Clearly in this case, what is said is not the same as what is meant. In his attempt to explain how we can mean more than what we say, Grice (1975) used implicature to refer to what is meant or implied. In the example just given, although what is said is "Oh quite well . . .", what is meant is "Not well at all!" But how is it possible that we can compute what is meant from what is said, or in this particular case, "Not well at all" from "Oh quite well, he hasn't been to prison yet?" What enables this possibility, according to Grice, is the Cooperative Principle (CP) that we are expected to observe.

> **Cooperative Principle (CP)**: "Make your conversational contribution such as is required, at the stage at which it occurs, by the accepted purpose or direction of the talk exchange in which you are engaged," (Grice, 1975, p. 45).

The CP comes with four attendant conversational maxims: Quantity, Quality, Relation, and Manner (Grice, 1975, p. 45).

(1) Quantity:

    a. Make your contribution as informative as is required.
    b. Make your contribution not more informative than is required.

(2) Quality: Try to make your contribution one that is true.

    a. Do not say what you believe to be false.
    b. Do not say that for which you lack adequate evidence.

(3) Relation: Be relevant.
(4) Manner: Be perspicuous.

    a. Avoid obscurity of expression.
    b. Avoid ambiguity.
    c. Be brief (avoid unnecessary prolixity).
    d. Be orderly.

It is important to remember that these maxims are not empirical generalizations, that is, they do not describe what people do. They do, however, articulate the "rules" participants are *expected* to observe, like the traffic lights we are expected to heed but don't always do. The very existence of traffic lights, however, enables a baseline orderliness of traffic flow. Like Austin and Searle's Speech Act Theory, Grice's CP articulates a theoretical model for language use. Observing the CP and maxims, according to Grice (1975, p. 49), is a matter of being rational:

[A]nyone who cares about the goals that are central to conversation/ communication (e.g., giving and receiving information, influencing and being influenced by others) must be expected to have an interest, given suitable circumstances, in participation in talk exchanges that will be profitable only on the assumption that they are conducted in general accordance with the CP and the maxims.

Aside from enabling a baseline orderliness of traffic flow, the presence of traffic lights also allows us to produce or interpret certain nonconforming behavior as "in a hurry," "reckless," "city people," and the like. In a similar vein, the conversation maxims are the traffic lights we sometimes choose to disregard. They may, according to Grice (1975), be "flouted" (as one blatantly fails to fulfill it) or "exploited" to generate a conversational implicature (p. 49).

When consulted on the quality of food in an Italian restaurant in the neighborhood, one of my colleagues who frequents the restaurant and is known for his expert judgment on food says, "The artichoke is good." His response clearly flouts the maxim of quantity. By commenting only on the artichoke rather than the overall quality of the food, he provides less information than is required. There is no reason for me to believe that he does not have access to information on other items on the menu or is not qualified to offer any assessment. I assume that he is observing the CP and its maxims even though the actual words he utters appear to flout them. He must, then, be inviting me to entertain the inference that the rest of the items on the menu are not particularly praiseworthy. He is, in other words, conveying the implicature that the overall quality of the food is less than desirable. In a similar vein, after having observed someone break up all the furniture, the remark *He is a little intoxicated* invites the implicature of the exact opposite of what is said, and this is done by flouting the maxim of quality. In the case of *Oh quite well . . . he hasn't been to prison yet*, the maxim of relation is being flouted as "prison" is not typically a measure for one's well-being. Assuming that the speaker is observing the CP, the implicature of *Not well at all* may be generated. Finally, parents spelling out words such as i-c-e-c-r-e-a-m to each other in front of small children are exploiting the maxim of manner to produce the implicature that what is being discussed must be done in secrecy that excludes the small children who may have gone wild at the sound of "ice cream."

Task 6: Give one example each: (1) flouting maxim of quantity; (2) flouting maxim of quality; (3) flouting maxim of relation; (4) flouting maxim of manner. In each case, consider what implicature is being generated and how.

If in a recommendation letter for graduate school, the professor writes *Mr. Smith's handwriting is excellent*, what would be its implicature? To generate the implicature that Mr. Smith is a weak candidate, according to Grice (1975), the following calculation needs to be applied (p. 50):

> He has said that *Mr. Smith's handwriting is excellent*; there is no reason to suppose that he is not observing the maxims, or at least the CP, he could not be doing this unless he thought that *This is a weak candidate*; he knows (and knows that I know that he knows) that I can see that the supposition that he thinks that *This is a weak candidate.* is required; he has done nothing to stop me thinking that; he intends me to think, or is at least willing to allow me to think, that *This is a weak candidate*; and so he has implicated that *This is a weak candidate.*

Grice (1975) made it very clear that in order to carry out such a calculation, both participants need to assume a common understanding of the conventional meaning of the words used, the CP and its maxims, and the context of the utterance along with other relevant background knowledge (p. 50) (cf. "common ground" in Clark, 1996).

Some scholars have questioned the universality of these maxims. As Keenan (1976) showed in her ethnographic study, members of a Malagasy society regularly provide less information than is required from the perspective of a middle-class white U.S. English-language speaker, and in answering a query of where one's mother is, the response *She's either in the house or at the market* is not interpreted as implying anything other than what is said because satisfying informational needs is not a basic norm in the Malagasy society (p. 70).

By now, it should have become clear that saying more or other than what we mean is a normal part of human communication, and that we convey and interpret such indirect meanings by addressing the felicity conditions of speech acts or by flouting Grice's conversational maxims. What has not been made clear is that oftentimes the resources of both Searle's felicity conditions and Grice's maxims need to be drawn upon to figure out what is meant by a speaker—indirectly (Searle, 1975, p. 63). Consider the following exchange:

A: Let's go to a movie tonight.
B: I have to study for an exam.

How is it that we have no difficulty figuring out that what B says amounts to a rejection? The answer is that it takes a two-stage process. First, Grice's CP allows us to detect that something indirect is going on:

(1) B is being cooperative. Her response is intended to be relevant.
(2) The relevant response should be acceptance, rejection, and so forth.
(3) What B says literally is not any of the above, that is, not relevant.
(4) By flouting the maxim of relation, B must mean more than what she says.

Second, the Speech Act Theory brings us to what that indirect speech act is:

(5) A preparatory condition on proposal acceptance is B's ability to do the act.

(6) Going to a movie takes time, and so does studying. One cannot do both.

(7) The preparatory condition on acceptance cannot be satisfied.

(8) The primary illocutionary force is rejection of the proposal.

Thus, to attribute the social action of rejection to the utterance *I have to study for an exam* calls for the application of both CP and Speech Act Theory. In other words, as philosophers of language, Grice and Searle have provided us an analytic heuristic for showing how the interpretation of such utterances might work. It is worthy of note that, although not addressed by either Grice or Searle, the sound of these utterances is also an important element for identifying their illocutionary forces, perlocutionary effects, or implicatures—an issue taken by John Gumperz and encapsulated in his concept of contextualization cue.

Contextualization Cue (Gumperz)

Contextualization cue is a term coined by the founder of interactional sociolinguistics John Gumperz (1982). It is a powerful resource for signaling what is going on. If your child says *I'm mad at you!*, she is not signaling anything. She is explicitly stating how she feels. Alternatively, she could signal being mad through such contextualization cues as curtness of her response, tone of voice quality, facial gestures, or body movement.

> **Contextualization cue** refers to any verbal or nonverbal form contributing to signaling what the activity is and how the talk is to be understood.

Contextualization cues carry certain formal and content properties (Auer, 1992; Gumperz, 1992a, 2003; Levinson, 2003). Formally, they tend to be non-segmental features (e.g., prosody) or a minor class or lexical or grammatical items (e.g., particles, adverbs), and such cross-channel features as prosody, lexicon, or gestures work in a cluster to signal any clear function. Content-wise, they tend to be non-propositional, out of one's awareness, cued but not coded, and they tend to invoke presuppositions that aid interpretation.

Discussions of contextualization cues often involve a set of related terms (Gumperz, 1992a, 1992b; Gumperz & Cook-Gumperz, 2007). **Contextualization** refers to the use of any (non)verbal sign to retrieve the presuppositions that must be relied on to interpret what is intended. **Contextual presuppositions** are sociocultural assumptions (e.g., Dinner is intimate and lunch casual) underlying our interpretations in interaction. **Situated inference** is interpretation arrived at as a result of considerations of contextual presuppositions and the specific situational context. **Conversational inference** refers to the situated, context-bound process of interpretation by means of which participants in an exchange assess other participants' communicative intentions and on which they base their own responses.

Contextual cues can be nonverbal, prosodic, lexical, or discoursal. **Nonverbal cues** comprise proxemics, gaze, gesture, and body movement. Different degrees of proxemics, for example, signal levels of intimacy among participants or formality of occasions. A scowl can signal disapproval or puzzlement. **Prosodic cues** rely on such features as intonation, pitch, or volume. The Indian servers at a British airport were considered sullen and rude by customers because they would offer food in a falling intonation (e.g., *Gravy.*), which is the "normal" way of doing offering in their native language as opposed to the English norm of *Gravy?* in rising intonation (Gumperz, 1982). **Lexical cues** can also signal meanings that are nonpropositional. In responding to the question *Is this a good restaurant?*, a Russian speaker may say *Of course!* to mean *Indeed!* To an American, this sounds like a comment on the "stupidity" of the question (LoCastro, 2003). The different social meanings signaled by *I'm sorry* and *Excuse me* are often not recognized by learners of English. According to Borkin and Reinhart (1978), *Excuse me* is used as a remedy immediately before or after a minor infraction while *Sorry* is mainly used to express regret and dismay. *Excuse me* displays one's concern about breaking a rule, and *I'm sorry* about hurting another person. Address terms are important cues that signal relationships. "First name only" is a common usage among Americans but not so in Chinese, where such usage by an acquaintance or stranger can cause embarrassment (Scollon & Scollon, 1995). Questions such as *How are you doing?* or *Did you have a good weekend?* are part of ritual exchanges in English that are typically not produced to elicit extended responses, which learners of English often give (Liddicoat & Crozet, 2001). Conversational closing signals such as *Okay, Well,* or *Alright* are often missed by even advanced nonnative speakers, which can result in awkwardness in interaction; utterances such as *Let's have coffee* in English often serve to express friendliness and/or to close a conversation, but learners of English tend to take them as literal invitations (Wolfson, 1989; Wong & Waring, 2010). In an elementary classroom, an African American boy's response *I don't know* to the teacher's question is interpreted as being uncooperative while its delivery in rising intonation signals *I want encouragement* (Gumperz, 1982). A teacher's use or nonuse of contextualization cues such as *okay, well,* or decreased/increased volume to signal transitions in a kindergarten/elementary classroom turned out to affect the students' behavior in systematic ways (Dorr-Bremme, 1990).

Discourse cues include such practices as silence, backchannels, or story-structure. Backchannels or response tokens such as *mm hm* or *uh* *huh* can cause communication breakdowns. For Japanese, giving such backchannels indicates "I'm listening," whereas for Americans, it means "I agree." These tokens also vary in their frequencies and locations in different languages. Compared with Americans, Japanese and Koreans backchannel more frequently (and often in the middle of a sentence) while Chinese backchannel less frequently. As a result, for Americans, Japanese and Koreans can seem eager to talk or overly enthusiastic while Chinese may appear aloof and uninterested (Clancy, Thompson, Suzuki, & Tao, 1996; Iwasaki, 2009; Morita, 2008; Young & Lee, 2004). An African American girl's story was considered by her white teacher to be incoherent because it followed a topical instead of a temporal organization (Michaels & Collins, 1984). In an Australian university seminar, Japanese students' silence, which was used to save face when they did not know an answer, was interpreted by their Australian counterparts as disinterest and disagreement (Nakane, 2006).

Gumperz (2003) wrote about how contextualization cues may be researched and specified the following steps: (1) transcribe and analyze self-contained episodes of recorded interactions for what is intended and perceived; (2) play passages to listeners with and without similar backgrounds to test analysts' hypotheses by asking questions such as:

What is it about the way A says X that makes you think Y?
Can you repeat it just about the way he said it?
What is another way of saying it?
Is it possible that he merely wanted to ask a question?
How would he have said it if. . .?
How did the answers interpret what A said?
How can you tell that the answerer is interpreted that way?

(3) reanalyze the passages based on the interview; (4) work with additional data; and (5) develop more specific elicitation procedures.

Task 7: Give one example each of the following: (1) nonverbal cue, (2) prosodic cue, (3) lexical cue, and (4) discourse cue. For each example, explain what makes it contextualization cue in your opinion, using the formal and content properties discussed earlier.

Task 8: Pick one of the cues you discussed in Task 7 and conduct a mini-empirical study on it by following the previous steps suggested by John Gumperz.

Frame (Bateson, Goffman, and Tannen)

Unlike the works introduced so far that mostly manifest an utterance-by-utterance analytic disposition, Bateson's framing theory offers a way of specifying social actions relevant to a larger activity or stretch of discourse. Having written on a wide variety of subjects including anthropology, psychology, biology, family therapy, psychiatry, pathologies, and interpersonal communication, Gregory Bateson is best known among discourse analysts for his concept of "frame" as detailed in his classic *Steps to an Ecology of Mind* (Bateson, 1972/2000).

When Bateson went to observe the monkeys in the San Francisco Zoo in 1959, he tried to figure out how it was that it seemed clear to an observer and apparently to the monkeys themselves that the fight-like behavior they were engaged in was really play, that is, the monkeys were performing the social action of play. The conclusion was that since you cannot have two contradicting messages "This is play." and "This is fight." co-existing on the same plane, the only way to resolve this paradox is for "This is play." to function as a metamessage that defines a frame within which "This is fight" may be interpreted. According to Bateson, every metamessage is, sets, or defines a frame; it gives us instructions of how to understand the message inside that frame (Bateson, 1972/2000, pp. 188, 190). In the case of the monkeys, the metamessage of *play* instructs us to understand the *fight* within the frame of *play*.

Although Bateson made the proposal of "play" being the metamessage that defines a frame within which "fight" may be interpreted, he did not specify how such a metamessage gets constructed. It is the sociologist Erving Goffman (1974/1986) who specified the *how*: "fight" is keyed as "play" when patterns of "fight" are not followed fully but systematically altered. In other words, "Biting-like behavior occurs, but no one is seriously bitten" (p. 41). As such, the primary key/frame "fight" becomes the transformed key/frame "play" (p. 41).

Key is a set of conventions by which one activity is transformed into another patterned on the original activity (e.g., a playful key, a documentary key); **keying** is a systematic transformation of one activity into another patterned on the original activity.

The notion of frame is further developed by the interactional sociolinguist Deborah Tannen both conceptually and empirically. Conceptually, Tannen further clarified "frame" as the definitions of what is going on. Empirically, Tannen and her students considerably fleshed out the notion of frame by utilizing a ranging of framing terminologies in the analysis of actual social interaction.

> **Frame** is a metamessage that gives us instructions of how to understand the message inside the frame or the definition of what is going on (e.g., This is play.)

In an example of a driver stopping at an intersection to let a couple cross the street, Tannen (1986) noted that the driver establishes the "helping" frame, which the woman saves, but the man breaks. One can also embed one frame within another as mommy and child engage in role-reversals in pretend play, where the role-reversal is a frame nested inside the play frame (Gordon, 2002). In Tannen and Wallat's (1987) study of pediatric interaction, the pediatrician juggles the frames of examination (examining the child) and social encounter (building rapport with the mother and entertaining the child) by looking in the child's ear and teasing that she is looking for a monkey. While examining the child's stomach, she asks *Is your spleen palpable over there?* after *Any peanut butter and jelly in there?*, where the examination frame leaks into the teasing frame (also see reframing and blending frames in Chapter 5).

In sum, an important aspect of identifying what social actions are being performed in discourse involves recognizing that talk, text, or nonverbal conduct can signal meanings beyond what it literally conveys, and the concepts of implicature, contextualization cue, and frame offer us crucial analytical tools for illuminating such meanings.

Key Points

- The meaning of words resides in their use or the diversity of language games such as reporting an event or cracking a joke.
- We do things with words by performing speech acts such as greeting or complaining.
- There are five types of speech acts: representatives, commissives, expressives, directives, and declarations.
- Speech acts are judged by their success or failure rather than their truth value; meeting the felicity conditions of any speech act enables its successful execution.
- The felicity conditions for speech act include propositional content condition, preparatory condition, sincerity condition, and essential condition.
- Speech acts may be performed indirectly by addressing the felicity condition of the primary act.
- Conversation is made possible because participants assume cooperation with each other by observing the Cooperative Principle and its attendant maxims of Quantity, Quality, Relation, and Manner.
- Flouting the conversational maxims generates conversational implicatures.

- Contextualization cues, both verbal and nonverbal, signal what activity participants are engaged in and how their talk and gesture can be understood.
- Contextualization cues can be systematically researched.
- Frame is the definition of what is going on; frames can be saved, broken, blended, embedded, juggled, or redefined.

References

Auer, P. (1992). Introduction: John Gumperz' approach to contextualization. In P. Auer & A. di Luzio (Eds.), *The contextualization of language* (pp. 1–38). Amsterdam: John Benjamins.

Austin, J. L. (1962). *How to do things with words*. Cambridge, MA: Harvard University Press.

Bateson, G. (2000). *Steps to an ecology of mind*. New York: Ballantine Books. (Original work published 1972)

Biletzki, A., & Matar, A. (2014, Spring). Ludwig Wittgenstein. In E. N. Zalta (Ed.), *The Stanford encyclopedia of philosophy*. Retrieved from http://plato.stanford.edu/archives/spr2014/entries/wittgenstein/

Borkin, A., & Reinhart, S. (1978). Excuse me and I'm sorry. *TESOL Quarterly, 12*(1), 57–69.

Clancy, P. M., Thompson, S. A., Suzuki, R., & Tao, H. (1996). The conversational use of reactive tokens in English, Japanese, and Mandarin. *Journal of Pragmatics, 26*(3), 355–387.

Clark, H. (1996). *Using language*. New York: Cambridge University Press.

Dorr-Bremme, D. W. (1990). Contextualization cues in the classroom: Discourse regulation and social control functions. *Language in Society, 19*, 379–402.

Goffman, E. (1986). *Frame analysis*. New York: Harper and Row. (Original work published 1974)

Gordon, C. (2002). 'I'm mommy and you're Natalie': Role-reversal and embedded frames in mother-child discourse. *Language in Society, 31*(5), 679–720.

Grice, H. P. (1975). Logic and conversation. In P. Cole & J. L. Morgan (Eds.), *Syntax and semantics, Vol. 3: Speech acts* (pp. 41–58). New York: Academic Press.

Gumperz, J. J. (1982). *Discourse strategies*. Cambridge: Cambridge University Press.

Gumperz, J. J. (1992a). Contextualization and understanding. In A. Duranti & C. Goodwin (Eds.), *Rethinking context: Language as an interactive phenomenon* (pp. 229–252). Cambridge: Cambridge University Press.

Gumperz, J. J. (1992b). Contextualization revisited. In P. Auer & A. di Luzio (Eds.), *The contextualization of language* (pp. 39–53). Amsterdam: John Benjamins.

Gumperz, J. J. (2003). Response essay. In S. L. Eerdmans, C. L. Prevignano, & P. J. Thibault (Eds.), *Language and interaction: Discussions with John J. Gumperz* (pp. 105–126). Amsterdam: John Benjamins.

Gumperz, J. J., & Cook-Gumperz, J. (2007). Discourse, cultural diversity and communication: A linguistic anthropological perspective. In H. Kotthoff & H. Spencer-Oatey (Eds.), *Handbook of intercultural communication* (pp. 13–30). Berlin: Mouton de Gruyter.

Harris, R. (1988). *Language, Saussure and Wittgenstein*. New York: Routledge.

Iwasaki, S. (2009). Initiating interactive turn spaces in Japanese conversation: Local projection and collaborative action. *Discourse Processes, 46*(2), 226–246.

Keenan, E. O. (1976). The universality of conversational postulates. *Language in Society,* *5*(1), 67–79.

Levinson, S. C. (2003). Contextualizing 'contextualization cues.' In S. Eerdmans, C. Prevignano, & P. Thibault (Eds.), *Language and interaction: Discussions with John J. Gumperz* (pp. 31–39). Amsterdam: John Benjamins.

Liddicoat, A. J., & Crozet, C. (2001). Acquiring French interactional norms through instruction. In K. R. Rose & G. Kasper (Eds.), *Pragmatic development in instructional contexts* (pp. 125–144). Cambridge: Cambridge University Press.

LoCastro, V. (2003). *An introduction to pragmatics: Social action for language teachers.* Ann Arbor, MI: University of Michigan Press.

Michaels, S., & Collins, J. (1984). Oral discourse styles: Classroom interaction and the acquisition of literacy. In D. Tannen (Ed.), *Coherence in spoken and written discourse* (pp. 219–244). Norwood, NJ: Ablex.

Morita, E. (2008). Highlighted moves within an action: Segmented talk in Japanese conversation. *Discourse Studies, 10*(4), 517–541.

Nakane, I. (2006). Silence and politeness in intercultural communication in university seminars. *Journal of Pragmatics, 38*(11), 1811–1835.

Potter, J. (2001). Wittgenstein and Austin. In M. Wetherell, S. Taylor, & S. J. Yates (Eds.), *Discourse theory and practice: A reader* (pp. 39–46). London: Sage.

Scollon, R., & Scollon, S. W. (1995). *Intercultural communication: A discourse approach.* Malden, MA: Blackwell.

Searle, J. R. (1969). *Speech acts.* New York and London: Cambridge University Press.

Searle, J. R. (1975). Indirect speech acts. In P. Cole & J. L. Morgan (Eds.), *Syntax and semantics, Vol. 3: Speech acts* (pp. 59–82). New York: Academic Press.

Searle, J. R. (1976). A classification of illocutionary acts. *Language in Society, 5*(1), 1–23.

Tannen, D. (1986). *That's not what I meant!: How conversational style makes or breaks relationships.* New York: HarperCollins.

Tannen, D., & Wallat, C. (1987). Interactive frames and knowledge schemas in interaction: Examples from a medical examination/interview. *Social Psychology Quarterly, 52*(2), 215–206.

Wittgenstein, L. (2009). *Philosophical investigations* (4th ed.). Malden, MA: Blackwell. (Original work published 1953)

Wolfson, N. (1989). *Perspectives: Sociolinguistics and TESOL.* Rowley, MA: Newbury House.

Wong, J., & Waring, H. Z. (2010). *Conversation analysis and second language pedagogy.* New York: Routledge.

Young, R. F., & Lee, J. (2004). Identifying units in interaction: Reactive tokens in Korean and English conversations. *Journal of Sociolinguistics, 8*(3), 380–407.

Yule, G. (1996). *The study of language.* Cambridge: Cambridge University Press.

5 Empirical Endeavors in Discourse and Social Action

Introduction

In the previous chapter, we considered some of the foundational works that inspired and influenced decades of research in discourse and social action. The linguistic philosophers (Wittgenstein, Austin, and Searle) did not work with naturally occurring data as discourse analysts do, but they were the pioneers who made the leap from a view of language as only representing thoughts and reality to an understanding of language as doing things—as performing social actions. They were the trailblazers who made the explicit proposal that we perform a wide range of social actions with what we say. The notion that we routinely mean more than what we say—in ways that go beyond what we literally and clearly say—is further developed with such concepts as implicature, frame, and contextualization cue proposed by Grice, Gumperz, and Bateson. How such linguistic and interactional acrobatics get executed in the actual use of language is the question that drives the work of most, if not all, discourse analysts. It is the question of this chapter: how are social actions accomplished?

A closer look at the work done in discourse and social action reveals that there are two ways in which this question can be approached. Some scholars begin with the conduct, that is, what participants say or do, and ask what social actions are accomplished by such conduct. What, for example, is being accomplished, when one produces repetitions, says *well*, or uses gaze or gestures in particular ways? Other researchers begin with a particular action such as balancing work and play in parent-child interaction, managing the nongranting of requests, achieving consensus, or doing reenactments, and ask: what discursive conduct is required to build these actions? In what follows, we offer illustrations of each approach.

Begin With Conduct

Repetition in Conversation

One type of conduct we routinely observe in human interaction is repetition, which begs the discourse analytic question: What does repetition do?

What social action does it accomplish? In this section, we offer two exemplars of how this question is answered first in interactional sociolinguistics and then in conversation analysis.

Based on 2.5 hours of a single dinner table conversation among six middle-class white friends (three from New York City, two from Los Angeles, and one from the UK), Tannen (2007) in her interactional sociolinguistic study identified five functions of repetition in an extended multiparty conversation: to participate, to ratify listenership, to produce humor, to stall, and to expand. She offered a range of examples as evidence for her claim. The following is a specimen of what she called "the most puzzling but also the most basic" type of repetition, where she (Deborah) and Chad are talking about what they read (p. 68). (Key: /??/ = indecipherable utterance.)

(1) Participation

01	Deborah:		Y'know who else talks about that?
02			Did you ever read R. D. Laing?
03			*The Divided Self*?
04	Chad:		Yeah. But I don't /??/
05	Deborah:		He talks about that too.
06	Chad:	→	He talks about it too.

Chad's immediate repetition of Deborah's utterance, according to Tannen, is simply a way of showing listenership and acceptance, that is, doing participation. Ratifying listenership, on the other hand, can be seen in a case such as the following, where the participants are talking about a promotional whistle-stop train tour (Tannen, 2007, p. 70). (Key: two dots = perceptible pause of less than half a second; three dots = half second of pause; extra dots = extra half second of pause.)

(2) Ratifying listenership

01	Chad:		they all wanna touch this . . . silly little mouse.
02	Steve:		At five o'clock in the morning on the train station.
03	Chad:		Yeah.
04	David:		In New Mexico.
05	Chad:	→	In New Mexico.
06			With ice on the . . . ice hanging down from things. . . .

While David displays listenership in line 04, Chad's repetition of that display ratifies David's listenership as he integrates the phrase into his narrative.

Repetition, according to Tannen, is also a resource for producing humor. In the following example (Tannen, 2007, p. 71), upon receiving the comment that his dog Rover *is being so good*, Peter in line 03 does a repetition of the

"X's been + adjective" structure with a different adjective. In so doing, he accepts the compliment humorously.

(3) Humor

01	Deborah:		Rover's being so good.
02	Steve:		I know.
03	Peter:	→	He's being hungry.

As Tannen (2007) pointed out, the humor resides in the fact that the same grammatical frame is used to "convert a common construction into an odd one" (p. 71).

In addition, repetition fulfills the function of what Tannen (2007) called stalling, as one repeats a prior speaker's question with a simple pronoun change without actually answering the question (p. 73). Here, Peter and David are talking about American sign language. (Key: three dots = pause of half a second or more.)

(4) Stalling

01	Peter:	But how do you learn a new sign.
02	David:	. . . How do I learn a new sign?

As Tannen noted, the analysis of the repetition as stalling is in part grounded in the pause preceding the repetition. It was also confirmed during playback that David had found the fast pacing of the questioning uncomfortable.

Expanding is the final function of repetition described by Tannen (2007, p. 73). Here, Deborah and Peter are talking about reading habits, where Deborah's *Do you read?* in line 01 is expanded upon via repetition in line 03.

(5) Expanding

01	Deborah:		Do you read?
02	Peter:		Do I read?
03	Deborah:	→	Do you read things just for fun?
04	Peter:		Yeah.
05			Right now I'm reading *Norma Jean the Termite Queen*.

Note that Deborah in line 03 reformulates her initial question with elaboration, which leads to Peter's further expansion with the addition of the title of the book.

Task 1: Consider the five functions of repetition proposed by Tannen (2007). Offer an example for each from your own data or experience.

1. To participate:

2. To ratify listenership:
3. To produce humor:
4. To stall:
5. To expand:

A very different approach of studying repetition is found in Wong's (2000) conversation analytic study, where the focus is on a particular form of repetition—a "second saying" after a "first saying" within the same turn—and how it is used to accomplish resumption in storytellng. Note that while Tannen analyzed conversations of which she was a participant for the most part, Wong was not part of the conversation she analyzed. In the following extract, Bee is telling a story about seeing Adele's husband as she was trying to park her car (pp. 410–411). (Key: hih-hih = laugh tokens.)

(6) First and second saying:

```
01  Adele:                            [Ugh: hih-hih
02               (h) oh:: he ordered new glasses today.=he's getting
03               wire [(frame:es) tch his mother is buying'im=
04  Bee: →       [Oh yeah.
05  Adele:   =(for [him)
06               [I thou:ght I saw: him=it was frea:ky .h I
07               was drivin' arund my- yih you school trying to
08               get parked.=I dunno if it was today or yesterday.=
09  Adele:   =yeah ((uttered softly))
10  Bee: →   .h an' I THOUGHT I SAW HIM ((crescendo
11               effect)) in a mov- I'm STA::RIN' at this GUY::
12               [hih hih .h
12  Adele:   [( ) hih::
14  Bee:     [I said GEE:: that looks like my girlfriend's husband.
15  Adele:   [hih::
16  Bee:     I said no ca:::n't be
```

Here, we observe the presence of *first saying* (line 06) + *insertion* (lines 05–09) + *second saying* (line 10), and the question is: what is this second saying or the repetition doing? Wong's answer is grounded in a conversation analytic account. It is notable, as Wong pointed out, that Bee manages to go past the first saying (*I thought I saw him*), the end of which can be a place for the earliest next start for Adele (Sacks et al., 1974). She does so with a latched utterance *it was freaky* (line 06), which in itself projects a story about what is freaky, and Adele displays her understanding of the "story" nature of Bee's talk by producing the only minimally responsive token *yeah* in a soft voice in line 09. At the same time, however, the inserted talk (lines 05–09) also renders Bee's right to the floor vulnerable as they can "change the shape and character of the upcoming talk and action—even lead to a change of speakership" (Wong, 2000, p. 413). The production of the second saying, then, preempts that possibility by retrospectively marking the inserted materials as parenthetical rather than just the next bit of talk. As Wong (2000) wrote,

> The first saying offers information that might have been produced "later" in the developing turn than it was. However, having already uttered the first saying in the turn-so-far, the current speaker then deploys a self-corrective technique, inserting an utterance (or utterances) that, temporally speaking, is hearable as information that might have been produced "earlier" in the turn. This might explain further why the first saying is "doable" later as a second saying.
>
> (p. 413)

The second saying, in other words, allows the speaker to resume the story without losing control of the extended turn.

Task 2: Compare Tannen (2007) and Wong (2000). How are the two approaches to studying repetition in everyday conversation similar to and/or different from each other?

In sum, repetition as a phenomenon has been of great interest to discourse analysts, and such interest has yielded important insights into how repetition is used across genres, age groups, and languages (e.g., Johnstone, 1994) as well as the variety of functions it is deployed to achieve (e.g., Hellermann, 2003; Norrick, 1987; Schegloff, 1996).

Discourse Markers

Of great interest to discourse analysts is also the question of what those little words such as *oh, so, well, okay, mhm, right, anyway, actually, like, you know, I mean*, or *whatever* do in interaction (cf. "little words that matter" in Bolden, 2006). These little words are typically referred to as discourse markers in the literature although scholars have not always agreed upon the exact definition of discourse markers (e.g., Fox Tree, 2010; Maschler, 2002; Schiffrin, 1987). In this book, we use the term simply to highlight the interactional functions of these small words and phrases.

Discourse marker refers to a range of words or expressions that rise above their semantic/referential meanings to take on complex interactional duties or "discourse meanings" (Waring, 2003, p. 416).

For illustrative purposes, we show how the marker *well* has been studied from, again, two different approaches: interactional sociolinguistics and conversation analysis.

Task 3: Consider the following exchange taken from Schiffrin (1987, p. 108). What is the function of *Well* in Lon's turn? Spell out your reasoning. (Key: . . . . = noticeable pause or break in rhythm.)

01 Sally: Are there any topics that you like in particular about school,
02   or none.
03 Lon: Well. . . . . . . .gym!

Schiffrin (1987) in her interactional sociolinguistic study reviewed the many functions of *well* already established mostly by the conversation analytic literature: beginning a turn without giving away the content of the rest of the turn; doing preclosing (e.g., *Well . . . I'll see you next week then*); as a means of shifting talk toward topics of mutual concern; for canceling a presupposition of a prior question; and prefacing disagreements, insufficient answers to questions, noncompliance with a request, or rejection of an offer. Based on her own audio-recorded data collected from sociolinguistic interviews (Labov, 1984; Tagliamonte, 2006) with three middle-aged couples and a younger neighbor in a lower-middle class urban Jewish Philadelphia neighborhood, Schiffrin's analysis of *well* confirms the prior findings while specifying its additional function as a response marker.

Sociolinguistic interview is a well-developed tool for recording conversation in such a way that mitigates the Observer's Paradox and captures the participants' vernacular, where the interviewer moves from general questions about one's neighborhood and community to more personal ones.

As Schiffrin (1987) pointed out, participants of conversation work hard to build coherence in interaction, and when such coherence is somehow not immediately visible, *well* becomes a resource for showing "the speaker's aliveness to the **need** [bold in original] to accomplish coherence" (p. 126). In various ways, according to Schiffrin (1987), the responses following *well* "temporarily upset the expectation of upcoming coherence" (p. 126). For example, in paired actions such as question-answer or request-compliance, what fits the upcoming coherence would be "answer" or "compliance," and anything that diverges from such "options of coherence" (Schiffrin, 1987, p. 107) is likely to be prefaced with *well*. In the following excerpt, Zelda's questions projects a *yes* or *no* answer, and Sally's response, which is anything but a clear *yes* or *no*, is marked with *Well* (Schiffrin, 1987, p. 106).

(7) Question–answer

01	Zelda:		Are you from Philadelphia?
02	Sally:	→	**Well** I grew up uh out in the suburbs. And then I
03			lived for about seven years in upstate New York.
04			And then I came back here t'go to college.

As can be seen, Sally precedes her nonbinary answer to a binary question with *Well*.

In the next excerpt, the author Debby's utterance in line 03 seeks a confirmation or disconfirmation (Schiffrin, 1987, p. 115).

(8) Request-confirmation

01	Ira:		And I've been working for the federal government
02			ever since. Thir-thirty six years hhhh
03	Debby:		So you must like them as an employer then.
04	Ira:	→	**Well** I like my job now.

Notice that Ira's response offers neither confirmation nor disconfirmation, and it is again prefaced with *well*.

In their conversation analytic study on *well*, Schegloff and Lerner (2009) examined its use in the turn-initial position in a second pair-part (see Chapter 2) response to a *wh*-question. Some of their data support the common understanding of *well* as "an indicator of incipient disaffiliation, rejection, misalignment, and the like" (p. 98). In the following segment, for example, Debbie has called her friend Shelley to express her frustration that Shelley is no longer going on a pre-planned trip with her (Schegloff & Lerner, 2009, pp. 97–98). Immediately prior to the extract, Debbie suggested that Shelley changed her plan because of her boyfriend Mark (i.e., the reference of *he* in lines 01–02). (Key: ↑ = raised pitch; number in parentheses = length of silence in seconds.)

(9) Marker of disaffiliation

01	Shelley:	So: I mean its not becuz he's- he's-I mean its not
02		becuz he:s not going its becuz (0.5) is money's not
03		(0.5) funding me.
04	Debbie:	Okay?
05	Shelley:	So an ↑when other time have I ever [done that?]

```
06   Debbie:   →                              [.hhh well]
07                       I'm jus say:in it jus seems you- you base alot of things
08                       on- on guy:s.(.) I do'know:, it just- a couple times
09                       I don- I don- .hh its not a big deal.
10                       (.)
11   Debbie:             it's [rea:lly. ]
12   Shelley:                  [thats no]t true Debbie [the onl-] the only time=
13   Debbie:                                           [its not]
14   Shelley:            =It- ↑N-Now your talkin about like (.) me
15                       not goin to your party because of Jay an you're
16                       right that wuz becuz of him..hh and that was
17                       pro[bly
18   Debbie:               [↑NO I under-stood tha:t,
19                       I don'care 'bout tha:t.
```

Note that Debbie's disaffiliative move of self-defense in line 07 in response to Shelley's challenge in line 06 is prefaced with *well*.

Beyond this common understanding of *well* as a disaffiliative marker of some sort, however, Schegloff and Lerner (2009) also described it as a practice for marking the upcoming response as non-straightforward. In the following phone conversation, for example, Ilene has called Lisa, who took care of Ilene's dog while she was away, to make arrangements to get the dog back, and in line 08, Lisa makes the announcement that she thinks she's broken her ankle (Schegloff & Lerner, 2009, p. 98). (Key: ↓ = lowered pitch; heheheh = laugh tokens; degree signs = quiet speech.)

(10) Marker of nonstraightforwardness

```
06   Ilene:    A:nd um then I've just got tih go tih the hospital trolley,
07             .hh uh: fro:[m two:
08   Lisa:                 [I think I've broken me a:nkle.
09   Ilene:    ((nasal)) Oh:: w't'v you do:ne,
10             (0.2)
11   Lisa:  →  We:ll I fell down the step- eh e-haa ↑as (.) a matter of
12             fact it wasn' any'ing tih do with Kizzy, .hhhh I: came ou:t
13             of the bah:throom en down those two little steps in
14             (the[hall) 'n kicked meself on my a:nkle.
15   Ilene:        [Mm::,
16             Oh:. [( ).
17   Lisa:          [↑Very badly [e n I-  ]     [I t h : o u]:ght=
18   Ilene:                      [It's prob]a'ly [a ↓brui:se]
19             =°Yeh,°=
20   Lisa:     =↑No it's ↑(not I think it'll be sprained)=
21             =.hh The do[ctor says he wozn't worried so that's
22                        alri[:ght=
```

23	Ilene:	[°Oh°	[°Yeh°
24	Lisa:	=I'm: glad he's not worried I'm the one who's living	
25		with it.	
26	Ilene:	ehhh Yheh-heh-heh-[hh-hh=	

Ilene's wh-question *What have you done?* in line 09 receives the seemingly straightforward response *I fell down* (line 11). The authors argue that the *well*-preface "alerts the recipient not to analyze it that way, that the response will not be straightforward" (p. 102). As can be seen, Lisa's response is indeed not a straightforward one, as she goes on to offer a detailed account of the fall.

> Task 4: Compare Schegloff and Lerner (2009) and Schiffrin (1987). How are the two approaches to studying *well* in everyday conversation similar to and/or different from each other?

In sum, discourse analytic research on discourse markers has been wide ranging, illuminating their use across different contexts (e.g., Heritage & Sorjonen, 1994), in different languages including learner language (e.g., Golato, 2010; Müller, 2005), as well as their development in interaction (e.g., Kyratzis & Ervin-Tripp, 1999) (for a useful overview of discourse markers, see Maschler & Schiffrin, 2015).

Gaze, Gesture, and Body Movement

The role of gaze, gesture, and body movement in interaction has received increasing attention in discourse analysis. Much of the work on embodied actions has been done in the conversation analytic (CA) tradition perhaps in part because of CA's prevalent use of videorecordings. As noted in Chapter 3, while gaze concerns where speaker and recipient direct their eye gaze during an interaction, gesture encompasses head (e.g., nod), facial (e.g., "thinking" face), as well as hand (e.g., pointing) movements in interaction. Body movement, on the other hand, would involve larger span changes such as turning one's torso or jumping up and down.

Gaze

Gaze has been found to highlight or draw attention to gesture (Streeck, 1993), to signal action completion (Olsher, 2005), and to do closing (Goodwin & Goodwin, 1992). In addition, gaze shift has also been found during "toddler harassment" (i.e., toddlers harassing each other) to manage caregiver intervention as both the victim and the harasser orient to the types of gaze shift (i.e., *looking to, noticing,* or *searching out*) as signs of the caregiver's availability for intervention (Kidwell, 2009). The following is an example of gaze doing the work of closing. Nancy and Tasha are talking about the asparagus pie made by Jeff (Goodwin & Goodwin, 1992, p. 79). Note that lines 03 and 04 happen at the same time as indicated by the brackets.

(11) Gaze withdrawal as closing

```
01   Nancy:    Jeff made an asparagus pie.
02             It was s:: so [: goo:d.
03   Tasha:              [I love it. Y] [eah I love that.
04                       [ ((nods))  ] [((starts to withdraw gaze))
```

As shown, at the very same time Tasha closes the sequence with *Yeah I love that,* she starts to withdraw her gaze as well.

Gesture

Research on gestures has shown that head movements can be used to elicit or display recipiency (Heath, 1992) or to initiate repair (Seo & Koshik, 2010), facial gestures to facilitate word search (Goodwin & Goodwin, 1986) and turn-taking (Streeck & Hartge, 1992), and hand gestures to manage co-participation and to enhance, complete, or perform an action (Goodwin & Goodwin, 1992; Olsher, 2005, 2008; Streeck & Hartge, 1992).

In the following doctor-patient interaction taken from Heath (1992) that involves talk about how long a patient needs to take some tablet medication, for example, the vertical head movement is used by the doctor to elicit, and by the patient to display, recipiency (Heath, 1992, p. 105). Again, note the simultaneous occurrence of the verbal and the nonverbal as indicated by the brackets (see Chapter 1).

(12) Manage recipiency

```
01   Doctor:                        [((head nods))]
02             until they're:: all::: gone >th[at'll ta[ke a]we e ]:k (.)
03             alright?
04   Patient:                             [((head nods))]
```

The doctor nods as he explains the duration of the medication (*that'll take a week*), which seems to have succeeded in immediately obtaining the patient's recipiency as the latter nods in return.

In the next segment, the "thinking face" as a facial gesture is displayed by the speaker while searching for the word *crabmeat* (Goodwin & Goodwin, 1986, p. 58). Again, lines 01 and 02 co-occur as indicated by the brackets.

(13) Thinking face

01   A: [He pu:t uhm, (0.7) tch!] Put crabmeat on the bottom.
02   [((*thinking face*))   ]

In the next two extracts, hand gestures are used to first enhance a verbal action and then to complete an unfinished verbal action in managing delicacy. In the following data from an ESL class, the students in a small group are engaged in a map-making project, and in line 02, Junko seeks clarification of Aiko's prior turn (Olsher, 2008, p. 119). (Key: large/raj = 'large' pronounced as 'raj'.)

(14) Gesture to enhance verbal action

((*J rubs arms and resumes coloring*))

01   Aiko: Because your area is (large/raj).
02   Junko: What?
03   (.) ((*A moves hand toward J's map area, then retracts*))
04   Aiko: → [((*A's hand sweeps across J's area of the map*))
05   [L[a:rge.]
06   Junko: [Ah::::] ((*A's arm returns before end of turn*))

Note that Junko's initiation of repair is responded to by Aiko with the repair *Large* (line 05) enhanced by the co-occurring "large" gesture of sweeping across J's map area (line 04). Rather than enhancing a verbal action, gesture can also be deployed to complete one.

In contrast to Aiko's gesture that enhances her action of repair, the focal gesture in the next segment is used to complete an action. A group of graduate student physicists are practicing for their upcoming conference presentations with their professor, Ron. Miguel has just finished his conference rehearsal as the segment begins (Olsher, 2005, pp. 224–225 taken from Jacoby, 1988, pp. 432–441).

(15) Gesture to complete verbal action

01   Ron: Okay. ((*sits back in chair*)) uh:m first of all
02   that was <u>ex</u>cellent. You covered a hu:ge amount
03   →   of materials, but [you are g- ((*points to stopwatch*))
04   Miguel: [((*hitches up pants, sits on table*))
05   Ron: (Y' know? [by my watch it was-
06   Miguel: [Well I was thirty seconds: uh::
07   Ron: That's disastrous. (I mean uh) (.)
08   I was yer (0.2) chairman I would stand up
09   an' (.) just cut you off.
10   Miguel: ((*nods head*))=

Note that in line 03, Ron's very delicate verbal action of critiquing Miguel's time management prefaced by the discourse marker *but* is, initially, completed with the hand gesture of pointing to his watch. In line 06, Miguel's *well*-prefaced response further marks the delicate nature of the interaction.

Perhaps not surprisingly, gesturing alone can perform independent actions as well. Parents of young children must be familiar with their babies' gesture of turning away from food as a sign of rejection. Goodwin and Goodwin (1992) detailed a case where one participant mimics another's (rapidly shaking) hand movements during storytelling, and such mimicking is produced and received as heckling. In a remarkable exhibit of how a stroke victim Chil manages to communicate with only three words, *Yes*, *No*, and *And*, Goodwin (2003) showed how Chil at the breakfast table uses pointing to propose an alternative as Chuck (author of the study) repeatedly tries to figure out what Chil wants (Goodwin, 2003, p. 227). (Note: Images of pointing embedded in the original transcript not reproduced here.)

(16) Gesture to propose alternative

```
01   Peggy:       It's very nice outdoors, you want to walk a little bit.
02   Chil:        Yes.
03                No No Nuh dih dah
04        →       (0.9)
05   Chil:        uhm,
06        →       (2.9)----------------((image of pointing)
07   Chuck:       Aww: Bagel?
08   Chil:        No no
09        →       (0.4)
10   Chuck:       Put this away?-------((image of pointing))
11   Peggy:       Scuse [me.
12   Chil:              [Nah.
13   Chuck:       Chocolate?
14   Chil:        Naw no.
15   Chuck:       Do you want something to eat?
16   Chil:    →   (1.5)------------------((image of pointing))
17   Chuck:       Aw oh look at the movies. ((referring to listing in
18                the newspaper))
19   Chil:        Yes.
20   Chuck:       Yeah I'm trying. There's this um (0.2) uh
```

As can be seen, using a series of pointing gestures, Chil repeatedly rejects Chuck's guesses and is finally able to lead Chuck to the targeted item.

Body Movement

Body movement can be used to manage multiple courses of action (Schegl-off, 1998) or to constitute and enhance an action. In the following tutoring session that is being videorecorded for research purposes, we observe some preliminary interaction among the physics tutor, Emily, her tutee, Grace, and the manager of the taping session, Marjorie, who is positioned to the left of the pair off-camera. They appear to be joking about this "laboratory" set-ting, and body torque (see Chapter 2) is being used by Grace to attend to both Emily and Marjorie (Schegloff, 1998, p. 548). (Key: .hh = inbreath.)

(17) Body torque to multitask

01	Emily:		I'll do my best to ignore this whole system
02			ha [ha ha
03	Grace:		[ha [ha ha
04	Marjorie:		[Yeah, good idea [( )?
05	Emily:		[(telling just sort of)
06			weird looking.
07	Grace:		.hh haha [ha
08	Marjorie:		[We're going to just lo:ck you in here.
09	Emily:	→	Okay, ha ha ha-((*arms planted on desk with body*
10			*turned to M*))
11	Marjorie:	→	so you can't go away.

As Schegloff (1998) pointed out, "Grace's arms remain planted in the forward-facing body position that was established for 'doing tutoring'" (p. 550). By turn-ing only her upper body toward Marjorie, Grace is able to sustain the tutoring activity and "treat Marjorie's talk as an 'insert' into it" (p. 552). A screen shot of lines 09–10 is included in Schegloff (1998) to illustrate the body torque, which, unfortunately, cannot be reproduced here due to the low image quality.

Body movement can also constitute and enhance an action (Goodwin, 2000). In an episode that involves three young girls playing hopscotch (see Figure 5.1), Carla thrusts her finger gesture ("four") in front of Diana's face and walks into the grid as Diana is in the process of jumping. Her body movement as such constitutes and enhances her action as a challenge. Note that the data were originally in Spanish.

Finally, in a fascinating study on videorecorded dance instructions in Swed-ish, Estonian, and English, Keevallik (2010) showed that her dance instructors use what she calls "bodily quoting" as part of the corrective activity, that is, as evidence for what needs correction.

Task 5: As can be seen, nonverbal conduct can be represented in a vari-ety of different ways ranging from verbal descriptions to drawings and to screen shots. Consider these differences in representation and the advantages and disadvantages of each, if relevant.

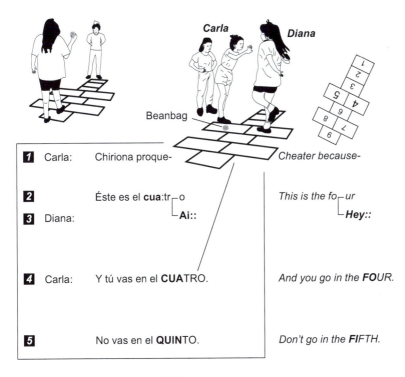

Figure 5.1 Body Movement as Challenge

Adapted from Goodwin, 2000

In sum, work on gaze, gesture, and body movement has demonstrated how such nonverbal resources can be drawn upon to accomplish a variety of social actions among different age groups, in different settings, and across different cultures.

Task 6: What practical implications can we draw from the research on the functions of gaze, gesture, and body movement? Are there other areas of nonverbal conduct that would warrant further investigation?

Begin With Action

Balancing Work and Play

In her interactional sociolinguistic study on parent–child interaction based on audio-recorded and transcribed conversations involving members of three families (consisting of two parents and one young child each), Gordon (2008) showed how parents are able to balance work and play through blending frames and reframing (see Chapter 4 on framing). Immediately prior to the following segment (Gordon, 2008, p. 330), Clara and Neil have been trying to get their 4-year-old son Jason to go to a coffee shop with them so they could hear a guitarist who was playing there. Jason wanted them to buy him a toy (Silly String) instead. The segment begins with Jason whining about wanting the toy. Note that vocal noises, intonation information, and manner of speaking are included as they function as what Gumperz (1982) called contextualization cues (see Chapter 4) (Key: each new line = an intonation unit; arrow at the end of a line = the intonation unit continues onto the next line; angle brackets = descriptions of vocal noise or the manner in which an utterance is spoken.)

(18) Reframe work into play

01	Jason:		<*whimpers*>
02			<*whiney*> I want it.>
03			((*short pause*))
04			<*whiney*> I wanna get (the) Silly String.>
05	Neil:		[(You won't ??)]
06	Clara:	→	[<*high-pitched*> Lemme see] if I get this straight.
07			YOU,
08			want ME,
09			to jump outta my chair,>
10	Jason:		<*laughs*>
11	Clara:		<*high-pitched*> go all the way to the mall,
12	Jason:		<*laughs*>
13	Clara:		just for the simple purpose,
14			of getting Silly String for you.>
15	Jason:		<*laughs*>
16			<*laughing*> Yeah.>
17	Clara:		<*high-pitched*> And then come ALL THE WAY BACK.
18			Just with this little bottle of Silly String.>
19	Jason:		<*laughing*> Yea:h.>
20	Clara:		[<*high-pitched*> It sounds a little] silly to me!>
21	Neil:		[I told him that-]
22			I told him we should bring a uh →
23			his coloring book and crayons,
24			to the Starbucks,

In line 06, Clara begins to reframe the situation, changing the definition of the situation from conflict into play, by using a high-pitched voice and exaggerated intonation contours to tease Jason about the silliness of his request, and Jason responds with laughter and *Yeah* (lines 10, 12, 15–16, 19). The conflict is thus deftly diffused rather than escalated.

In the next segment, Janet and her almost-3-year-old daughter Natalie are engaged in pretend play where Natalie is playing the role Blue Fairy, and Janet is pretending to be Natalie. The segment begins with Natalie asking for her mother's yogurt inside the play frame (Gordon, 2008, p. 339). In other words, Natalie enacts the Blue Fairy role to get the yogurt and addresses her mother as "Natalie."

(19) Blending work and play

01	Natalie:		Hi Miss Natalie.
02			May I have some of y- that yogurt.
03			I guess I'll get some.
04	Janet:	→	*<high-pitched>* Blue Fairy why are you trying→
05			to eat my yogurt.
06			Why are you trying to eat my yogurt Blue Fairy.>
07			Mnm mnm. ((*negative*))
08			[Do- do not grab,]
09	Natalie:		[(I want ??)]
10	Janet:		Blue Fairy should know better manners than to grab.
11	Natalie:		Blue Fairy can I grab.
12	Janet:		*<high-pitched>* Blue Fairy don't you have→
13			some good manners.>
14	Natalie:		Please?
15	Janet:		*<high-pitched>* Didn't they teach you manners→
16			at fairy school?>.
17	Natalie:		They didn't teach me manners at fairy school.
18	Janet:		*<high-pitched>* You're kidding!>

In line 04, Janet's response is produced in a **blended frame**, where she attends to the play frame by addressing Natalie as *Blue Fairy* in a high pitch but at the same time blends in the work frame of parenting Natalie by chastising her for helping herself with the yogurt without permission. As shown, the blended frame continues for multiple turns, and Natalie in line 14 finally uses her manners and says *Please?*

In sum, Gordon investigated how work and play are balanced, and in so doing, identified the practices of reframing and blending, where discursive strategies such as address terms, high pitch, and exaggerated intonation are engaged to signal play, and those such as directives and chastising are used to do parenting work.

Managing Nongranting of Requests

While Gordon's (2008) interactional sociolinguistic study answers the questions of how parents balance work and play in their interactions with young children, Lee's (2011) conversation analytic study specifies how airline agents manage the nongranting of customer requests. Based on 169 audiotaped calls (collected in 2002–2003) made to an airline in South Korea, Lee found that airline agents shape customer requests toward a grantable direction through implicit substitution or embedded restriction.

Implicit substitution involves implicitly rejecting a customer's nongrantable request by offering substitutes, thus responding as if the customer's request had been granted when in fact it has not. In the following call (Lee, 2011, p. 118), for example, the agent is clearly not able to grant the customer's request for a *half past nine* flight (line 04), and yet, she responds to the request with a *yes* and proceeds to offer *eight thirty* as the available option (line 08). Note that the data were originally in Korean, and the following transcripts offer an idiomatic English translation. (Key: (x)/(y) = not clear which is said or heard; number in parentheses = length of silence in seconds.)

(20) Implicit substitution

01	Customer:		Monday December twenty third:?
02	Agent:		Yes:?
03	Customer:		Uh: a flight going down to Wulsan would there
04			be uh: a schedule at **half past nine** by any chance,
05	Agent:		And the departure is from Seoul Kim:po: going to
06			Wulsan?
07	Customer:		Yes:=
08	Agent:	→	=Yes.<.h<**we have eight thirty**: in the morn-
09			ing and the next is te:n thirty?
10	Customer:		Eight thirty: and the next at ten thir[ty?
11	Agent:		[Yes yes::
12			(0.5)
13	Customer:		(Oh::)/(Uh::) about ha::lf past nine::- .ss then I'll
14			make a reservation for eight thi::rty:=
15	Agent:		=How many people,
16	Customer:		One person.

Note that the customer's *about ha::lf past nine:* in line 13 displays her understanding of the agent's offer as not fitted to her original request, and yet, he proceeds to request the alternative, thus acquiescing to the agent's implicit substitution. As Lee (2011) wrote, implicit substitution is enabled by the knowledge asymmetry between the customer and the agent, as the latter has the full airline schedule at his or her disposal to offer the various specifications. It is also driven by a concern for efficiency since an unfulfilled request typically leads to requesting and offering alternatives—a step that the agent bypasses by combining rejecting and offering into one move. Finally, implicit substitution maximizes the fulfillment of customers' requests, as it pushes the customers into the direction of making more grantable requests.

Agents can also manage the nongranting of requests through **embedded restriction**, which involves embedding a restriction on a not-yet-specified component of a request into a response that is addressed to a customer's inquiry about a different component of the request. For instance, agents may embed a restriction on seat availability when responding to a customer's inquiry about flight schedules, as shown in the following extract (Lee, 2011, pp. 119–120).

(21) Embedded restriction

01	Agent:		Yes=from Pusan to Cheju around what time do
02			you go:?
03	Customer:		Yes=today after this time:- uh- what time do you
04			have?
05			(2.0)
06	Agent:	→	We have one seat at twelve thirty fi:ve, and one seat at
07			one twenty f:iv[e
08	Customer:		[What time?
09			(0.5)
10	Agent:		Twelve thirty five one twenty five we have one seat
11			for each:=
12	Customer:		=You don't have anything before that:¿
13			(.)
14	Agent:		No::.

((lines omitted: A and C talk about the unavailability of previous flights.))

15	Customer:	Yes okay. ↑You said you have one seat at twelve thirty
16		five?
17	Agent:	Yes:.
18	Customer:	(Oh)/(Uh) I'll make a reservation for that.

In lines 06–07, without asking the customer for the number of passengers, the agent embeds the specification of seat availability into her response of departure times, thus preempting the possibility of the customer asking for more than one seat for these particular flights and sidestepping the potential of having to reject a forthcoming customer request. As shown, the customer eventually made a grantable request in accordance with the agent's specifications.

In answering her question of how airline agents manage situations where customers' requests cannot be granted then, Lee demonstrated how the agents highlight what is grantable in their response through implicit substitution and preempt potentials for nongrantable requests through embedded restrictions, thereby minimizing dissatisfaction and enhancing efficiency.

Task 7: Consider the similarities and differences between Gordon (2008) and Lee (2011) in their approaches to answering the "how" question of discourse and social action. What social action in the world might you choose to study? How might you collect and analyze your data?

Achieving Consensus

Critical discourse analysis is yet another methodology used by discourse analysts to address the question of how social actions are accomplished (see Chapter 8 for a further discussion on critical discourse analysis). By examining transcripts of interviews and meetings (along with confidential company documents) over six months in a senior management team of a single business unit in a multinational defense company in Australia, Wodak, Kwon, and Clarke (2011) in their critical discourse analysis study showed how, to facilitate consensus building, the same chief executive officer (CEO) in two key meeting genres (regular management team meetings and "away-days") discursively enacts authoritarian or egalitarian leadership through a choice of strategies that include:

(1) Bonding: a strategy that supports motivation to reach consensus and a decision.
(2) Encouraging: a strategy that stimulates the participation of others.
(3) Directing: a strategy that brings the discussion toward closure and resolution.
(4) Modulating: a strategy that aims for a balance between Encouraging and Directing.
(5) Re/committing: a strategy that moves from a consensual understanding toward a commitment to action.

Task 8: Consider whether the following talk (data from Wodak et al., 2011) illustrates any of the five discursive strategies listed previously. If yes, what are some of the linguistic devices/language choices that can be used to realize the strategy?

1. What do you think, Will and Charlie?
2. . . . I'm just putting the concerns on the table, I'm not saying they're insurmountable, but we just need to be aware of them.
3. . . . . the default position is two buildings, then if we need to do anything else around some of this other stuff to refurnish, we'll do that, but let's get the second building.

According to the authors, their analysis went through four stages that oscillated between the micro and the macro, creating constant dialogs to "reconcile hypotheses arising from the text with broader contextual understandings derived from direct ethnographic observations of the organization" (Wodak et al., 2011, p. 597). In the first stage, corpus linguistics analysis was used to identify two meetings as the most salient in containing topics related to the broader organizational strategic mandate (note that corpus analysis has become an increasingly popular tool in critical discourse analysis; see example in Chapter 9). The second stage focused on identifying the overall structure and dynamic of the two meetings. The third stage involved a detailed analysis of specific discursive strategies and related linguistic/pragmatic/rhetorical devices. During the final stage, the analysts synthesized findings of the prior stages and identified how transformational and transactional leadership styles are discursively deployed to achieve consensus. While transformational leadership refers to a style where the leader specifies goals and rewards the followers when such goals are achieved, transformational leadership involves offering inspiration to build a collective identity, stimulating intellectual discussions, and attending to individual needs (Wodak et al., 2011, p. 594). Both of the following extracts involve Mike the CEO. In the first instance, he forcefully argues for the "two buildings" plan. (Note that no transcription keys were provided in the original published article, which I hope will not distract the reader from appreciating the main analytical points that are being proposed.)

(22) Authoritarian

01	Mike:	→	So in my head is, is, the default position is two
02			buildings, then if we need to do anything else
03			around some of this other stuff to refurbish, we'll
04			do that, but let's get the second building.
05	Adam:		So what would you say for the size of the Adelaide
06			site 800, 600 people?
07	Mike:	→	Say, it's going to be somewhere over 800 and less
08			than 1,100.
09	Will:		and a 150 after these numbers were ready.
10	Adam:		Why don't we, sort of, suggest making this unmade,
11			and giving growth in [unclear]?
12	Mike:	→	Because the capability's there, you can't just make it
13			smaller!
14	Bradley:		It's just not sensible to do that.
15	Mike:	→	You just can't make this smaller by wanting to put it
16			somewhere else because it's sensible. Thing is we should
17			be growing there—his design capability, the design
18			capability around the falcon training aids business,
19			is all in Adelaide.
20	Adam:		Hang on, we've started this—OK, fine. We've started
21			this conversation by all of us, I think, recognizing
22			attrition and retention issues we've got in Adelaide.
23			And what we need to do is address that. We're now
24			saying 'Well, too bad, we have the projects in
25			Adelaide—
26	Mike:	→	No, no, what I'm saying is—Realistically if you're
27			going to grow the business you need more people

28			in Sydney, more people in—but a minimum of 800
29			or so /
30	Bradley:		Core capability/
31	Mike:	→	in Adelaide.

As the authors noted, Mike's insistence on "two buildings" is done directly and forcefully through summarizing and reformulating his opinions in declarative ways. By contrast, in the following extract taken from the second meeting, Mike engages different strategies to emphasize that there are enough specialists available to support the implementation of the second project.

(23) Egalitarian

01	Mike:	→	So are we talking about Hobson's choice here, really?
02			Do we have any other option what to do, this way,
03			other than saying we're not going to take the PER
04			EGRINE contract? That's the two options.
05	Will:		I believe what Larry's saying about sharing the resources
06			across the projects is fundamental. If we don't do
07			that, we will fail.
08	Mike:	→	Right, and then at some level of abstraction I agree
09			with that, and absolutely. But now we've got this
10			[bangs table for emphasis] cast-iron, concrete case that
11			we have to do something about.
12	Harris:		Do we know today what the resources overlay is
13			between the new Avionics re baseline and the
14			globalization—
15	Will:		No, my issue was that we don't have/
16	Harris:		[indistinct]
17	Will:		/a baseline for Avionics, and unlikely to have a formed
18			baseline until the end of May, but I will have one that's
19			90 percent accurate at the end of April.
20	Harris:		So you don't really know what sort of demands or
21			tensions there's going to be in terms of this resource.
22	Larry:		Except that the people are not likely to—the key
23			people are not going to change.
24	Mike:	→	Well, what I thought I was hearing last week was that
25			we will build sufficient and backfilled and shadow
26			in order to have—if you take a very prudent view of
27			this, we will have enough people to cover that. /
28	Larry:		Well/
29	Harris:		/Right, to mobilize PEREGRINE and to run with
30			OSPREY.
31	Mike:		That was the plan. That was the plan.

As Wodak et al. (2011) pointed out, Mike listens to others without disagreeing with them immediately (lines 08–11), he employs the strategy of Modulating to reduce the complexity of the problem (e.g., Hobson's choice in lines 01–03), and he offers reasoning of his view (as opposed to declarative statement) (lines 24–27) that succeeds in gathering Harris's agreement (lines 29–30).

In sum, in answering the question of how consensus is achieved then, Wodak and her colleagues were able to show that while the authoritarian leadership style characterized by Directing and Summarizing in the first meeting (November) only led to superficial consensus (extract 22) (p. 607), the egalitarian style that featured Encouraging as demonstrated in the second meeting (April) facilitated the achievement of consensus with greater efficacy (extract 23) (p. 609). This difference between superficial and true consensus is in part evidenced in the rapid changing of topics (topic breath) in the November meeting and the development of topic depth in the April meeting.

Reenactments in Conversation

A good example of how social action can be accomplished nonverbally can be found in Thompson and Suzuki's (2014) conversation analytic study on reenactments, where "a speaker re-presents or depicts a previously occurring event, often dramatically" (p. 816). Based on videorecordings of three- and four-party conversations in Japanese and English among close friends and family members, the authors showed how the participants use gaze to (1) portray the gaze of the characters in the original event and to (2) "designate their recipients to stand in for characters in the original event" (Thompson & Suzuki, 2014, p. 841). In the following segment, Jennifer, in a conversation with her friends Bonnie and Teresa, reenacts her encounter with a customer who "begs" for a cup of coffee before the shop opens. (Key: S>>>> = gazes at mid-space; ^ = eyebrow flash; $ = shrug; T>>>> = moves gaze to, and gazes to, Teresa; B>>>> = moves gaze to, and gazes at, Bonnie; @ = laughter; number in parentheses = length of silence in seconds. Note that three screen shots were also provided at various points in the extract, which are not reproduced here.)

```
(24)  Gaze in reenactment
                        S>>>>>>>
      01    Jennifer:    .hhh and um,
      02                 (0.2)
                        >>>>>>>>>>>>>>
      03                 then he's like Well-
                        >> ^ T>>>>> B>>>>>>>>
      04        →        I know you're not open yet,
                        >>>>>T>>>>>>>>>>>>>>>B>>>>>>>>>>
```

05		→	but I would <u>really</u> just w<u>a</u>nt a cup of c<u>o</u>ffee.
			S>>>>
06			I'm like,
07			(0.6)
			>>>> $ T>>>>>>>>>>>>>>>>>>>
08		→	Alright, but you still have to wait til
			>>>>>>>>>>>>
09			s<u>e</u>(h)ven o(h)clock.
10	All:		@@@

The authors noted that in lines 04–05, as Jennifer reenacts the guy, she gazes first at Bonnie and then at Teresa to invite them as *stand in* for herself in the original story, and when she plays the role of herself in line 08, she designates Teresa as the "guy" in the original story via her gaze. As such, part of the social action of enactment is accomplished through gaze (also see Sidnell, 2006).

Approaches to Discourse and Social Action

As shown, the issue of discourse and social action can be addressed via a variety of approaches such as conversation analysis, interactional sociolinguistics, and critical discourse analysis. Working within such varying frameworks, discourse analysts have offered illuminating answers to questions such as what social actions are accomplished via discursive resources such as repetitions and discourse markers as well as gaze, gesture, and body movement. They have also produced important insights into how specific social actions are accomplished discursively—how work and play are balanced in parent-child interaction, how the nongranting of requests is handled by airline agents, how consensus is built in team meetings, and how reenactments are managed through gaze.

The previous presentation may have given the impression that doing discourse analysis is a matter of offering illustrative excerpts of a particular phenomenon of interest, which is certainly an integral part of presenting the outcome of discourse analytic work, but not the entirety of the work itself, which entails the systematic collection and analysis of data. In fact, the reader might have already noticed some differences in the various approaches in addressing the same type of questions—differences in their ways of describing, transcribing, and interpreting the data. One obvious difference lies in the different conventions and the level of detail in which transcriptions are done. While both attend to the linguistic details that capture not just what is said, but how it is said, conversation analysis and interactional sociolinguistics differ in such details as how pauses (with numbers or dots) are captured or whether each line of transcript composes a single intonational unit. Critical discourse analysis, on the other hand, is less attentive to the details of delivery. The approaches also differ in the extent to which participants' backgrounds are documented and reported. While participants' background information is largely absent in conversation analytic (CA) studies (Lee, 2011; Wong, 2000), it tends to be carefully described in both interactional sociolinguistic (IS) (Gordon, 2008; Schiffrin, 1987; Tannen, 2007) and critical discourse analysis (CDA) (Wodak et al., 2011) studies. In addition, while the analyst's interpretation tends to preside in critical discourse analysis studies, CA analysis privileges participants' understandings of each other's talk as displayed in the minute details of moment-to-moment interaction, which requires greater attention to the interactional particulars that evidence such understandings. Although this attention to details to demonstrate participants' understandings is also evident in IS studies (though perhaps not to the same extent as conversation analysis), interactional sociolinguistics is also open to multiple interpretations, as evidenced in the common practice of playback, where an analyst's interpretations are checked with the participants.

One by-product of these differences might be the trade-off between breadth and depth. With the repetition studies, for example, Tannen (2007) addressed a wide range of functions while Wong (2000) delved into one single feature with greater specificity. It is also noticeable that the analysis of nonverbal conduct in social interaction has been mostly taken up in conversation analytic studies (Goodwin, 2003; Schegloff, 1998; Streeck, 1993; Thompson & Suzuki, 2014). Finally, it should not come as a surprise that different approaches would invoke different analytical tools in the analysis of data. While framing is a key analytical concept in Gordon's (2008) study on parent-child interaction, for example, concepts such as turns and repair tend to feature in conversation analytic studies (Olsher, 2008; Schegloff & Lerner, 2009; Wong, 2000). Of course, all these observable differences are rooted in underlying theoretical frameworks from which these differences are derived. For our purposes, however, I hope understanding the differences in the actual execution of discourse analytic work among the various approaches can provide an initial entry point for a beginning student of discourse to appreciate the affordances of a wide range of discourse analytic work and begin to assemble an analytical toolbox tailored to his or her specific research question.

Task 9: What would you consider to be some of the advantages and disadvantages of employing the various approaches to discourse and social action?

Despite their differences, analysts interested in discourse and social action formulate their projects in search of either what social actions a particular item of talk, text, or nonverbal conduct (e.g., *well*) in discourse performs (i.e., what does X do?) or how a particular action (e.g., balancing work and life) is accomplished in discourse (i.e., how is Y done?). In either case, analysts strive to answer their questions by grounding their findings in actual instances of social interaction. In reading a discourse analytic study on social action then, one is well advised to ask the following questions:

a. Is the starting point of the study a specific type of conduct (text/talk/nonverbal), or is it a specific social action?
b. What kinds of data were collected to answer the research question?
c. What kinds of evidence are pointed to in grounding the answers?
d. How is the analytical reasoning done?
e. Are the analyses convincing?

Task 10: Read Waring (2012) (see References) or any study on discourse and social action of interest to you and answer the previous questions.

Task 11: Consider the following interview excerpt between the television journalist Charlie Gibson and the 2008 U.S. vice presidential candidate Sarah Palin. Using all the analytical resources discussed so far, offer an analysis of what Charlie's remark in line 05 is doing (i.e., what social action does it perform?). (Key: > < =quickened pace; number in parentheses = length of silence in seconds; degree signs = quieter speech.)

```
01  Charlie:         >D'y agree with the< Bush Doctrine?
02                   (1.5)
03  Sarah:           In what respect Charlie,
04                   (0.8)
05  Charlie:    →    Bush- wh- wh- what d'y- what d'y interpret it to be.
06                   (0.2)
07  Sarah:           his wo:rld vie:w?
08                   (0.2)
09                   [(°y' mean,°)      ]
10  Charlie:         [>No.=the< Bush] doctrine. enunciated September
11                   (.) two thousand two.
12                   °for the Iraq war.°
13                   (0.8)
14  Sarah:           I believe that what (.) President Bush has (.) attempted
15                   to do, i:s hh
16                   rid this world (0.5) of (.) >Islamic extremism,<
17                   ((continues))
```

Key Points

- Discourse analysts approach the issue of discourse and social action by asking (1) what action is accomplished by specific conduct (i.e., begin with conduct) or (2) what resources are deployed to accomplish a specific action (i.e., begin with action).
- Repetition in conversation can be used to display participation, ratify listenership, produce humor, stall, expand, or resume a story without losing an extended turn, among other functions.
- The discourse marker *well* may be used to indicate that the upcoming response upsets the expectation of coherence or to mark the non-straightforward nature of the upcoming response.
- Gaze may be used to highlight gesture, signal action completion, and do closing.
- Gestures may be used to elicit or display recipiency; facilitate word searches and turn-taking; manage co-participation; and enhance, complete, or perform an action.
- Body movement may be used to manage multiple courses of action or to constitute and enhance an action.
- Work and play may be balanced through reframing and blending frames in parent-child interaction.
- The nongranting of requests may be managed by airline agents through implicit substitution and embedded restriction.
- Consensus building may be facilitated through an egalitarian leadership style characterized by strategies such as bonding, encouraging, and modulating.
- Reenactments in conversation may be managed through gaze.
- The question of discourse and social action may be addressed from a variety of analytical approaches.

References

Bolden, G. (2006). Little words that matter: Discourse markers 'so' and 'oh' and the doing of other-attentiveness in social interaction. *Journal of Communication, 56*(4), 661–688.

Fox Tree, J. E. (2010). Discourse markers across speakers and settings. *Language and Linguistics Compass, 4,* 269–281.

Golato, A. (2010). Marking understanding versus receipting information in talk: *achso* and *ach* in German interaction. *Discourse Studies, 12*(2), 147–176.

Goodwin, C. (2000). Action and embodiment within situated human interaction. *Journal of Pragmatics, 32*(10), 1489–1522.

Goodwin, C. (2003). Pointing as situated practice. In S. Kita (Ed.), *Pointing: Where language, culture and cognition meet* (pp. 217–241). Mahwah, NJ: Lawrence Erlbaum.

Goodwin, C., & Goodwin, M. H. (1992). Context, activity and participation. In P. Auer & A. di Luzio (Eds.), *The contextualization of language* (pp. 77–99). Amsterdam: Benjamins.

Goodwin, M. H., & Goodwin, C. (1986). Gesture and coparticipation in the activity of searching for a word. *Semiotica, 62*(1–2), 51–76.

Gordon, C. (2008). A(p)parent play: Blending frames and reframing in family talk. *Language in Society, 37*(3), 319–349.

Gumperz, J. J. (1982). *Discourse strategies.* Cambridge: Cambridge University Press.

Heath, C. (1992). Gesture's discreet tasks: Multiple relevancies in visual conduct and in the contextualisation of language. In P. Auer & A. di Luzio (Eds.), *The contextualization of language* (pp. 101–128). Amsterdam: John Benjamins.

Hellermann, J. (2003). The interactive work of prosody in the IRF exchange: Teacher repetition in feedback moves. *Language in Society, 32,* 79–104.

Heritage, J., & Sorjonen, M.-L. (1994). Constituting and maintaining activities across sequences: And prefacing. *Language in Society, 23*(1), 1–29.

Johnstone, B. (Ed.). (1994). *Repetition in discourse: Interdisciplinary perspectives* (Vols. 1–2). Norwood, NJ: Ablex Publishing.

Keevallik, L. (2010). Bodily quoting in dance correction. *Research on Language and Social Interaction, 43*(4), 401–426.

Kidwell, M. (2009). Gaze shift as an interactional resource for very young children. *Discourse Processes, 46*(2–3), 145–160.

Kyratzis, A., & Ervin-Tripp, S. (1999). The development of discourse markers in peer interaction. *Journal of Pragmatics, 31,* 1321–1338.

Labov, W. (1984). Field methods of the project on linguistic change and variation. In J. Baugh & J. Sherzer (Eds.), *Language in use: Readings in sociolinguistics* (pp. 28–53). Englewood Cliffs, NJ: Prentice Hall.

Lee, S.-H. (2011). Managing nongranting of customers' requests in commercial service encounters. *Research on Language and Social Interaction, 44*(2), 109–134.

Maschler, Y. (2002). The role of discourse markers in the construction of multivocality in Israeli Hebrew talk-in-interaction. *Research on Language and Social Interaction, 35*(1), 1–38.

Maschler, Y., & Schiffrin, D. (2015). Discourse markers: Language, meaning, and context. In D. Tannen, H. E. Hamilton, & D. Schiffrin (Eds.), *The handbook of discourse analysis* (2nd ed.) (pp. 189–221). Malden, MA: Wiley Blackwell.

Müller, S. (2005). Discourse markers in native and non-native English discourse. Amsterdam: John Benjamins Publishing.

Norrick, N. R. (1987). Functions of repetition in conversation. *Text, 7,* 245–264.

Olsher, D. (2005). Talk and gesture: The embodied completion of sequential actions in spoken interaction. In R. Gardner & J. Wagner (Eds.), *Second language conversations* (pp. 221–245). New York: Continuum.

Olsher, D. (2008). Gesturally-enhanced repeats in the repair turn: Communication strategy or cognitive language-learning tool? In S. G McCafferty & G. Stam (Eds.), *Gesture: Second language acquisition and classroom research* (pp. 109–132). New York: Routledge.

Sacks, H., Schegloff, E. A., & Jefferson, G. (1974). A simplest systematics for the organization of turn-taking for conversation. *Language, 50*(4), 696–735.

Schegloff, E. A. (1996). Confirming allusions: Toward an empirical account of action. *American Journal of Sociology, 102*(1), 161–216.

Schegloff, E. A. (1998). Body torque. *Social Research, 65*(3), 535–596.

Schegloff, E. A., & Lerner, G. (2009). Beginning to respond: Well-prefaced responses to wh-questions. *Research on Language and Social Interaction, 42*(2), 91–115.

Schiffrin, D. (1987). *Discourse markers.* Cambridge: Cambridge University Press.

Seo, M. S., & Koshik, I. (2010). A conversation analytic study of gestures that engender repair in ESL conversational tutoring. *Journal of Pragmatics, 42*(8), 2219–2239.

Sidnell, J. (2006). Coordinating gesture, talk, and gaze in reenactments. *Research on Language and Social Interaction, 39*(4), 377–409.

Streeck, J. (1993). Gesture as communication: Its coordination with gaze and speech. *Communication Monographs, 60*, 275–299.

Streeck, J., & Hartge, U. (1992). Previews: Gestures at the transition place. In P. Auer & A. di Luzio (Eds.), *The contextualization of language* (pp. 135–158). Amsterdam: John Benjamins.

Tagliamonte, S. A. (2006). *Analysing sociolinguistic variation.* New York: Cambridge University Press.

Tannen, D. (2007). Talking voices: Repetition, dialogue, and imagery in conversational discourse (2nd ed.). New York: Cambridge University Press.

Thompson, S. A., & Suzuki, R. (2014). Reenactments in conversation: Gaze and recipiency. *Discourse Studies, 16*(6), 816–846.

Waring, H. Z. (2003). Also as a discourse marker: Its use in disjunctive and disaligning environments. *Discourse Studies, 5*(3), 415–436.

Waring, H. Z. (2012). Doing disaffiliation with now-prefaced utterances. *Language and Communication, 32*, 265–275.

Wodak, R., Kwon, W., & Clarke, I. (2011). 'Getting people on board': Discursive leadership for consensus building in team meetings. *Discourse Society, 22*, 592–644.

Wong, J. (2000). Repetition in conversation: A look at 'first and second sayings.' *Research on Language and Social Interaction, 33*(4), 407–424.

Part IV

Discourse and Identity

6 Classics in Discourse and Identity

Introduction

We have so far considered two major issues that occupy the pursuits of discourse analysts: (1) discourse and structure and (2) discourse and social action. In this and the next chapters, we consider a third question that is of abiding concern for many discourse analysts: How are identities negotiated in discourse? As will become evident throughout the chapter, contrary to the "everyday" notion of identity that tends to be fixed labels for individuals or groups (e.g., woman, expert, middle-class white Americans), identity, as repeatedly revealed by discourse analysts, is a complex, nuanced, and negotiable phenomenon in discourse.

While social actions encapsulate what we do in and with discourse, identities display who we are to each other (Benwell & Stokoe, 2006). Gee (2000) defined identity as "[b]eing recognized as a certain 'kind of person' in a given context" (p. 99), and "[a]ny combination that can get one recognized as a certain 'kind of person' is what he calls Discourse with a capital 'D'" (p. 110):

> A Discourse is a sort of "identity kit" which comes complete with the appropriate costume and instructions on how to act, talk, and often write, so as to take on a particular role that others will recognize.
>
> (Gee, 1989, p. 7)

Although identity and social action are not entirely separable in principle, discourse analysts often foreground one or the other in the framing of their works, and there are certain classic concepts developed by sociologists and anthropologists that tend to be invoked in the analysis of discourse and identity, to which we now turn. We organize the ensuing discussion into what may be conceptualized as three broad sets of identities: universal, social, and interactional. These labels are by no means unproblematic in terms of what they cover and how they are distinguishable from each other. They merely serve as a convenient, and undoubtedly imperfect, heuristic for imposing a rough structure upon a complex set of materials. For the purpose of this chapter, "universal" is used to reference identities relevant to any person

regardless of situational or local contexts (e.g., age), "social" to refer to identities that highlight one's social roles in specific situations (e.g., teacher and
student), and "interactional" to refer to identities tied to specific interactions
in a local context (e.g., speaker and hearer). In other words, the collection
of classic concepts related to identity can approximately be arranged along
a progression of increasingly narrower dimensions—moving from broad
"universal" identity concerns to specific identity relevancies in a particular
interaction. The chapter ends with a schematic staging of these classic concepts as a "pyramid" that synthesizes their relative standings.

Universal Identities

The notion that certain kinds of identities may be applicable to any human
being has been captured in a number of terms devised by discourse analysts
from different perspectives. Zimmerman (1998), for example, uses **transportable identities** to refer to identities such as age and gender that travel
with individuals across contexts. A similar term is Gee's (2000) **nature-
identity** (N-identity), which refers to one's natural state not as a result of
individual achievements or social control (e.g., identical twin). In membership categorization analysis (see discussion later in the chapter) (Schegloff,
2007), there is a collection of categories called **Pn-adequate MCDs** (membership categorization devices) that apply to all populations (e.g., age and
gender). The analytical usefulness of these concepts is nicely illustrated in
Richards's (2006) study of classroom interaction, where introducing transportable identities such as "nature lover" into the classroom offers the potential of making conversation possible in teacher-student talk.

Aside from this range of labels that acknowledges the existence of such
"universal" identities, two broad identity concerns that appear relevant to
all human interaction regardless of context are such considerations as face
and politeness. In what follows, we first discuss Goffman's (1967) notions of
face and face-work and then Brown and Levinson's (1987) concepts of face-
threatening acts and politeness.

Face and Face-Work (Goffman)

Largely based on keen observations of face-to-face interaction, Goffman
(1967) proposed that face figures centrally in social interaction, where we
present to each other positive images of ourselves, showcasing, for example,
our competence, kindness, or beauty through verbal or nonverbal behavior
(p. 5).

> **Face** is the positive image one claims for oneself by a pattern of behav-
> ior displayed to others during an encounter.

Being in face captures a state where one's behavior presents an image that is internally consistent (e.g., a disciplined person meeting deadlines). One can also be in wrong face, on the other hand, when the behavior is out of sync with the image (e.g., *It's just so unlike him.*), or out of face when one participates in an encounter without being prepared (e.g., being called on to give an impromptu speech). The latter two states may also be described as shamefaced or loss of face. Losing face, in other words, entails failure to keep with the positive self-image one claims. An example of being in wrong face may be seen in the following e-mail addressed to me by a student in response to my complaint about some behavior issues:

(1) In wrong face

Dear Professor Waring,

Thank you so much for your understanding and for your advice. **I've been a bit out of character because of the stress recently** [bold added], and I promise this won't happen again for this and any other classes. Thanks again. I really appreciate your help.

Sincerely,

Dana (pseudonym)

In this e-mail, Dana characterizes her own behavior as *out of character,* that is, failing to match the positive image she claims for herself. By characterizing her failure as such and promising future remedy, Dana is also engaging in what Goffman calls face-work.

Task 1: What would be the positive image that you claim for yourself? What do you do to keep up that image? What are the kinds of face-work that you engage in?

Face-work refers to the measures taken to make one's actions consistent with one's face. It involves the avoidance process and the corrective process (Goffman, 1967). The avoidance process is carried out through either defensive measures to attend to one's own face (e.g., keep distance, stay off certain topics, or withhold feelings) or protective measures to attend to others' faces (e.g., use discretion, use circumlocution, or neutralize offensive acts). The corrective process is typically done through an interchange such as the following:

(2) Interchange as corrective process

A: You're late. (Challenge)

B: Sorry. (Offering)
A: Okay. (Acceptance)
B: Thanks. (Thanks)

Another way to think of face-work, according to Goffman (1967), is its execution through "ceremonial activity" (i.e., proper conduct), which includes deference and demeanor. Deference refers to the appreciation shown to another, and demeanor to deportment, dress, and bearing. While demeanor is the communication of respect for self, deference is the communication of respect for others. Deference is done through either avoidance rituals (i.e., acts of keeping distance such as avoiding first names) or presentation rituals (i.e., acts of demonstrating regard such as giving compliments).

Task 2: Consider this passage taken from a 19th-century book of etiquette (Goffman, 1967, p. 62). What kinds of ceremonial activity are manifested here? Do they involve deference or demeanor? Is there any evidence of avoidance or presentation ritual?

Issue your commands with gravity and gentleness, and in a reserved manner. Let your voice be composed, but avoid a tone of familiarity or sympathy with them. It is better in addressing them to use a higher key of voice, and not to suffer it to fall at the end of a sentence. The best-bred man whom we ever had the pleasure of meeting always employed, in addressing servants, such forms of speech as these—'I'll thank you for so and so,'—'Such a thing if you please.'—with a gentle tone, but very elevated key. The perfection of matter, in this particular, is, to indicate by your language, that the performance is a favor, and by your tone that it is a matter of course.

Face-Threatening Acts (FTAs) and Politeness (Brown and Levinson)

While Goffman's theory of face and face-work is largely based on his own keen observations of face-to-face interaction, Brown and Levinson's (1987) large-scale empirical work yields further specifications of face, which culminates in a theory of politeness that accounts for how different types of face are managed in social interaction. Drawing from an extensive database that includes firsthand tape-recorded usage in English, Tzeltal (a Mayan language spoken in a community in Mexico), and South Indian Tamil (from a village in the Coimbatore District of Tamilnadu) as well as examples from native speaker intuitions for English, elicited data in Tzeltal and Tamil, and occasional examples from secondhand sources for Malagasy, Japanese, and other languages, Brown and Levinson (1987) posited that participants manage two types of face in social interaction: negative and positive.

Negative face refers to the desire to be left alone and **positive face** to the desire to be liked.

The speaker (S) and the hearer (H) (or writer and reader) may experience threats to both types of face. The hearer's negative face may be threatened, for example, when receiving a request, and his or her positive face may be threatened when receiving disapproval. On the other hand, the speaker's negative face may be threatened when he or she is put in a position to give thanks, and his or her positive face may be threatened when he or she is put in a position to confess wrongdoings. Such acts as requesting, expressing disapproval, thanking, and confessing are therefore called face-threatening acts (FTAs).

Face-threatening act (FTA) is an act that threatens either the positive or negative face of either the speaker or the hearer.

In carrying out such FTAs, participants employ a variety of politeness strategies, which include the choice of not doing the FTA in the first place. As Figure 6.1 shows, by including both polite and not-so-polite activities (e.g., when you do an FTA on record without redressive actions), Brown and Levinson's politeness seems broader than our everyday notion of politeness. The FTA can be implemented either on or off record, and going on record can be done with or without redressive actions. Much of Brown and

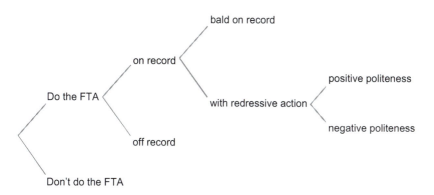

Figure 6.1 Politeness Strategies for Doing FTAs

Based on Brown & Levinson, 1987

Levinson's attention is devoted to specifying what these redressive actions, that is, positive or negative politeness, may look like.

Positive politeness refers to strategies that partially satisfy the addressee's positive face by communicating that one's own wants are in some respects similar to the addressee's wants.

More specifically, positive politeness becomes manifest when one claims common ground (e.g., uses in-group markers, avoids disagreement), conveys that S and H are cooperators (e.g., makes offers or promises, assumes or asserts reciprocity), and fulfills H's want for some X (e.g., gives gifts such as goods, sympathy, understanding, and cooperation).

Negative politeness refers to strategies that partially satisfy the addressee's negative face by communicating respect.

Negative politeness is implemented through not presuming, not coercing, communicating S's want to not impinge on H, and redressing H's other wants. As Brown and Levinson (1987) wrote, negative politeness is "the heart of respective behavior, just as positive politeness is the kernel of 'familiar' and 'joking' behavior" (p. 129). In short, positive politeness is approach based and involves the assurance that S wants at least part of what H wants. Negative politeness, on the other hand, is avoidance based and entails practices such as self-effacement, formality, restraint, impersonalizing, and softening. The former features such practices as showing interest in H, seeking agreement, and giving sympathy, and the latter such practices as being conventionally indirect, giving reasons, begging forgiveness, and showing deference.

Task 3: Consider the FTAs of request and criticism. What types of face do they threaten, and for whom? What kinds of politeness strategies would you be using when performing these acts? A good place to start may be to think of the kinds of wording you would employ in doing requests or criticism and, from there, identify what kinds of politeness strategies are exemplified in those wordings.

One might use negative politeness by stating, for instance, *I'm so sorry to bother you, but I was wondering if you'd mind doing X* to mitigate the threat to the hearer's negative face. Positive politeness is evidenced when a speaker says *I thought the content of your talk was fantastic* before launching a critique of the delivery in order to mitigate the threat to the hearer's positive face. In a study on the use of politeness strategies in refusal letters in business settings, Jansen and Janssen (2010) showed how the negative politeness strategy of giving a reason plays a significant role in ensuring customer satisfaction while the positive politeness strategy of giving a compliment or asserting knowledge (of the problem) does not. When the latter two actions are done but no reasons are given, it even has a negative effect on the recipients' evaluation of the letter.

> Task 4: Consider the following text taken from a manuscript review. What kinds of politeness strategies are employed to conduct the FTA of rejection?
>
> > I very much enjoyed the clarity of your writing. Your data are fascinating, and I think the overall claim of shifting footing in tutor-tutee interaction is a valid one. I was also glad to see your focus on tutee initiatives in subverting the asymmetry, which I believe is an important issue that has far-reaching implications for improving the efficacy of advising encounters and understanding the mystery of learning in general. My main problem is with the analysis. It seems to me that the data are mostly glossed and paraphrased rather than actually analyzed. I'm not left with any clear understanding of the two practices: X & Y. To turn the paraphrase into analysis, we need to see much more detailed accounts of the turn designs, sequential environments, and actions of these practices. My more specific comments are listed below: (24 points to follow)

A face-threatening act may also be performed by going off record—flouting the Gricean maxims (see Chapter 4) of Relevance, Quantity, Quality, and Manner (Brown & Levinson, 1987):

(1) Flouting maxim of relevance

    a.   give hints/clues (e.g., *It's cold in here.*)
    b.   presuppose (e.g., *I washed the car again today.*)

(2) Flouting maxim of quantity

    a.   understate (e.g., *I was pretty horrified.*)
    b.   overstate (e.g., *I called a hundred times.*)
    c.   use tautologies (e.g., *Boys will be boys.*)

(3) Flouting maxim of quality

    a.   use contradictions (e.g., *Well, John is here, and he isn't here.*)
    b.   be ironic (e.g., *John's a real genius.*)
    c.   use metaphors (e.g., *Henry's a real fish.*)
    d.   use rhetorical questions (e.g., *How many times do I have to tell you . . .*)

(4) Flouting maxim of manner

    a.   be ambiguous (e.g., *John's a pretty smooth cookie.*)
    b.   be vague (e.g., *Perhaps someone did something naughty.*)
    c.   overgeneralize (e.g., *Mature people sometimes help do dishes.*)
    d.   displace H (e.g., direct request to someone else other than the intended target)
    e.   be incomplete/use ellipsis (e.g., *If reading is not finished by 7 p.m., . . .*)

When facing the possibility of doing an FTA, then, one is presented with the following five choices:

(1) Do the FTA bald on record.
(2) Use positive politeness.
(3) Use negative politeness.
(4) Do the FTA off record.
(5) Don't do the FTA.

The choices of which strategy to use for a particular FTA (x), according to Brown and Levinson (1987), may be based on the weight of the FTA (x) calculated from the relative power (P), distance (D), and rank of imposition (Rx) involved in each act: $Wx = P (S, H) + D (S, H) + Rx$, a formula which takes into consideration the power of H over S, the distance between H and S, and the degree of imposition of the specific act. The heavier the weight, the higher the number of the strategy (see earlier: (1) being "Do the FTA bald on record and (5) being "Don't do the FTA). In other words, a non-FTA can be done bald on record whereas an act with the most serious face threat may lead to the person not doing it at all.

Task 5: Calculate the weight (i.e., risk to face) of the following FTAs using 1–3 (least to most risk), and decide on which strategy you would use in each case.

(1) Ask for a recommendation letter from your professor.
(2) Ask your sister to babysit for the weekend.
(3) Critique a classmate's presentation.
(4) Complain to your boss about her misbehavior.

Clearly, there are advantages and disadvantages associated with each choice for doing the FTA. An on record strategy features clarity, and one that is bald on record boasts efficiency. Going on record with redress, on the other hand, allows the speaker to attend to the hearer's face wants. Finally, an off-record strategy directs greater attention to the hearer's negative face and is deniable.

Brown and Levinson's politeness theory has received some criticism over the years (see Jansen & Janssen, 2010 for a review). Some have questioned the universality of the claims; some have argued that a politeness theory should be built inductively to capture how participants themselves would character-ize their strategies rather than deductively from the theoretical notion of *face*; and some have pointed out that Goffman's *face* is a form of deference, not a desire to be unimpeded as suggested by Brown and Levinson's *negative face*.

Nevertheless, it remains unquestionable that Goffman's face and face-work as further developed in Brown and Levinson's politeness theory provide a useful vocabulary for understanding and describing at least one aspect of identity and identity work managed by participants in interaction. Scollon and Scollon (1995), for example, described face as the "interpersonal identity of individuals in communication" (p. 34). The positive image one claims for oneself (i.e., face) is, after all, the identity one strives to project, and the range of politeness strategies (i.e., face-work) one exercises is the work of maintain-ing certain identities for oneself and for one another.

Task 6: To what extent does Brown and Levinson's politeness model res-onate with your own experience? Have you ever visited a place where the politeness norm is noticeably different from your own? Explain.

Social Identities

While Brown and Levinson (1987) and Goffman (1967) address an aspect of identity that is more or less universal, some aspects of identity exhibit spe-cific ties to social roles (e.g., parent) or groups (e.g., Republican) as well as institutional positions (e.g., customer service representative). Gee (2000), for example, used **institution-identity** (I-identity) to refer to one's social posi-tion (e.g., professor) and **affinity-identity** (A-identity) to one's experiences with certain "affinity groups" (e.g., a Yankees fan) (p. 101). Similarly, Zim-merman (1998) used **situated identities** as a cover term for those particu-lar identity sets specific to an institutional context, such as teacher-student, doctor-patient, or emergency call taker-citizen complainant.

Efforts have also been made to develop systematic means for considering how these identities are built or used in actual interaction. In what fol-lows, we consider three such efforts in a roughly chronological order: Sacks's (1972) membership categorization, Erickson and Shultz's (1982) performed social identity and co-membership, and Ochs's (1993) social act and stance.

We end this section with an exemplar from Zimmerman (1998) that illustrates the negotiability of these identities in interaction.

Membership Categorization (Sacks)

As alluded to earlier, membership categorization is in fact a broader framework that accounts for identity categories such as age or gender (i.e., our reference to "universal" identities). Its placement in this section of the chapter is therefore somewhat arbitrary although much of the work conducted within membership categorization analysis (MCA) does indeed address what we refer to as "social identities" here. As will be shown, by pointing to attributes of specific identities, membership categorization makes important contributions to our understanding of how identities may be used in interaction to achieve particular interactional goals. The notion of membership categorization was developed in ethnomethodology and conversation analysis and initially explored by Harvey Sacks in the 1960s in two of his classic papers on *Search for Help* and *Baby Cries*. The central concept in membership categorization analysis is membership categorization device (MCD) (Hester & Eglin, 1997; Sacks, 1972; Schegloff, 2007).

Membership categorization device (MCD) is a collection (e.g., gender, age, nationality, family) of membership categories that go together (e.g., man, woman, professor) along with its **rules of applications**, where categories are classifications of social types that may be used to describe persons.

Before we explain rules of application, here are some MCD types (Hester & Eglin, 1997; Schegloff, 2007; Stokoe, 2012):

(1) Pn-adequate MCDs: Collections that apply to all populations (e.g., age and gender)
(2) MCDs with different organizations

    a.   team-type ("duplicatively" organized) MCDs: family, soccer team, and so forth.

    b.   positioned category MCDs (hierarchically organized): stage of life (baby, teenager, adult).

    c.   standardized relational pair (SRP) MCDs: husband-wife, parent-child, friend-friend, cousin-cousin, stranger-stranger, neighbor-neighbor, doctor-patient, lawyer-client, teacher-student and so forth.

According to Schegloff (2007), categories exhibit three features. First, they are **inference rich**, that is, each category comes with its associated commonsense knowledge, which presumably applies to all members of that category. For example, if one follows the statement *I'm 48*, with *but I look much younger*, it is because the category of 48 carries such inferences as being middle aged and certainly not very young, and *I look much younger* is designed specifically to address that inference. Second, categories are **protected against induction**: the knowledge about each category does not get revised on the basis of new/ unfitting information, which is treated instead as an exception. Third and perhaps most important for the purpose of analysis, categories come with **category-bound predicates**. There are, for example, prototypical activities associated with the categories of mother, teacher, playboy, princess, or physicist. These categories can invoke their associated activities and vice versa.

Category-bound activities (CBAs) are activities that are "expectably and properly done by persons who are the incumbents of a particular category. The category and the activity are **co-selected**" (Hester & Eglin, 1997, p. 5).

Subsequent researchers have observed that category-bound activities are just one class of predicates which "can conventionally be imported on the basis of a given membership category. . . . Other predicates include rights, entitlements, obligations, knowledge, attributes and competencies" (Hester & Eglin, 1997, p. 5). Pomerantz and Mandelbaum (2005) also spoke of "activities, motives, rights, responsibilities, and competencies associated with incumbents of particular relationship categories" (p. 152).

There are four rules of application when it comes to the MCD (Hester & Eglin, 1997; Sacks, 1995; Schegloff, 2007; Stokoe, 2012): the economy rule, the consistency rule, the hearer's maxim, and the viewer's maxim. According to the **economy rule**, a single category term can do adequate reference. When introducing someone at a party, it is enough to say "This is my friend X" or "X is a dancer," and not necessary to say that X is a white middle-aged dancer, a vegetarian, *Star Wars* fan, and so forth. According to the **consistency rule**, if one person has been referred to by one category, subsequent persons may receive the same category or categories from the same MCD. If one person has been referred to by occupation, the rest may be too: "Jim is our assessment specialist" should be followed not by "Howard is an amazing cook," but by "Howard is our resident linguist." The **hearer's maxim** states that "if two or more categories are used to categorize two or more members of some population, and those categories can be heard as categories from the same collection, then: hear them that way" (Sacks, 1995, volume 1, p. 239), and the **viewer's maxim** that "if a Member sees a category-bound activity being done, then, if one sees it being done by a member of a category to which the activity is bound, see it that way" (Sacks, 1995, volume 1, p. 258). What both the hearer's maxim and viewer's maxim seem to be saying is: if the connection is obvious, make it. In the case of *The baby cries. The mommy picks it up*, the hearer's maxim allows us to see the mommy as the baby's mommy (i.e., *baby* and *mommy* from the same collection of *family* as opposed to *baby* from the *stage of life* collection), and the viewer's maxim allows us to see that the baby is doing the normal category-bound activity of crying as attached to the category of baby.

Baker (2004) outlined three steps in doing membership categorization analysis: (1) locate the central categories, (2) work through the activities and inferences associated with each category, and (3) look at the category-predicate connection to find the social actions implied. In other words, the goal is to establish how particular categories are invoked to accomplish particular social actions—by consulting the category-bound predicates associated with those categories. A simple illustration may be found in Pomerantz and Mandelbaum (2005), who used an excerpt from the Suicide Prevention Center (Sacks, 1972):

(3) Relatives, friends

01	Call Taker:		You don't have anyone to turn to?
02	Caller:		No.
03	Call Taker:	→	No relatives, friends?
04	Caller:		No.

Here, the call taker invokes the categories of "relatives" and "friends" to perform the action of pursuing a different response to the initial inquiry based on the category-bound activities (of relatives/friends) of offering comfort, advice, help, and so forth.

Task 7: Consider the following anecdote taken from Baker (2004, p. 164). What resources (e.g., category, category-bound activity, hearer's maxim, viewer's maxim) did the woman behind the counter use to generate her "mistake"? Explain.

A woman, a young male child holding a screwdriver, and a man entered a bakery, the woman behind the counter greeted them and then addressed the child as follows: "Have you been helping Daddy?" There was a pause that I distinctly remember. The woman customer then spoke: "This is not Daddy."

Thus, membership categorization specifies the ways in which identity categories become usable in interaction for accomplishing social actions—through category-bound predicates.

Performed Social Identity and Co-Membership (Erickson)

While the focus of membership categorization is on how identity categories become a resource for performing social actions in interaction, the issue of how specific social identities are made relevant in an encounter is taken up in Erickson and Shultz's (1982) proposal of *performed social identity*—a concept initially designed to highlight the attributes made relevant by students and counselors during gatekeeping interactions (pp. 16–17).

> **Performed social identity** refers to an aggregate of participant attributes (e.g., ethnicity, interest, experience) made relevant during the course of interaction.

Erickson (2011) offered an elaborate example of how, during an after-hours pediatric clinic visit, the mother of an infant enacts the performed social identity of a "good mother" by producing a remarkably well-formed complaint that details her observation of her baby's fever over a 40-hour period (pp. 445–449). As Erickson (2011) wrote, "She was precise in identifying the various amounts of fever . . . with an overall pattern of increase over time. . . . She was also precise in identifying the kind of medication the child was given (Tylenol), and the amounts and timing of administration of the doses the baby had received" (p. 447).

One instance of performed social identity is what Erickson (2004, 2011) called co-membership or situational comembership (Erickson, 1975).

> **Co-membership** refers to shared attributes of participants that are invoked implicitly or explicitly in interaction.

Co-membership, according to Erickson (personal communication), "establishes a frame of generous interpretation of others' communicative behavior." In a curious gatekeeping interchange in school counseling, a student reports on having received an "F" grade in his major area of study without any hedging, and the counselor responds lightheartedly with sarcasm and irony (Erickson, 1975). Erickson (2011) attributed the apparent strangeness of the interaction to the high co-membership between the participants, who were both Italian Americans with a shared history beyond that particular interchange. In short, the notion of co-membership offers us a useful way of considering how social identities become relevant in actual interaction.

Task 8: Consider the following language classroom interaction taken from Waring (2014, p. 63). How is co-membership established? What is the effect, if any, of such co-membership for language learning? Refer to the details of the interaction in your response and be as specific as you can. (Key: degree signs = lower volume; > < = quickened pace; number in parentheses = length of silence in seconds; .hhh = inbreath; heheheh = laughter; (h) = laugh particle inside a word; dash linking verbal and nonverbal = co-occurrence of the two.)

168	Hiromi:	=and also:: she's also attending (.) music schoo:l
169		°an' she's violinist° .hh °an:° in the morning
170		I went to: grocery- Japanese grocery sto:re in
171		New Jerse:[y I don't g]o so often but-
172	Teacher:	[.hhhhhhhh]
173		[Yes.]
174	Hiromi:	[I] went the:[re,]
175	Teacher: →	[I kno]w what grocery store
176		[>you're talking about.<]
177	Hiromi:	[Yeah. big.]
178	Teacher:	>yeah very big in< Edgewater.=
179	Hiromi:	=Yes. Edge[water. Edgewater.-((*nods*))]
180	Teacher: →	[m:hm? mhm >mhm<] I go
181		there >once a month.<
182	Hiromi:	((*nods*)) I happened to see- uh meet- uh:
183		my daughter's frie::nd (0.2) mothe:r hheheh
184		[there.]
185	Teacher:	[Oh g↑](h)ood.

Social Act and Stance (Ochs)

Rather than focusing on how social identities are used or become relevant in interaction, Ochs (1993) devised a framework for systematically tackling how such identities are constructed linguistically through social acts and stances. By social identities, Ochs (1993) is referring to "social statuses, roles, positions, relationships, and institutional and other relevant community identities one may attempt to claim or assign in the course of social life" (e.g., mother, teacher, boss) (p. 288).

Social act refers to socially recognized, goal-oriented behavior, such as requesting, contradicting, or interrupting.

> **Stance** is a display of socially recognized point of view or attitude, which includes **epistemic stance** (i.e., degrees of certainty) and **affective stance** (i.e., intensity or kinds of emotions).

Ochs's goal is to provide a systematic way for us to understand the relationship between language and identity. In other words, how are social identities such as parent, teacher, middle-class person, provost, or community organizer constructed linguistically? As she wrote, "I may attempt to build my identity as a professional academic by performing a range of professional acts such as hypothesizing, claiming, instructing, and assessing, and displaying stances such as objectivity, knowledgeability, and intellectual flexibility" (Ochs, 1993, p. 289).

Ochs (1993) took great care to emphasize that the relationship between language and social identity is *mediated* by the conventions through which particular social acts and stances are realized (p. 289). The act of instructing, for example, may find different manifestations in different social or cultural groups, as does display of a stance of knowledgeability. As such, shared conventions are necessary for particular social identities to take hold. In addition, certain acts and stances do not invariably map onto certain identities but are related in complex ways to achieve these identities (p. 290).

Drawing upon data collected from traditional West Samoan communities, for example, Ochs showed how children are socialized into the "curser" identity by having their earliest meaning sound *tae* (literal meaning: *eat shit!*) "interpreted and ratified as a particular social act, namely a conventional curse" (Ochs, 1993, p. 293). Family identities in America, on the other hand, may be constructed through the social act of co-narration at the dinner table (Ochs & Taylor, 1992). Finally, how particular acts and stances are linked to particular identities can vary cross-culturally. According to Schieffelin and Ochs (1986), for example, the identities of caregivers and children are constructed differently across societies. While in middle-class America caregivers display a great deal of cognitive accommodation toward children by using a simplified register, in Papua New Guinea and the Samoan society, the direction of the accommodation is reversed so that the identities of caregivers and children are constructed through children displaying accommodation to their caregivers.

Task 9: Consider the following social identities. What social acts and stances may be plausibly engaged to enact these identities?

(1) Leader
(2) Graduate student
(3) Mother.

Notably, Ochs's (1993) framework not only provides a way of specifying the construction of social identity through social acts and stances but also foregrounds social and cultural variations in such identity construction. As shown, acts and stances deployed to build particular social identities may vary across social and cultural groups.

Negotiability of Social Identities

As might have become evident so far, social identities are not *a priori* fixed categories but resources that can be built and used and become relevant in interaction. Zimmerman (1998), for example, made a point of emphasizing that situated identities are interactionally negotiated rather than unilaterally secured, as shown in the following emergency phone call that involves the call taker (CT) and the caller (C) (pp. 88–89). (Key: number in parentheses = length of silence in seconds.)

(4) Riddle call

01	CT:	Mid-city police and fire.
02	C:	(YA:H) This is the ( ) ((*voice slurred*))
03		(1.5) ((*loud background noise*))
04	CT:	Hello:?
05		(0.4)
06	C:	YEA:H?
07	CT:	What do you want?
08		(0.5)
09	C:	Yea:h we- we wan' forn'ca:y (h) heh
10		(0.6) ((*background voices, noise*))
11	CT:	About wha:t?
12		(5.3) ((*noise; voice: Hey give me that.*))
13	C:	Hey=I've=a ri:ddle for ya::
14		(0.3)
15	CT:	HU::H?
16	C:	I have a ri:dle for ya.
17		(0.3)
18	CT:	I don't have ti:me for riddles-do-ya wanna squa:rd or not=
19	C:	=NO: just a simple que:stion. (0.4)
20		What fucks and leaks like a ti:ger,
21		HUH? ((*background noise*))
22	CT:	Good bye.
23		((*disconnect*))

As can be seen, the participants exhibit great difficulty aligning with the situated identity sets that the other attempts to establish. The call taker strives to align with the identity set of call taker–citizen complainant by soliciting a request for assistance (line 07), refusing to engage in any casual chat while reasserting the kind of assistance that may be provided (line 18), and ending the call (line 22). The caller, on the other hand, resists such alignment by offering a riddle to be solved (line 16) and proceeding to present that riddle (lines 19–20) despite the call taker's rejection.

In sum, our understanding of how social identities work in discourse is facilitated by such frameworks and concepts as membership categorization, performed social identity, and social acts and stance. A common theme appears to be this: social identity is something one *does* in interaction— whether through the construction of social acts or stances, the performance of particular narratives, or the invoking of category-bound attributes. Given that social identity is an accomplishment rather than an irrevocable inheritance, much of the work of a discourse analyst involves describing its negotiability in talk, text, and nonverbal conduct.

Interactional Identities

In many ways, the negotiability of social identity observed so far is amplified in the concept of interactional identity, where the roles of speaker and hearer, for example, are constantly shifting. The distinction between social identity and interactional identity, therefore, is not a clear-cut one (especially when it comes to the discussion of positioning theory later). Roughly, however, while the identity categories dealt with in the prior section under the umbrella of "social identities" (e.g., mommy, caretaker, counselor, emergency call taker) evoke one's role or position in society, interactional identities are local phenomena situated within specific interactional encounters. A useful term would be Gee's (2000) **discourse-identity** (D-identity), which refers to one's individual accomplishments as "interactionally recognized by others" (e.g., a charismatic person) (Gee, 2000, p. 101). Zimmerman (1998) also used **discourse identities** (without the hyphen) as a cover term for identities such as current speaker, question asker, or complainer that are observed in the turn-by-turn organization of interaction. Such local and interactional identities are further elucidated in Goffman's (1981) footing, alignment, and participation framework and Davies and Harré's (1990) positioning theory.

Footing, Alignment, and Participation Framework (Goffman)

Goffman (1981) offered us a set of tools for capturing identities on an interactional level, where the notion of footing, which he introduces with the following scene (p. 124), becomes relevant:

> After a bill-signing ceremony in the Oval Office, the President stood up from his desk and in a teasing voice said to UPI's Helen Thomas:

"Helen, are you still wearing slacks? Do you prefer them actually? Every time I see girls in slacks it reminds me of China."

. . . Nixon asked Miss Thomas how her husband liked her wearing pants outfits.

"He doesn't mind," she replied.

"Do they cost less than gowns?"

"No," said Miss Thomas.

"Then change," commanded the President with a wide grin as other reporters and cameramen roared with laughter.

The shift from official bill-signing to small talk is described by Goffman as a change of footing, as evidenced in a change of tone, "an alteration in the social capacities in which the persons present claim to be active," as well as a shift in addressee and posture (Goffman, 1981, p. 126). In the previous episode, as Nixon rises from his desk and singles Thomas out as the addressee, his tone of voice changes from formal to casual, and Nixon and Thomas shift out of their social capacities as president and journalist to engage in a conversation as a man and a woman in a social, rather than an official, setting.

One can think of footing then as a participant's constantly shifting interactional identity. Goffman (1981) used footing, alignment, and frame in roughly interchangeable ways as shown in the following:

A change in footing implies a change in the alignment we take up to ourselves and the other present as expressed in the way we manage the production or reception of an utterance. A change in our footing is another way of talking about a change in our frame for events.

(p. 128)

Footing is one's standing in an interaction at any given moment as signaled by the totality of tone, posture, and participants' relative positionings toward each other.

Changes in footing, according to Goffman (1981), find their "structural underpinnings" in the concept of participation framework (p. 128), which specifies a set of speaker and hearer roles or "a set of positions that individuals within perceptual range of an utterance may take" in relation to the production and reception of a particular utterance (Schiffrin, 1994, p. 104).

Participation framework refers to a set of speaker and hearer roles in relation to a particular utterance within its perceptual range.

Goffman called attention to the multiparty, multimodal nature of social interaction decades before full-blown research programs were developed in these areas. His dissatisfaction with the unanalyzed notions of "speaker" and "hearer" begins with the observation that sound is not the only cue that matters in face-to-face interaction. Once visual cues are taken into consideration, one realizes that an utterance may be produced within the aural and visual range of those who are not the intended recipients. In other words, a hearer might not be the intended hearer, and given certain visual cues, an intended hearer might not be hearing at all. As Goffman (1981) wrote, "the terms 'speaker' and 'hearer' imply that sound alone is at issue, when, in fact, it is obvious that sight is organizationally very significant too, sometimes even touch" (p. 129). Simple notions such as speaker and hearer then become insufficient to precisely characterize the shifting identities in interaction. As such, Goffman (1981) took issue with "global categories (speaker and hearer)" and embarked on "decomposing them into smaller analytically coherent elements" (p. 129).

The smaller hearer categories or participation statuses, according to Goffman, compose those who occupy the official status of a ratified participant (addressed and unaddressed recipients) and those who don't (bystanders). Students in a classroom, for example, may at times be unaddressed but ratified participants when the teacher is directing her talk to one particular group. As Goffman (1981) pointed out, "this structurally important distinction between official recipients is often accomplished exclusively through visual clues" (p. 133). The bystanders may be either overhearers or eavesdroppers depending on whether any intent or effort is involved in obtaining the hearing.

Goffman's decomposition of "speaker" yields the following categories or production formats: animator, author, and principal. The animator voices the talk; the author formulates the talk; and the principal is the one whose positions and beliefs are represented in the talk. Our daily usage of "speaker" often implies the convergence of the three roles. Goffman (1981) also used "figure" to refer to the character featured in the talk. The spokesperson for the White House, for example, would be the animator of a statement authored by the president's speech writers, while the president is the principal whose positions are represented in the statement.

How is the notion of participation framework, with its ensemble of interactional identities, useful for our understanding of discourse? For one thing, it gives us a more acute sense of what is being done with discourse. In rejection letters which are written by editors and addressed to submitting authors but carbon copied to the reviewers, reference to "the level of the engagement of the reviewers" and "the depth of scholarship" brought to the evaluation of the manuscript are formulated not just for the benefit of the author as the addressed recipient but also for the reviewers as "overhearers" whose work is now being complimented.

Task 10: Explain the participation frameworks in the following scenarios. How does the concept of participation framework help us understand what is going on?

(1) Use of carbon copy and blind carbon copy in e-mail
(2) Listserv mishaps
(3) Working with OPOL (one parent one language approach in bilingual families)
(4) Oscar acceptance speeches
(5) Talk directed to family pets
(6) Self-talk.

In his critique of Goffman's participation framework, Goodwin (2007), in a chapter entitled "Interactive Footing," observed a lack of complexity and nuance in Goffman's decomposition of the recipient category compared with that of the speaker. Using an example of reported speech, Goodwin (2007) illustrated how, as opposed to using static recipient categories,

> participation can be analyzed as a temporally unfolding process through which separate parties demonstrate to each other their ongoing understanding of the events they are engaged in by building actions that contribute to the further progression of these very same events.
>
> (pp. 24–25)

Positioning Theory (Davies and Harré)

Goffman's idea of footing is treated by the social psychologist Rom Harré and poststructural feminist Bronwyn Davies as a promising alternative to the notion of positioning in their own positioning theory (Davies & Harré, 1990, p. 54)—another influential framework for analyzing discourse and identity (also see Kendall, 2008). Positioning theory was proposed as a critique of the concept of "role" in dominant social psychology, which the authors regard as highlighting "static, formal and ritualistic aspects" rather than "dynamic aspects of encounters" (Davies & Harré, 1990, p. 43).

Positioning is a discursive process whereby participants locate themselves and each other in relation to values, qualities, and social categories in jointly produced storylines.

According to Davies and Harré (1990), positioning is done through **discursive practices**—"all the ways in which people actively produce social and psychological realities" (p. 45), and such positioning can be **interactive,** where one person positions another, or **reflexive**, where one positions one-self (p. 48). The fairytale storyline of romantic love, for example, may include a prince who performs some heroic act and a princess who relies on the prince to be saved. Two people may position each other within this story-line by engaging in a specific set of discursive practices. The prince and the princess are the two **subject positions** within this story—another central notion of the positioning theory which Davies and Harré (1990) regarded as "[t]he closest one might come conceptually to role" (p. 58).

Davies and Harré (1990) emphasized that positions shift in line with the "narrative/metaphors/images through which the positioning is being con-stituted" (p. 58). In other words, what position is assigned or taken up at any given moment very much depends on what storyline one subscribes to, and two people in the same interaction can follow very different storylines. As an illustration of their theory, Davies and Harré (1990) offered an example of an exchange between a man and a woman (the authors themselves at a confer-ence), who went all over town to look for some medicine for the woman on a cold, wintry day—but to no avail.

(5) drag

01	Man:	I'm sorry to have dragged you all this way when you're not well.
02	Woman:	You didn't drag me. I chose to come.

By positioning himself as the responsible party, the man inadvertently, according to the woman (as reported elsewhere in the author's discussion of the example), positions her as incapable of making decisions for her-self. Meanwhile, her protest in turn positions him as sexist and paternalistic, which he then finds offensive. The two, in other words, live in diverging storylines with diverging subject positions: him being a caretaker vs. a sexist, and her being an accessory vs. a feminist.

Task 11: Consider how the participants position each other in the fol-lowing interaction among the 3-year-old Zoe and her parents. What discursive practice(s), subject position(s), and storyline(s) are involved? (Key: ↑ = raised pitch; number in parentheses = length of silence in seconds.)

```
01   Zoe:    ((runs to kitchen door, with arm akimbo)) ↑Zoe to the
02           REScue. Are YOU in TROUble?
03   Dad:    No:. I'm Not. I'm okay. [what about you.]
04   Zoe:                           [((runs away))    ]
05           (1.2)
06   Zoe:    [are you] in ↑trouble?-((to Mom))
```

```
07  Mom:   [are you]-
08         a little bi:t.
09  Zoe:   then I'm gonna save you from the Drago::n.
10  Mom:   Alri::ght. I'm looking for- can you solve a problem for me?
11  Zoe:   Yeah.
12  Mom:   I'm looking for my daughter's chair. for her to eat dinner.
13  Zoe:   What's the problem.
14  Mom:   That's the problem. I can't find my daughter's chair.
15  Zoe:   I'll help you. ((goes into kitchen)) Right here.
16  Mom:   Oh my Go:d. Thank you. Super Zoe?
17  Zoe:   ((walks out bending forward))
18  Mom:   ((gets chair from Dad))
```

Thus, compared with social identities that are also negotiable in actual interaction, interactional identities entail more or less local categories specifiable by virtue of the structure of interaction (e.g., speaker or hearer) and the issue of the particular interaction (e.g., someone incapable making decisions for herself). While Goffman (and Goodwin) offers powerful analytical tools for explicating the myriad speaker and hearer roles that are constantly in flux, Davies and Harré's positioning theory provide us a useful vocabulary for characterizing the open-ended set of identity possibilities enabled in and through interaction.

Pyramid of Identities in Discourse

The relationships among the different types of identities we have discussed so far may be visualized as a three-tier system that captures a progression from identities tied specifically to interactional moves to those of broader relevance to human interactants. At the bottom of the pyramid are "universal" concerns such as face and politeness and transportable identities that are potentially relevant across contexts (e.g., age or gender). The mid-tier of the pyramid absorbs "social" identities, such as mother or doctor, applicable to specific contexts and specific groups of people. The top of the pyramid represents identities in the most local interactional terms such as "speaker" or "question asker." It is important to reiterate that these tiers are not mutually exclusive, and in any spate of interaction, identities at all three tiers may be made relevant by the participants (see Figure 6.2).

In his discussion of nature-identity, institution-identity, discourse-identity, and affinity-identity, for example, Gee (2000) pointed out that these identities are not distinct from one another but "interrelate in complex and important ways" (p. 101). To illustrate such interrelatedness, he offered a telling example of the ADHD (attention-deficit/hyperactivity disorder) identity, which may be viewed from all four perspectives. When an unusually active child whose attention often wanders receives the diagnosis of ADHD, this condition is often treated as part of the child's nature, that is, his N(ature)-identity. When the child then becomes a client who continuously seeks monitoring and treatment of this condition, he takes on the I(institution)-identity of an ADHD patient. The same child may be recognized as having ADHD even without the official diagnosis in one setting but as normal and creative in another; his discourse identities may vary, in other words. Finally, there are ADHD groups made up of people with or without the official diagnosis of ADHD along with advocates who share certain experiences and practices and the A(ffinity)-identity of ADHD.

For any given identity, according to Gee (2000), we may ask the (1) macro-question of what instutition(s) or group(s) enable the recognition of a particular Discourse in a particular way (e.g., the institutional category of ADHD seeps into folk usage of the term as a teacher attributes the D-identity to a child) and the (2) micro-question of how the moment-to-moment interaction works to sustain the recognition of a particular Discourse in a certain way (e.g., an "intelligent" academic may very well not be recognized as such in other kinds of Discourses) (p. 111).

One might imagine that the interrelatedness among the various identity categories is applicable to Zimmerman's framework of discourse identity (interactional), situated identity (social), and transportable (universal) identity as well (see definition in various prior sections).

Task 12: In the following advanced ESL class, where a discussion on gender-based behavior and shopping is under way, Sarah is describing the different shopping styles of her and her husband (Waring, 2013). Consider what kinds of identities (discourse, situated, or transportable) are made relevant by Sarah in her telling and explain how. (Key: ↑ = raised pitch; > < = quickened pace; $ = smiley voice; (hh) = laugh tokens; dash linking verbal and nonverbal = co-occurrence of the two.)

```
01   Sarah:     I think I could reme(hh)mber wh(hh)at
02              w(hh)e nee(hh)ded. What we needed, and
03              what- what- what to ↑bu:y, ((sniff)) so:,
04              UM:: t! uh- a::nd- a:nd also um:: t! If ↑I
05              y'know, if I um:: just g- got into the store:,
06              I: >I was like,< I said like,
07              $↑Okay, let's ↑start.$—((pumps arms))
08              from the ↑first ↑floor.
09              [HH S(hh)o the(hh)re w(hh)as]=
10   Teacher:   [   hah hah hah hah hah        ]
```

11	Students:	[((*smiles*))]
12	Sarah:	=nothing hh n(hh)othing at first foor– floor,
13		so um, w– for us, but (.) I just wanna (.)
14		checked out, y' know, but this is exactly the
15		difference between my husband and I,
16		or (.) men and women, ((*nods*))=
17	Teacher:	=Mhm

As you worked through the transcript in the previous task, you might have noted, for example, Sarah's discourse identity as a storyteller, her situated identity as a student as she responds to the pedagogical task of discussing gender-based behaviors, and her transportable identity as an obsessive shopper.

Task 13: Discuss the similarities and differences between Zimmerman's (1998) discourse identity, situated identity, and transportable identity on the one hand, and Gee's (2000) nature–identity, institution–identity, discourse–identity, and affinity–identity on another. How is Zimmerman's discourse identity similar to and/or different from that of Gee's? Explain with examples.

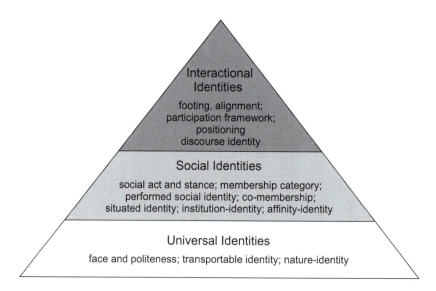

Figure 6.2 Pyramid of Identities in Discourse

Task 14: Consider how the various identity categories discussed in this chapter may apply to the following interaction.
((In a preschool morning meeting among 4-year-olds, Zoe is showing her finger puppets.))

01 Zoe: I'm ready to take questions.
02 Isa: What is that little orange thing?
03 Zoe: The little orange thing, which animal do you think it is?
04 Isa: A lion.

Key Points

- Participants in social interaction attend to their own and each other's face and engage in face-work.
- Face-threatening acts may be performed off record or on record with positive or negative politeness strategies.
- Membership category analysis focuses on how categories (or identities) are invoked in discourse to accomplish social actions.
- Social identities may be made relevant in interaction through performed social identity such as co-membership.
- Social identities may be constructed through social acts and stances.
- Footing or alignment is one way to capture interactional identities.
- Participation framework comprises a set of speaker and hearer categories and is the structural underpinning of footing.
- Positioning is one way of conceptualizing the dynamic nature of social encounters where the participants discursively position themselves and each other in particular subject positions along particular storylines.
- Participants may orient to discourse, situational, or transportable identities in interaction.
- Identities as conceptualized in the big D(iscourse) include nature-identity, institution-identity, discourse-identity, and affinity-identity.
- The various types of identities in discourse may be visually represented through a pyramid featuring increasingly narrowing domains.

References

Baker, C. D. (2004). Membership categorization and interview accounts. In D. Silverman (Ed.), *Qualitative research: Theory, method and practice* (2nd ed.) (pp. 162–176). London: Sage.

Benwell, B., & Stokoe, E. (2006). *Discourse and identity*. Edinburgh: Edinburgh University Press.

Brown, P., & Levinson, S. (1987). *The universals of politeness*. Cambridge: Cambridge University Press.

Davies, B., & Harré, R. (1990). Positioning: The discursive production of selves. *Journal for the Theory of Social Behavior, 20*(1), 43–63.

Erickson, F. (1975). Gatekeeping and the melting pot: Interaction in counseling encounters. *Harvard Educational Review, 45*, 44–70.

Erickson, F. (2004). *Talk and social theory: Ecologies of speaking and listening in everyday life.* Malden, MA: Polity Press.

Erickson, F. (2011). The gatekeeping encounter as a social form and as a site for face work. In C. N. Candlin & S. Sarangi (Eds.), *Handbook of communication in organisations and professions* (pp. 433–454). Berlin: Mouton de Gruyter.

Erickson, F., & Shultz, J. (1982). *The counselor as gatekeeper: Social interaction in interviews.* New York: Academic Press.

Gee, J. P. (1989). Literacy, discourse, and linguistics: Introduction. *Journal of Education, 171*(1), 5–176.

Gee, J. P. (2000). Identity as an analytic lens for research in education. *Review of Research in Education, 25*(1), 99–125.

Goffman, E. (1967). *Interaction ritual.* New York: Pantheon Books.

Goffman, E. (1981). *Forms of talk.* Philadelphia, PA: University of Pennsylvania Press.

Goodwin, C. (2007). Interactive footing. In E. Holt & R. Clift (Eds.), *Reporting talk: Reported speech in interaction* (pp. 16–46). Cambridge: Cambridge University Press.

Hester, S., & Eglin, P. (1997). Membership categorization analysis: An introduction. In S. Hester & P. Eglin (Eds.), *Culture in action: Studies in membership categorization analysis* (pp. 1–24). Washington, DC: University Press of America.

Jansen, F., & Janssen, D. (2010). Effects of positive politeness strategies in business letters. *Journal of Pragmatics, 42*(9), 2531–2548.

Kendall, S. (2008). The balancing act: Framing gendered parental identities at dinnertime. *Language in Society, 37*, 539–568.

Ochs, E. (1993). Constructing a social identity: A language socialization perspective. *Research on Language and Social Interaction, 26*(3), 287–306.

Ochs, E., & Taylor, C. (1992). Family narrative as political activity. *Discourse & Society, 3*(3), 301–340.

Pomerantz, A., & Mandelbaum, J. (2005). A conversation analytic approach to relationships: Their relevance for interactional conduct. In K. Fitch & R. E. Sanders (Eds.), *Handbook of language and social interaction* (pp. 149–171). Mahwah, NJ: Lawrence Erlbaum Associates.

Richards, K. (2006). Being the teacher: Identity and classroom conversation. *Applied Linguistics, 27*(1), 51–77.

Sacks, H. (1967). The search for help: No one to turn to. In E. S. Schneidman (Ed.), *Essays in self destruction* (pp. 203–223). New York: Science House.

Sacks, H. (1972). On the analyzability of stories by children. In J. J. Gumperz & D. Hymes (Eds.), *Directions in sociolinguistics: The ethnography of communication* (pp. 325–345). New York: Rinehart & Winston.

Sacks, H. (1995). *Lectures on conversation* (Vols. 1–2). Malden, MA: Blackwell.

Schegloff, E. A. (2007). A tutorial on membership categorization. *Journal of Pragmatics, 39*, 462–482.

Schieffelin, B. B., & Ochs, E. (1986). Language socialization. *Annual Review of Anthropology*, *15*, 163–191.

Schiffrin, D. (1994). *Approaches to discourse*. Cambridge, MA: Blackwell.

Scollon, R., & Scollon, S. W. (1995). *Intercultural communication: A discourse approach*. Malden, MA: Blackwell.

Stokoe, E. (2012). Moving forward with membership categorization analysis: Methods for systematic analysis. *Discourse Studies*, *14*(3), 277–303.

Waring, H. Z. (2013). Doing being playful in the language classroom. *Applied Linguistics*, *34*, 191–210.

Waring, H. Z. (2014). Managing control and connection in the adult ESL classroom. *Research in the Teaching of English*, *49*(1), 52–74.

Zimmerman, D. H. (1998). Discourse identities and social identities. In C. Antaki & S. Widdicombe (Eds.), *Identities in talk* (pp. 87–106). London: Sage.

7 Empirical Endeavors in Discourse and Identity

Introduction

In the previous chapter, we introduced a range of frameworks and concepts in discourse and identity: Goffman and Brown and Levinson's face and facework; Sacks's membership categorization; Erickson's performed social identity and co-membership; Ochs's social act and stance; Goffman's footing, alignment, and participation framework; Davies and Harré's positioning theory; Zimmerman's discourse, situated, and transportable identities; and Gee's nature-identity, institution-identity, discourse-identity, and affinity-identity. Collectively, this background constitutes some of the foundational thinking in our conceptualization of discourse and identity. To a certain extent, many of the concepts have also become a common set of vocabulary that appears to be referenced as a matter of fact (often without quotation marks) in the actual analysis of discourse and identity. It is to such actual analysis that we now turn.

As we survey the empirical landscape of discourse and identities, endeavors made by scholars using a variety of approaches appear to cluster around (1) individual identities such as urban father, teenage boy, and heterosexual man and (2) institutional identities such as novice teachers, fellow physicians, students, and academics. For the purpose of this chapter, I use "individual" as a cover term for any identities not defined by an institutional setting, which hosts "institutional" identities. In many ways, "individual" is an awkward term especially given the deeply social nature of identity in discourse. I have purposely avoided the more attractive alternative of "social," however, to minimize any confusion with what was referred to as "social identities" in the previous chapter, which is a broader term that would include what is referred to as "institutional identities" in this chapter as well. I hope it is clear to the reader that the individual vs. institutional division is an entirely arbitrary one as there can be many different ways to frame the empirical landscape, and I have simply adopted one such possibility for ease of presentation.

Discourse and Individual Identities

Individual identities (i.e., identities not defined by institutional settings) would encompass, in my case, being recognized as a woman, a mother, an Asian American, a ballet lover, and the like. How such identities are negotiated in discourse has been a subject of great interest for discourse analysts. In this section, I offer four exhibits of how the negotiation in and through discourse of such identities as parent, child, host, guest, or heterosexual young man has been investigated by analysts employing approaches as wide ranging as conversation analysis, interactional sociolinguistics, linguistic anthropology, and critical discourse analysis.

Operative Identities at Meal Time

The notion of operative identity (cf. "performed social identity" in Erickson & Shultz, 1982) comes from Sacks's lecture where a recently widowed man repeatedly rejects the offer of some herring by his stepson and daughter-in-law (Sacks, 1995, volume 2, p. 327). It is through these repeated offering and rejections that such identities as an old stubborn man and a burden is made relevant or operative (Sacks, 1995, volume 2, pp. 318–331).

Operative identity is an identity made relevant over the course of an action in interaction.

An operative identity then is closely tied to the actions that are being implemented in interaction, which is the essence of membership categorization analysis (part of conversation analysis) (see Chapter 6). The focus is on finding grounds for how categories or identities are enacted through and deployed in the service of actions rather than treating them as *a priori* variables that affect the interaction. A nice illustration can be found in Butler and Fitzgerald's (2010) study on operative identities during a family meal based on a videorecording of a breakfast that involves a 2- to 3-year-old child, Jason, with his parents (Eric and Sara) and grandparents (Bob and Kate) (p. 2466). In line 05, Kate the grandmother asks if Jason needs a separate plate but directs her question to the table (Eric and Sara). (Key: number in parentheses = length of silence in seconds; ↑= raised pitch; degree signs = quieter speech; hih heheh = laughter.)

(1) Separate plate

```
01   Eric:         D'you have breakfast with daddy? ((gaze to Jason))
02                 (.)
03                 Big break↑fast?
04   Jason:        Oh (0.6) [(        )
05   Kate:    →              [○Now-○ <Do you want a s:eparte plate
06                 him? ((gaze at table))
07            →    (1.2) ((Eric gaze to Jason; Jason nods; Eric nods))
08   Sara:         O:h let's: yeah [let's give him a plate.]
09   Bob:                          [He-        he nod]ed.
```

10		Hm he[h he
11	Sara:	[↑ihih hih hih
12	Bob:	He[y?
13	Sara:	[Okay.

As the authors observed, by initiating the offer of a plate, Kate makes relevant her membership category or identity as a host, which may be an omni-relevant category throughout this meal interaction. At the same time, by addressing her offer to the table rather than Jason, she specifically assigns (1) to Jason the membership category of a child through the *stage of life* membership categorization device (see Chapter 6)—a child who can't make decisions for himself and (2) to Eric and Sara the membership category of parents who are commonly expected to make decisions for their child. In other words, Kate is invoking the *family* device that entails rights and responsibilities for parents and children.

Just because the identities of parents and child have become operative through Kate's speaker selection in line 06 does not mean such identities will therefore sustain throughout the rest of the interaction. In fact, by directing his gaze to Jason in the very next line (line 07) and predicates his nod of acceptance on that of Jason's, Eric, as does Jason, implicitly challenges the identity ascription of Jason being a child not capable of making his own decision. Meanwhile, Sara's subsequent response of *Let's give him a plate* (line 08) includes Kate as a co-member along with Eric and Sara as decision makers for Jason, thus repartitioning the membership categories set up by Kate's offer. Finally, without noticing that Jason has in fact been invited to respond, Bob's treatment of Jason's "uninvited" self-selection as humorous (lines 09–10) hinges upon Jason's membership as a child in the *stage of life* device, who is displaying responsibilities for an activity that falls within the realm of his parents.

Thus, operative identities, as Butler and Fitzgerald (2010) wrote,

> are not simply invoked and displayed . . . , but are transformed, challenged and perhaps even undermined in the fine detail of talk-in-interaction—through a gaze (Erik's selection of Jason), a reference form (Sara's *let's*), and a nod (Jason's response).
>
> (p. 2467)

Treating identities as action relevant categories that are enacted, invoked, and subject to change over the course of moment-to-moment interaction is a hallmark of membership categorization analysis.

Task 1: Consider the following phone call from a mediation center for neighborhood disputes taken from Stokoe (2009, p. 76) (C = caller; M = mediator). The caller is complaining about excessive noise from her next-door neighbor's child. What identity or membership category is made relevant in the interaction, and how is it tied to the specific action that is being implemented? (Key: number in parentheses = length of silence in seconds.)

```
01  C:  An,=
02  M:  =yeah.
03      (0.3)
04  C:  By that ti- a- cos I'm a single mother,
05  M:  M:mm.=
06  C:  =By that time, (0.3) I'm ti:red.
07      (0.2)
08      .hhh
09  M:  Yeah.=
10  C:  An' I don't have many resources left for co:ping with things.
```

In sum, in the conversation analytic framework, or membership categorization analysis more specifically, the relevance of identity is a production and accomplishment of interaction, where identity can be displayed, developed, claimed, recast, resisted, and transformed (Antaki & Widdicombe, 1998; Benwell & Stokoe, 2006).

Gendered Parental Identities at Meal Time

A very different approach to identities at meal time can be observed in Kendall's (2008) interactional sociolinguistic study on gendered parental identities. Based on four audiorecorded dinners that involves a 10-year-old girl, Beth, with her mother (Elaine) and father (Mark), Kendall employed the framing (see Chapter 4) approach as well as the framework of discursive positioning (see Chapter 6) to show how mother and father created gendered parental identities by taking up different positions in different frames. Notably, Kendall combined the previously two unconnected notions of frame and positioning in her analytical framework. As she wrote, "In my model, positions are mutually constitutive components of frames" (Kendall, 2008, p. 545). Put simply, who we are is intricately connected to what we do in and through talk. "Doing dinner" (or creating and maintaining the frame of) dinner, for example, makes relevant such positions as head chef, host, and director of cleanup while "doing socialization" requires positions that monitor etiquette, behavior, and language (see Table 7.1). In addition, positions are characterized by functions of talk or speech acts (e.g., order), linguistic registers (e.g., imperatives), footing (e.g., participant structure, social capacity,

Table 7.1 Frames and Positions

Dinner Frame	Caregiving Frame	Socialization Frame	Managerial Frame	Conversational Frame
head chef	assistant	etiquette monitor	planner	journalist
host	teacher	behavior monitor	social secretary	moral guardian
director of cleanup	caretaker	language monitor		facilitator
				comedian

Note: Based on (Kendall, 2008)

alignment between self and other such as power and solidarity), and relation to surrounding talk (p. 548).

As Kendall (2008) reported, Mother takes up more and, in fact, all the positions observed in the data. In addition, Mother takes up more managerial and caretaking positions; whereas Father takes up more playful positions, thus yielding a clear gendered distribution of parental identities. The following interaction takes place shortly after Mark, the dad, picked up Beth from her horseback riding lesson as Elaine, the mom, is preparing for dinner (Kendall, 2008, p. 550). As the segment begins, Beth attempts to engage Elaine in a conversational frame on the topic of horseback riding lesson in which Mark participates (lines 01–05).

(2) Head chef

01	Beth:		Mom you know what John said?
02			He said even if you're on the correct ( ) you're on the
03			wrong diagonal. You can change it.
04	Mark:		Oh yeah he says- he said to change 'em when you
05			think you're on the wrong one.
06	Elaine:	→	Beth help me carry this over.
07	Mark:		And that he you know without him asking and telling
08			him all this that he wants you to-
09	Elaine:	→	And then you can bring the plate over to Daddy.
10	Mark:		uh keep yourself on the right diagonal by changing
11			when you need to.
12	Beth:		Hopefully tomorrow I'll get it right.

As Kendall observed, despite the ongoing conversational frame maintained by Beth and Mark, Elaine asserts her *head chef* position within the dinner frame through directives such as orders, requests, and instructions (lines 06, 09).

In Kendall's study then, identities are built by taking up particular positions within particular frames through specific features of talk such as speech acts, footing, and the like.

Task 2: Consider the following extract taken from Kendall (2008), where Mark offers Beth more food (p. 561). What frame(s) are in play, and what positions are being maintained? How so? Ground your responses in the specific lines of the transcript. Consult Table 7.1 if necessary. (Key: 'text' = direct quote; <*manner*> text> = the manner in which an utterance is spoken.)

01	Mark:	You want another bowl?
02	Beth:	Ew.
03	Mark:	Hm?
04	Beth:	No! They're disgusting.
05	Elaine:	Excuse me.
06	Beth:	Sorry!
07	Elaine:	Just say 'no thanks'.
08	Beth:	No thanks!
09		((6 seconds))
10	Mark:	<chuckling whispered> Disgusting.>
11	Beth:	<scoffs>
12	Elaine:	Go take your vitamin.

Being a Responsible Urban Father

Positioning theory (see Chapter 6) is also employed in Wortham and Gadsden's (2006) linguistics anthropological explication of the identity construction of an urban father, but through a different type of data—an interview with an African American man Robert who became a father as a teenager. By focusing on one specific narrative within that interview, the authors showed how Robert engages four layers of narrative positioning to construct his identity as a responsible father. Their analysis is situated within the larger context gained from the interview data—one in which the street is dangerous, home is nurturing, and the system is biased. Their specific analytical tools involve four layers of narrative positioning: (1) narrative events, (2) voicing, (3) evaluation (of the voices), and (4) interactional positioning with the interlocutor.

Voicing is a practice through which a narrator characterizes oneself or others as being recognizable types of people, a voice being "a recognizable social type, associated with a character primarily through indexical cues in a narrative" (Bakhtin, 1981; Wortham & Gadsden, 2006, pp. 320–321).

In the following extract, Robert uses both narrative events and voicing to position himself as a responsible father (Wortham & Gadsden, 2006, p. 320).

(3) Have a system

```
01  Robert:   okay, well my typical day starts at about five thirty a.m.
02            I get up, hit the showers, I have to be at work by seven.
03            so I hit the shower and either Natasha or I will fix her
04            something to eat, fix her something to eat before we
05            wake her up, because she's hard to wake up in the morning.
06            so, we have to have a system. the initial wake up, then the go
07            in there and take your shower. and then the, she actually
08            comes out of the shower, then the wake-up to get your
09            clothes on, get ready, and then go to school. we have to
10            get her two to three times in the morning before she's
11            actually awake.
```

As observed by the authors, Robert positions himself as a responsible and accommodating parent in a functioning relationship by narrating his typical morning routine that involves working together with his girlfriend to get his daughter ready. Within this same extract, Robert also engages in voicing, where his *we have to have a system* is an indexical cue that presupposes the voice of "organized, planful, responsible people" (p. 321). The idea of voicing then appears very much related to the notion of category-bound predicates in membership categorization analysis, where having a system would be an attribute bound to such a category as organized, planful, and responsible people.

Narrative positioning is also done through taking a position toward particular voices. Elsewhere in his narrative, for example, Robert voices her mother as a demanding *drill sergeant* but evaluates that voice with *She gave the best to her kids and expects the best from her kids* (p. 323). In so doing, Robert positions himself as aligning with that value system that respects hard work and responsibilities. Finally, one way to self-position as a hardworking responsible parent is through interactional positioning *vis-à-vis* his interlocutor the interviewer (Wortham & Gadsden, 2006).

Interactional position is a position taken up in interaction *vis-à-vis* one's interlocutor (e.g., as friendly, hostile, kindred spirit, different species).

Task 3: Consider the following extract taken from the author's interview with Robert (Wortham & Gadsden, 2006). Where do you see evidence of interactional positioning, and how does this interactive positioning contribute to Robert's self-positioning as a responsible father? (Key: *italics* = stress.)

01	Interviewer:	. . . we appreciate, when I say *we*, NCOFF (National
02		Center on Fathers and Families), we really appreciate
03		your taking <u>your</u> time out of your busy schedule to
04		come in here. although twenty-five dollars is not a
05		<u>lot</u>, we at least want to show that we respect your <u>time</u>.
07	Robert:	it's like I was telling Lisa, I said <u>twenty-five</u> dollars, I
08		could work <u>half</u> a day to make that, so it's plenty to
09		<u>me</u>, so it's <u>more</u> than enough.
10	Interviewer:	oh, okay. so I'm going to start with some back
11		ground information. . .

Heterosexual Masculinity

Finally, breaking away from the theme of various family identities in our discussion of "individual" identities, we take up one of the most researched identities in the discourse literature—that of gender, and we sample a critical discourse analytic account of how heterosexual masculinity is performed through young men's talk. As a critique of discourse analytic work that perpetuates such gender stereotypes as men's talk being competitive and women's being cooperative, Cameron's (2006) work is based on a tape-recorded, casual conversation that takes place as five white, middle-class American 21-year-old men who attend the same university watch sports on television. The following conversation involves gossiping about another young man who is not present (Cameron, 2006, p. 424). (Key: [talk] = turn completely contained within another speaker's turn; *italics* = emphatic stress.)

(4) Antithesis of man

01	Bryan:	uh you know that really gay guy in our Age of
02		Revolution class who sits in front of us? he wore
03		shorts again, by the way, it's like 42 degrees out he
04		wore shorts again [laughter 1 [Ed: That guy] it's like
05		a speedo, he wears a speedo to class (.) he's got
06		incredibly skinny legs [Ed: it's worse] you know=

```
07   Ed:                                                    =you know
08            like those shorts women volleyball players wear?
09            it's like those (.) it's l[ike
10   Bryan:                            [you know what's even more
11            ridicu[lous? when you wear those shorts and like a
12            parka on . . .
13   Ed:           [French cut spandex]
```

((five lines omitted))

```
19   Bryan:   he's either got some condition that he's got to
20            like have his legs exposed at all times or else he's
21            got really good legs=
22   Ed:                         =he's probably he'[s like
23   Carl:                                         [he really likes
24   Carl:    his legs=
25   Bryan:     =he
26   Ed:         =he's like at home combing his leg hairs=
27   Bryan:   he doesn't have any leg hair though=    [yes and oh
28   Ed:                                 =he real[ly likes
29            his legs=
30   Al:             =very long very white and very skinny
31   Bryan:   those ridiculous Reeboks that are always (indecipherable)
32            and goofy white socks always striped=    [tube socks
33   Ed:                                       =that's [right
34            he's the antithesis of man
```

As Cameron (2006) observed, to establish that a certain individual is the "antithesis of man," the group paradoxically "engages in a kind of conversation that might well strike us as the antithesis of 'men's talk'"—gossiping on such conventionally feminine topics such as clothing and bodily appearance (p. 424). Moreover, according to Cameron, the talk exhibits such "female talk features" as (1) *you know* (e.g., lines 01, 06, 07) and *like* (e.g., lines 03, 04, 08, 09) that highlight common ground and attend to the hearer's face, (2) the latching (e.g., lines 07 & 21) and repetition (e.g., lines 23–28) that are often taken as markers of cooperation, as well as (3) the joint, highly cooperative, production of discourse as shown in their discussion of the "gay" guy's legs (lines 21–29)

By identifying such "female" talk features in these young men's talk, Cameron showed that dichotomies such as cooperative vs. competitive is unproductive in getting at what is really going on when it comes to the analysis of gender and language. For Cameron, what the young men are doing is performing their gender identity as heterosexual males by gossiping about gay men being the "antithesis of men" (p. 430). In this particular context, the urgency of asserting heterosexual masculinity in an all-male group, according to Cameron, appears to override the danger of sounding "feminine."

Task 4: Cameron's analysis is based on the data collected by Danny—one of the five young men in the group—who wrote a course paper for the author entitled "Wine, women, and sports" that confirms the stereotype of male interaction being completive, hierarchically organized, and so forth. While acknowledging that Danny's analysis was not inaccurate and his conclusions not unwarranted, Cameron questioned the partiality of Danny's description of data. On the basis of extract (4), do you find Cameron's argument convincing? To what degree do you agree with her assessment? Explain.

Discourse and Institutional Identity

Aside from individual identities such as being a multitasking mother, an urban father, a stubborn old man, or a heterosexual young man, institutional identities such as a novice teacher, a fellow physician, a boy in a literacy classroom, and an academic have also been the object of inquiry for discourse analysts with a particular interest in identity. We offer four exhibits showcasing how the analysis of such identities as instantiated and negotiated in and through discourse is conducted by analysts utilizing a variety of approaches.

Being a Novice Teacher

We begin with a study done by Vásquez and Urzúa (2009) on novice teacher identity based on 39 audiotaped mentor-teacher meetings in TESOL (Teaching English to Speakers of Other Languages) that involve 17 teachers and three mentors. In particular, the authors ask: what roles do directly reported speech (DRS) (e.g., *I said . . .*) and directly reported mental states (DRMS) (e.g., *I thought . . .*) play in the performance of the novice teacher identity?

Task 5: Consider the following utterances taken from Vásquez and Urzúa (2009). Identify the directly reported speech (DRS) and directly reported mental states (DRMS). Do they engage in different types of identity work? If yes, how so? (Key: [. . .] = omitted data, usually minimal responses produced by interlocutor.)

a. I gave them a sheet that had those options and I said "Some of them will not have every form so you have to remember that." I said "Try your best to fill in the forms. If you can't do it it's OK."
b. . . . sometimes I was like "Why are we graduate assistants teaching these classes, are we really qualified" you know . . .

c.   . . . my thing was like "Oh we're not gon-" initially "we're not gonna have enough time. We're gonna- we don't really have enough activities for the amount of time that we have."

d.   . . . so I had to make a speech [. . .] yeah basically I told them "if you are not prepared just don't come."

e.   . . . several people have dropped off since midterm. Like they went from a B or an A to a D and I'm gonna tell them in their meetings this week "You have major issues now," even though they should know . . .

f.   I'm not like taking my aggression out on him but I find myself becoming frustrated and I think it's with my own self like "How do I include him?"

Vásquez and Urzúa (2009) identified a total 180 instances of DRS and 96 instances of DRMS in their data and argued that the novice teachers use DRS to foreground competence and DRMS to highlight uncertainty. In the following extract, for example, the teacher demonstrates great confidence in a hypothetical future job interview by directly reporting what she might actually say in that interview (Vásquez & Urzúa, 2009, p. 13).

(5) Show it in interview

I think it's a rich resource. you can show it to- You can say "Look." you can show it in an interview like "Here. Let me leave you with my portfolio of all these lessons that I created for a certain class. You can see some of my own work.

By contrast, the insecurity and inability with regard to time management issues are expressed through DRMS (Vásquez & Urzúa, 2009, p. 15)

(6) Got a little nervous

Yea I got a little nervous then, just because we were- and this is probably, I don't really notice when I'm being observed that much until something's kind of not going exactly right, and then I was like "I'm not gonna be able to finish this!"

Overall, the authors showed that the teacher uses DRS of what was said or clearly unsaid (e.g., would have liked to say) to position herself as (1) skilled instruction giver and (2) successful classroom manager, and DRMS of feelings and attitudes to convey (1) general negative appraisals of their teaching, (2) nervousness and insecurity when being observed, (3) problems of time management, and (4) inability or lack of knowledge in responding to specific problems. They also pointed out that linguistically, DRS is usually done in imperatives and "need" (i.e., *You need to do X.*) statements and DRMS in interrogatives. The identity of a novice teacher then is discursively reflected and enacted in the two seemingly contradictory aspects of asserting competence on the one hand through DRS and acknowledging uncertainty on the other through DRMS.

Being a Fellow Physician

A different type of identity and identity work is addressed in Erickson's (1999) microethnographic study on the interaction between a clinically experienced attending physician (preceptor) and a clinically inexperienced physician (intern) (who has just graduated from medical school with an M.D.) during residency—a 3-year period during which he undergoes preparation for board certification in a medical specialty under the supervision of an attending physician. The supervision or precepting session involves a three-stage process: (1) the intern interviews the patient independently, (2) the intern presents the case to the preceptor, and (3) the intern accompanies the preceptor back to the patient, where the preceptor reexamines the patient and determines the final diagnosis and treatment. The goal of the precepting session is to ensure patient safety and to teach the beginning physician at the same time. Erickson's study focuses on the intern's identity work during the second, case presentation stage.

According to Erickson, case presentation is a medium for physician self-presentation and requires complex identity work because the event is inherently face-threatening (see Chapter 6) where the intern strives to maintain his face as being clinically competent while dealing with ambiguities in diagnosis and treatment in the real medical world. At the same time, the intern also has to manage the complex footing (see Chapter 6) *vis-à-vis* the preceptor as a novice, a colleague who shares expertise, or as a colleague who shares common background beyond medical expertise. The question is: how does the intern negotiate these identity issues in his interaction with the precept?

To answer this question, Erickson collected data that included transcripts of videotaped precepting sessions as well as focus-group interviews. He engaged in interpretative analyses where particular and sometimes multiple interpretations are proposed for a given discourse feature and arguments are made on the basis of noting the features in the transcript and relying on ethnographic information to attribute meanings to those features. He began by detailing the ethnographic background of the precepting session, and for each analytical point, he first made a claim: for example, the use of *x* signifies *y*, he then showed where and how x is used in the transcribed extracts of discourse and, finally, he used the ethnographic information from the literature, focus-group interviews, and his own prior work and experience to attribute *y* to *x*. The particular case presentation Erickson focused on concerns the "irritable bowel syndrome"—a condition (based on ethnographic information) typically regarded as medically uninteresting among medical professionals, which makes it difficult for the intern to display his competence, let alone the kind of medical machismo (e.g., "[c]lutching certainty out of the jaws of uncertainty") doctors strive for.

Erickson's analysis shows, for example, that the intern's fellow physician identity is in part co-constructed through the informal register and the footing of collegiality employed by both the intern and the preceptor. The following is an exemplar of the intern's use of the informal register (Erickson, 1999, pp. 117–118). (Key: most utterances transcribed as breath groups with syllable of tonal nucleus appearing at the left margin; two dots = approximately half a second pause; four dots = full second pause; / = abrupt termination of speech or latching.)

(7) Bag

01	Intern:	. . . . um . . family
02		history is . . he said his
03	→	father had co/cancer . . he's not sure
04		what cancer but his father wore a
05	→	bag so we can assume perhaps he had large
06		bowel cancer/

As Erickson observed, the more formally projected "colorectal cancer" in line 03 is replaced with simply *cancer*, and in line 04, the everyday term *bag* is used in lieu of the technical term "colostomy bag." Such informality or use of quasi-medical terms is the contextualization cue (see Chapter 4) that generates the inference of collegiality or co-membership (see Chapter 6), where the intern positions himself as a fellow physician rather than an apprenticing novice. The connection between informality and collegiality is grounded in the ethnographic information that part of becoming a "real" doctor is learning to talk in ways that breaks the frame (see Chapter 4) of seriousness from time to time and alternate between formal and informal registers. Strict, textbook-like formality can make someone sound like a medical student with no medical experience in the real world. Engaging in informal talk then is one way for the precept to treat the intern as an experienced physician and for the intern to display his learning and to act as a fellow physician rather than an apprenticing novice.

In Erickson's data, both the preceptor and the intern can initiate the informal register. There are, however, two cases where the preceptor's initiation is not taken up by the intern, and Erickson attributes the discrepancies to the racial backgrounds of the participants (the intern and the patient being African American young men of roughly the same age, and the preceptor being white and middle aged) and the potential for stigma and embarrassment. Following is one such case that concerns the patient's drug use (Erickson, 1999, p. 118).

(8) Shoot up

01	Intern:	otherwise he's not aware of any other . . problems. . . .
02	Preceptor:	((*shakes head slightly back and forth in negation*))
03	→	he doesn't shoot up.
04	Intern:	((*picks up notes from chart and shakes head slightly in*
05		*negation*))
06	→	he has no history of IVDA ((*turns pages of notes*))
07	Preceptor:	OK . . physical exam,

Note that the preceptor's informal reference to intravenous drug use is responded to by the intern with what Erickson called the hyper-formal *he has no history of IVDA*. As Erickson pointed out, "race is still stigmatizable and hence a source of worry in self presentation, even for African-Americans who are professionals" (p. 124). The preceptor's reference to *shoot up* as a contextualization cue then may have inadvertently positioned the intern (or at least taken by the intern as such) as sharing co-membership with the patient in his familiarity with the practice of illegal drug use—just because he too is African American. By not taking up the informal register, the intern actively resists that categorization. Note that this extract also appears in Chapter 5 of Erickson's (2004) *Talk and Social Theory*, the video of which can be accessed through Erickson's faculty website at UCLA (https://pages.gseis.ucla.edu/faculty/ferickson/resources/talk.html)

In sum, the intern's performance of the situated social identity as a fellow physician and as someone not sharing certain racial stereotypes of a patient of the same race is in part negotiated through the use and non-use of informal register by the participants.

Task 6: How does the preceptor-intern relationship compare with that of the mentor-teacher? How are the identity concerns similar or different? Ground your explanations in the data we have presented from Erickson (1999) and Vásquez and Urzúa (2009), if possible.

Being a Boy in a Literacy Classroom

The question of how the identity of masculinity shapes literacy practices in the classroom and vice versa is the focus of Marsh and Lammers's (2011) critical discourse analytic study of adolescent literacy classrooms. Their data include interviews with Chavo, the focal student, his mother, and his teacher along with observations of Chavo in the classroom over 6 months and in the sports arena over several years, and their analysis employs Gee's (2005) theoretical tools (see Chapter 8) of (a) Discourse, (b) social languages, (c) situated meanings, and (d) figured worlds.

Task 7: Match Gee's four theoretical tools with their definitions.

A. Discourses

a. typical stories about the world (cf. mental models, frames, scripts)

B. social languages

b. meaning within a specific context

C. situated meaning

c. style of language associated with particular social identity

D. figured world

d. ways of being "kinds of people"

In talking to the interviewer about the humanities class, for example, Chavo uses the social language of an experienced student, calling it *isn't motivational*, from which the researchers infer the situated meaning that Chavo did not like the class but at the same time was playing it safe by not saying so directly, which might compromise his identity as a good student in front of a university professor. Interestingly, in speaking about the same classroom to a soccer teammate, Chavo uses the social language of a teenage athlete by saying that *it sucked*.

The authors' analysis involves constructing stories about Chavo's masculinity and literacy practices using the words of Chavo, his mother, and his teacher, where elements such as *um, ah,* and false starts are taken out along with the interviewer's questions to present a cleaner, more readable version of the text.

The figured world relevant to the mother, for example, is that being a boy has nothing to do with whether Chavo participates in school literacy and other academics literacy practice (Marsh & Lammers, 2011, p. 101).

(9) Mother's perspective

01	Mother:	I think that with Chavo, because of his really deep
02		love for learning,
03	→	I don't think that being a boy ever mattered to him.
04		what anyone would say, or kid him about doing
05		his homework, or being a good student.
06		He thrives on being a good student.
07		I mean, that is really big thing for him to be able to
08		accomplish.
09	→	But, when I think of him being male, I think that he
10		very early figured out that, first of all that he loved
11		to learn these things.
12		but second of all, because of his rules, he knew
13		that in order for him to play sports,
14		he was going to have to make the grades.
15		I think that made sense to him . . .

16	And I think the overall riding factor in that was
17	that he does have a real huge love for learning.

As shown, the mother explicitly denounces any connection between being a boy and learning in the case of Chavo (line 03), and she claims that the only way in which gender might have mattered is that Chavo understands he has to make the grades in order to play sports (lines 12–14).

Like Chavo's mother, the figured world relevant to his teacher, according to the authors, also seems to be one in which gender does not matter. For her, some kids are literature kids; some are not; being male or female has nothing to do with the distribution. Prior to the following segment, the teacher reported on her telling Chavo that he was just like her daughter, who didn't like the humanities class. As the segment begins, the teacher continues to establish Chavo's dislike of literature: he might be reading other genres such as a sports magazine or a soccer journal, but not literature (lines 04–06).

(10) Teacher's perspective

01	Teacher:	He must be so bored with this stuff.
02		He would never, you know, I don't know if Chavo
03		reads on his own,
04		but I would venture to guess if it's not a sports
05		magazine or a soccer journal,
06		he doesn't.
07	→	He is not a literature kid from my perspective.
08		He's gotta be in the class.
09		No, it's not an easy class.
10		And he does his work.

Note that this figured world of Chavo not being a literature kid is in part brought off precisely by the use of nominalization ("literature kid" in line 07) (Marsh & Lammers, 2011, p. 103).

Unlike his mother and his teacher, Chavo holds a different view of gender and literacy. His figured world is one in which boys and girls participate differently in literacy activities, and (boy) athletes don't read books (Marsh & Lammers, 2011, p. 106).

(11) Chavo's perspective

01	Chavo:	→	I think also once you get involved in sports like
02			you're s'posed to be known as like an athlete.
03			It's just like a lot of the [athletes] really don't even
04			want to like talk about reading or so don't even read.
05			So you just kind of get caught up into that somewhere
06			along the line, I guess.

. . . . .

07	→	I still tried to get good grades, got straight As in
08		middle school.
09	→	And I just wouldn't like be loud about it or brag
10		about it.

Clearly, Chavo seems to be fully aware that the Discourse of being a popular boy athlete is not one that meshes well with that of being a good student, and he has found a way to be both, which is evidenced in not only how he talks but also what he wears, who he sits next to, and so forth. His use of *I*-statements is noted by the authors as evidence of Chavo taking charge of the identity conundrum he finds himself in. In the final analysis, Marsh and Lammers (2011) argued that Chavo's identity of masculinity in relation to literacy is powerfully shaped by his figured world. The belief that being a good student is not part of masculinity, for example, makes him feign being less of a good reader than he actually is.

Being an Academic

It is important to keep in mind that identity is by no means an issue exclusively relevant to spoken interaction. Hyland (2012), for example, offered an in-depth analysis of how identity is implicated and negotiated in academic writing. With a specific focus on 50–100 word academic bios accompanying research articles, Hyland and Tse (2012) demonstrated how academic identities are constructed by not only what is said but also how it is said. Their data include 600 bios in six leading journals across three disciplines (200 each from applied linguistics, electrical engineering, and philosophy) written by an equal number of males and females with a random sampling of categories such as senior academic, junior academic, and postgraduate. These bios were coded according to rhetorical moves (see Chapter 3) and process types (see below). The range of moves represented in the data include employment, education, research interests, publications, community service (e.g., editorships and committee memberships, achievements (e.g., awards and honors), and personal data (e.g., hobbies and interests). Of all these moves, more than half compose employment and research interests. Notably, senior scholars are more likely to include research interests and publications (extract 12) while junior scholars and research students rely more on employment and education (extract 13) (Hyland & Tse, 2012, p. 159).

(12) Research and publication

Richard Janney is Professor Modern English Linguistics at the University of Munich. His current areas of interest are face-to-face interaction, the pragmatics of human communication, language and affect, and electronic discourse. He is co-author of InterGrammar: Toward an integrative model of verbal, prosodic, and kinesic choices in speech.

(Berlin: Mouton de Gruyter, 1987)

(13) Employment and education

    a. Qadri Ahmadi teaches Postcolonial Studies at the University of Minnesota.

    b. Liz Staggins is a Research student at the University of Manchester. She is currently working on a project about Aesthetic Psychology, the main theme of her PhD thesis.

Aside from rhetorical moves, identity is also constructed, according to Hyland and Tse (2012), via the various process types. The concept of process type comes from Systemic Functional Linguistics and refers to the different ways in which experience is expressed through verbs. A distinction is made, for example, between material and relational processes: material process is conveyed through verbs of *doing* such as *work*, *write*, or *study* and relational process through verbs of being such as the copula (Hyland, 2015). Interestingly, as one's academic rank rises, the use of relational forms increased and material forms decreased (Hyland & Tse, 2012, p. 162). Consider the following bios of three senior academics.

(14) Relational process

    a. Ruth Terry is Professor of Linguistics at UCL . . .

    b. She is the co-author of over 40 technical papers and is the holder of two patents.

    c. Dr. Desmond is the recipient of funding from various sources . . .

Here, the credible statue of the senior academics is in part conveyed through the relational process of *being* that highlights who they are as opposed to what they do—an aspect more observable in bios of junior academics, as shown in the next set of examples.

(15) Material process

    a. He has presented at many conferences.

    b. She regularly speaks at workshops and teacher education forums.

As Hyland and Tse (2012) pointed out, the authors of these bios are "trying to establish a credible academic identity through choices which foreground valued discoursal activities" (p. 162).

Overall, compared with junior academics, senior academics have access to a wider range of rhetorical moves (research, publication, employment, and achievement) and use far more relational processes to establish their unique positions. This does not mean, however, that junior academics are left without their own resources. As Hyland and Tse (2012) wrote, "in 50–100 words, authors are able to reflexively craft a narrative of expertise for themselves" and "construct a disciplinary aligned presence and shape a professionally credible self" (p. 155). Through these brief bios, in other words, authors find a space to present themselves as interesting, credible, and accomplished academics.

Task 8: Find an author bio in a research article of your choice and identify the specific ways in which the author's identity is being constructed in that bio.

Task 9: Consider the various illustrations so far of discourse analytic works addressed to the question of how identities are negotiated in discourse. What do they have in common? How do they differ from one another? What might be some of the strengths and weaknesses of the different ways of approaching the question?

Approaches to Discourse and Identity

So far, we have drawn upon portions of individual studies to illustrate how the issue of discourse and identity has been addressed by analysts of myriad empirical persuasions (also see Antaki & Widdicombe, 1998; Benwell & Stokoe, 2006; De Fina, Schiffrin, & Bamberg, 2006). Even within the small numbers of studies sampled in this chapter, one may observe how the methods differ in the range of data collected (e.g., audiorecordings or videorecordings, interviews, field notes, corpus of texts), the types of analytical concepts invoked (e.g., membership categorization, face, framing, contextualization cue, positioning, voicing, figured world, process type), and the extent to which local and larger social contexts are brought to bear in the interpretation of data. Despite these differences, all these analysts share the common goal of documenting how the participants do identity work in and through discourse by engaging in specific practices in the turn-by-turn talk (e.g., speaker selection, gaze and gesture, reference form), utilizing linguistics devices (e.g., repetition, informal register, direct reported speech or mental state, rhetorical moves), or deploying discursive practices (e.g., voicing, evaluating, interactional positioning, social language, ascribing and resisting membership categories).

The analytical reasoning typically involves (1) making claims about how the identity work is done (e.g., the identity of a fellow physician being negotiated through the use of informal register), (2) defining terms (e.g., narrative positioning), (3) establishing categories and subcategories regarding identities or identity work (e.g., DRS and DRMS), (4) showing and discussing specific portions of transcripts (e.g., what is said, how it is said, when exactly in the sequence something is said, how what is said is responded to by the participants in the data) that support the claims, (5) utilizing various analytical concepts to discuss data, and (6) using ethnographic data (if applicable) to bolster one's argument.

In reading a discourse analytic study on identity then, it would be useful to ask the following questions:

a. What (aspects of) identities are being managed or displayed?
b. How is the identity work done?
c. What kinds of data are gathered?
d. What concepts are invoked in the analysis?
e. How is the analytical reasoning built?
f. Are the analyses convincing?

> Task 10: Read Kiesling (2006) (see References) or any study on discourse and identity that is of interest to you and answer the previous six questions.

> Task 11: Consider the following extract taken from a tutorial interaction between a graduate student Priya and her tutor Liam at a writing skills center. Liam is a graduate of the International Education Program, and Priya is a doctoral student in Arts Education. Using all the analytical resources discussed so far, provide an account of how identities are negotiated within this brief extract. (Key: number in parentheses = length of silence in seconds; degree signs = quieter speech; > < = quickened pace).)
>
>   ((Liam is reading Priya's paper.))
>
> 01 Priya: Make sense?=
> 02 Liam: =Yea:h. It's very good.
> 03   (0.5)
> 04   I:s. The purpose of- °i::s°
> 05 Priya: Yeah I'll change all my typos [I want someone check ( ).
> 06 Liam: [ah::m
> 07   (1.0)
> 08 Priya: >Is it clear?<

Key Points

* Empirical endeavors have investigated how individual identities and institutional identities are negotiated in and through discourse.
* Identities can be enacted, invoked, and subject to change over the course of moment-to-moment interaction.

- Identities can be enacted as one takes up particular positions in particular frames.
- Identities can be constructed through narrative positioning (narrative events, voicing, evaluation, and interactive positioning)
- Heterosexual masculinity may be performed through talk that defies the cooperative vs. competitive gender stereotypes.
- Novice teachers display their identities of competence and uncertainty through the use of directly reported speech and directly reported mental state respectively.
- A medical intern negotiates his identity as a fellow physician through the use and non-use of the informal register in his interaction with the attending physician.
- Being a boy in the literacy classroom entails navigating the complex figured worlds in which boys and girls participate in literacy activities differently and that popular boy athletes are not good students.
- Academic bios provide a rhetorical space for senior and junior scholars to construct their professional identities through various rhetorical moves and process types.
- Empirical work on discourse and identity involves specifying what aspects of identity are under investigation and how the identity work is done, where various identity-relevant analytical concepts are used to illuminate the data and ethnographic background to enrich the analysis.

References

Antaki, C., & Widdicombe, S. (Eds.). (1998). *Identities in talk*. London: Sage.

Bakhtin, M. M. (1981). *The dialogic imagination*. Austin: The University of Texas Press.

Benwell, B., & Stokoe, E. (2006). *Discourse and identity*. Edinburgh: Edinburgh University Press.

Butler, C. W., & Fitzgerald, R. (2010). Membership-in-action: Operative identities in a family meal. *Journal of Pragmatics, 42*, 2462–2474.

Cameron, D. (2006). Performing gender identity: Young men's talk and the construction of heterosexual masculinity. In S. Johnson & U. H. Meinhof (Eds.), *Language and masculinity* (pp. 419–432). Oxford: Blackwell.

De Fina, A., Schiffrin, D., & Bamberg, M. (Eds.). (2006). *Discourse and identity*. Cambridge: Cambridge University Press.

Erickson, F. (1999). Appropriation of voice and presentation of self as a fellow physician: Aspects of a discourse of apprenticeship in medicine. In S. Sarangi & C. Roberts (Eds.), *Talk, work and institutional order* (pp. 109–144). Berlin and New York: Mouton de Gruyter.

Erickson, F. (2004). *Talk and social theory: Ecologies of speaking and listening in everyday life*. Malden, MA: Polity Press.

Erickson, F., & Shultz, J. (1982). *The counselor as gatekeeper: Social interaction in interviews*. New York: Academic Press.

Gee, J. P. (2005). *An introduction to discourse analysis: Theory and method* (2nd ed.). London and New York: Routledge.

Hyland, K. (2012). *Disciplinary identities: Individuality and community in academic discourse.* Cambridge: Cambridge University Press.

Hyland, K. (2015). Genre, discipline and identity. *Journal of English for Academic Purposes, 19,* 32–43.

Hyland, K., & Tse, P. (2012). 'She has received many honors': Identity construction in article bio statements. *Journal of English for Academic Purposes, 11,* 155–165.

Kendall, S. (2008). The balancing act: Framing gendered parental identities at dinnertime. *Language in Society, 37,* 539–568.

Kiesling, S. F. (2006). Hegemonic identity-making in narrative. In A. De Fina, D. Schiffrin, & M. Bamberg (Eds.), *Discourse and identity* (pp. 261–287). New York: Cambridge University Press.

Marsh, J., & Lammers, J. C. (2011). Figured worlds and discourses of masculinity: Being a boy in a literacy classroom. In R. Rogers (Ed.), *An introduction to critical discourse analysis in education* (2nd ed.) (pp. 93–116). New York and London: Routledge.

Sacks, H. (1995). *Lectures on conversation* (Vols. 1–2). Malden, MA: Blackwell.

Stokoe, E. (2009). Doing actions with identity categories: Complaints and denials in neighbor disputes. *Text & Talk, 29*(1), 75–97.

Vásquez, C., & Urzúa, A. (2009). Reported speech and reported mental status in mentoring meetings: Exploring novice teacher identities. *Research on Language and Social Interaction, 42*(1), 1–19.

Wortham, S., & Gadsden, V. (2006). Urban fathers positioning themselves through narrative: An approach to narrative self-construction. In A. De Fina, D. Schiffrin, & M. Bamberg (Eds.), *Discourse and identity* (pp. 315–341). New York: Cambridge University Press.

Part V

Discourse and Ideology

8 Classics in Discourse and Ideology

Introduction

In the previous chapters, we have considered how discourse analysts approach the questions of how discourse is structured, how social actions are accomplished in discourse, and how identities are negotiated in discourse. In this and the next chapters, we tackle the remaining big question that characterizes the pursuits of discourse analysts: how is ideology constructed in discourse? For that matter, what do we mean by *ideology*? As Dijk (1998) pointed out, there have been numerous definitions of ideology, yet its meaning remains "elusive and confused" (p. vii). To establish a general starting point for the time being, we use the following definition from the Merriam-Webster dictionary to facilitate our initial discussion on discourse and ideology.

> **Ideology** is a manner or the content of thinking characteristic of an individual, group, or culture.

We find evidence of how ideology is embedded in discourse all around us. When my daughter Zoe was 3 years old, we were having a conversation about who spoke Chinese to her at preschool. When I mentioned her teacher, Kwon, Zoe responded matter-of-factly, "Yeah, but he's a boy. He doesn't speak Chinese." In her developing system of language ideology, Zoe had somehow come to the conclusion that boys don't speak Chinese—perhaps based on her experience of having a father who doesn't speak Chinese and a mother who does. Recall also the exclamation "No one's mother works here!" in an office sign (see Chapter 1) designed as a cleaning reminder. The message underscores the ideology that mothers are cleaners. A medical insurance brochure picked up by one of my students demonstrates the ideology of pregnancy as sickness: "Medical care for pregnancy and delivery, and complications of pregnancy and delivery, will be reimbursed the same as any other sickness." Finally, in a report from *The New York Times* on the 2008 U.S. presidential election (Ericson, 2011), the words that speakers used at the two political conventions encoded the themes that each party highlighted.

Republicans talked about reform and character far more frequently than Democrats. Republicans were more likely to talk about businesses and taxes, and Democrats were more likely to talk about jobs or the economy. The frequency of each party's word usage is a reflection of the ideology upheld by each. Clearly, we see subtle traces or strong imprints of ideology in the use of language in a variety of contexts, and discourse analysts are interested in making evident such traces and imprints.

As will be shown in Chapter 9, answering the question of how ideologies are constructed in discourse can be done from a variety of perspectives using a variety of approaches. But first, in this chapter, we introduce two seminal efforts that explore the relationship between language and thought: Sapir and Whorf's linguistic relativism and Lakoff and Johnson's (1980) cognitive metaphor. Without generating any analytical vocabulary for discourse analysts such as footing and frame, these efforts nevertheless undergird some of the fundamental dialectics and struggles in our thinking of discourse and ideology. The bulk of this chapter is devoted to introducing three major frameworks that have in many ways defined the field of discourse and ideology: Fairclough's critical language studies, van Dijk's ideological analysis, and Gee's seven building tasks and four theoretical tools. We end the chapter with a brief note on critical discourse analysis. Although as a discourse analytic approach, critical discourse analysis does not hold any exclusive rights to the study of discourse and ideology (as will be shown in the next chapter), it is nevertheless the only approach that explicitly tackles issues of ideology as its stated aim. It is also the one most frequently associated with the study of discourse and ideology.

Language and Thought

Early influential work on the relationship between language on the one hand and thought and reality on the other were powerful precursors to systematic investigations into the intricate workings of discourse and ideology.

> Task 1: What do you think comes first, language or thought? In other words, do you have thoughts first and then express that thought through language, or is it the other way around?

Two different theories provide two opposing answers to the question in Task 1. In the theory of linguistic relativism, language determines or at least influences thought; in the framework of cognitive metaphor, thought begets language.

Linguistic Relativism (Sapir and Whorf)

Linguistic relativism was found in the writings of one of the preeminent American linguists of the 20th century Edward Sapir (1994–1939) and his student Benjamin Lee Whorf (1897–1941), an independent scholar of Native American languages who made his living as an insurance claim adjuster. Their thinking was later captured in what has come to be known as the Sapir-Whorf hypothesis, although neither had explicitly labeled it as such.

Sapir-Whorf hypothesis states that (1) language determines or at least influences cognition or perception and that (2) differences in language lead to differences in cognition and perception.

In other words, the medium *is* the message. As the Italian film director Federico Fellini (1920–1993) wrote, "A different language is a different vision of life." How a particular language categorizes things grammatically, according to the hypothesis, affects the way people categorize things in the world. The extreme version of the hypothesis proposes that categories of language determine categories of perception: one would not be able to imagine anything outside the bounds of what his or her language dictates. What has been presented as evidence of such linguistic determinism or linguistic relativity resides mostly in the domains of vocabulary and syntax. In Loftus and Palmer's (1974) experiment, for example, participants were shown the same video but asked questions with different verbs: *How fast were the cars going when they hit/smashed/collided/bumped/contacted (into) each other?* Interestingly, the respondents offered different answers, assigning different speeds to the car on the basis of how the question was formulated. Moreover, during a retest a week later, those previously exposed to the verb *smashed* were more likely to respond positively to the question of whether they had seen any broken glass.

Evidence for linguistic relativism can be found outside the laboratory setting as well. In a 2010 book entitled *Through the Language Glass: Why the World Looks Different in Other Languages*, the Israeli linguist Guy Deutscher argued that languages differ in the way in which they force us to register certain information—making certain information obligatory, and by making that information obligatory, they force us to attend to particular aspects of our environment. For instance, because the word "bridge" is grammatically feminine in German but masculine in Spanish, German and Spanish speakers would describe "bridge" in English very differently. German speaker use words such as *beautiful, elegant, fragile, peaceful, friendly*, and *slender*, whereas Spanish speakers use words such as *big, dangerous, long, strong, sturdy*, and *towering*. In an aboriginal community of about a thousand people who live some 30 miles north of Cooktown in Australia, the residents would refer to a person on a TV screen (when the TV faces north) coming toward the viewer as coming northward. In other words, they would know the geographic coordinates wherever they are (even without the sun or in a dark cave!) because their language forces them to encode this information, and by extension, to attend to environment cues that one would have otherwise never attended to.

Moving on to more familiar territories, children are often told not to use certain "bad words." Our objection toward bad words must be grounded in the belief that words hold certain sway over how we think and behave. We worry that bad words will lead to bad thinking and bad behavior. In a *New York Times* (Chan, 2007) report on the proposal to ban the use of "bitch" and "ho" following the New York City Council's symbolic resolution banning the use of racial slurs, the resolution is cited to state that "words, when misused, can lay foundations to legitimize the illegitimate and codify the unthinkable."

Task 2: Are there words in another language that cannot be directly translated into English, or vice versa? How might that affect our thinking and perception of the world?

Another somewhat related way of talking about linguistic relativity is *thinking for speaking*, which also observes the constraints language imposes on thinking. *Thinking for speaking* begins with the assumption that thought is always going to be richer than language that expresses those thoughts (Slobin, 2003).

Thinking for speaking is the level at which thought is forced into the linguistic resources afforded by a particular language.

The distinction between S-framed and V-framed languages is offered as an illustration of how *thinking for speaking* works. An S- or satellite-framed language is one in which the verb encodes manners of motion (*run* vs. *crawl*), and a V- or verb-framed language is one in which such encoding is done by the adverbial (*enter by crawling* as opposed to *crawling in*). The overall claim is that someone speaking an S-framed language such as English (as opposed to a V-framed language like French) will have richer memories and finer mental conceptualizations of manners of motion. In other words, the way your language represents manners of motion affects the way you think about manners of motion.

Cognitive Metaphor (Lakoff and Johnson)

So far, we have considered how language can affect thought, which has been most saliently captured in the Sapir-Whorf hypothesis. The effect of thought on language, on the other hand, is effectively embodied in the notion of cognitive metaphor (Lakoff & Johnson, 1980).

Task 3: Consider the following statements associated with the activity of argument taken from Lakoff and Johnson (1980, p. 4). Pay special attention to the italicized words. What images do these words conjure up in your head?

- Your claims are *indefensible.*
- He *attacked* every weak point in my argument.
- His criticisms were right *on target.*
- I *demolished* his argument.
- I've never *won* an argument with him.
- You disagree? Okay, *shoot!*
- If you use that strategy, he'll *wipe you out.*
- He *shot down* all of my arguments.

According to Lakoff and Johnson (1980), the previous statements constitute evidence for the existence of the cognitive metaphor of "Argument is war." The precise causal relationship between thought and language is articulated as such: "The concept is metaphorically structured, the activity is metaphorically structured, and, consequently, the language is metaphorically structured" (Lakoff & Johnson, 1980, p. 5). In other words, we speak or write metaphorically as a result of us thinking metaphorically.

Following this logic then, the cognitive metaphor of "life is a container" would engender formulations such as (Lakoff & Johnson, 1980, p. 51):

I've had a full life.
Life is empty for him.
There's not much left for him in life.
Her life is crammed with activities.
Get the most out of life.
His life contained a great deal of sorrow.
Live your life to the fullest.

The ubiquity of metaphors is documented in James Geary's book *I Is an Other*, where he claims that metaphors are not the rhetorical frills at the edge of how we think but at the heart of it (Brooks, 2011).

Task 4: What other cognitive metaphors can you think of? What is the linguistic evidence that such metaphors indeed exist?

Theoretical Frameworks for Studying Discourse and Ideology

While the proposers of linguistic relativism and cognitive metaphor have made important contributions to stimulating our thinking with regard to the relationship between discourse and ideology, they are not discourse analysts themselves. In what follows, we turn to the works of three influential scholars who are themselves discourse analysts and creators of important frameworks for conceptualizing and analyzing discourse and ideology: Norm Fairclough, Teun van Dijk, ann what follows, we turn to the works of three influential scholars who are thed James Paul Gee.

Critical Language Studies (Fairclough)

Critical language studies is a framework documented in Fairclough's (1989) seminal book *Language and Power*, the impetus of which was his dissatisfaction with the linguistic and sociolinguistic treatment of language and power at the time. As a linguist himself, Fairclough (1989) was deeply invested in going beyond mere descriptions of sociolinguistic conventions (e.g., standard vs. nonstandard dialects) that manifest unequal distribution of power to explain how such conventions are "a product of relations of power and struggles for power" (p. 1). As such, he proposes critical language study as an approach that highlights the "common sense" assumptions or ideologies implicit in the conventions beneath people's conscious awareness that legitimizes existing power relations. For Fairclough (1989), power is achieved through ideology and "the ideological workings of language" (p. 2).

In the conventions of traditional doctor-patient consultation, for example, the commonsense assumption (embedded in the use of language) is that the doctor is the medical authority who should be making all the treatment decisions with which the patient complies, and this assumption legitimizes the existing power asymmetry in ways that are not registered as problematic. Power can be exercised through coercion or the manufacturing of consent, and ideology, as Fairclough (1989) wrote, is "the prime means of manufacturing consent" (p. 4)—a process effectively captured in notion of hegemony (Gramsci, 1971).

Hegemony refers to ruling with the consent of the governed.

A familiar example of hegemony that might come to mind is how parental power over children is exercised. Although getting a child to do homework or play the piano can very well be a matter of coercion, such activities can also be constructed, to various degrees of success, as intrinsically fun and desirable for the child to willingly take on.

Task 5: What are some other examples of hegemony in your view and experience?

In Fairclough's critical language study (CLS), discourse is defined as language as social practice determined by social structures. In the following police interview of a witness, we observe multiple features of the unequal power relations between the two participants (Fairclough, 1989, p. 18). (Key: P = police; W = witness; dots = speaker about to go on but interrupted.)

(1) Police-witness interaction

01	P:	Did you get a look at the one in the car?
02	W:	I saw his face, yeah.
03	P:	What sort of age was he?
04	W:	About 45. He was wearing a . . .
05	P:	And how tall?
06	W:	Six foot one.
07	P:	Six foot one. Hair?
08	W:	Dark and curly. Is this going to take long?
09		I've got to collect the kids from school.
10	P:	Not much longer, no. What about the clothes?
11	W:	He was a bit scruffy-looking, blue trousers, black . . .
12	P:	Jeans?
13	W:	Yeah.

Task 6: What are some features of the previous interaction that offer evidence for the unequal relationship between the police interviewer and the witness?

As can be seen, it is the police interviewer who interrupts, who controls the course of the interview, and who interrogates without mitigation, acknowledgment, or appreciation of the witness's answers. What Fairclough did was to take a step beyond these observations and claim that such features of language use are an outcome of existing social conditions, that is, the relationship between the police and the public in the larger society. The fact that the witness does not treat the police interviewer's lack of any acknowledgment of his responses as problematic is evidence for her interpretation of the existing social conditions, that is, in this particular setting, it is natural for the police to exercise such institutional and discursive power. On the other hand, it is by routinely occupying such subject positions as police officer and police witness that the conventions of police-witness interview are sustained and reproduced. Insofar as the language use as observed in the previous excerpt reproduces the existing power relations between police and public, we are also observing, according to Fairclough (1989), a case of linguistic determination of the society.

Uncovering such, and often nonobvious, connections among language, power, and ideology is the goal of Fairclough's *critical language studies*. In particular, he proposed a three-stage analysis that begins with describing the formal properties of the text (e.g., police interviewer does the interrupting). Analysis of discourse, according to Fairclough, cannot stop at text as a product. It should also engage the processes for producing and interpreting that text, in which one might find traces of the productive process and cues of the interpretive process. The analysis of these processes or "interaction" would necessarily make evident a whole range of member resources (MRs) often glossed as background knowledge (e.g., it is normal that the police interviewer controls the discourse in a witness interview). The final stage of the analysis involves explaining how the productive and interpretative processes are socially determined by the larger social context (e.g., police-public relations in society). The analysis of discourse, in other words, is the analysis of language as a social practice at the level of text, interaction, and context for the purpose of revealing the complex relationships among language, power, and ideology, as shown in Figure 8.1 (Fairclough, 1989, p. 25).

If ideology is a prime means of manufacturing consent, and ideology is essentially a set of commonsense assumptions, it would be in the interest of the powerful to create the commonsense assumptions to their own advantage—to make arbitrary beliefs and practices look as if they were natural and legitimate, that is, to achieve naturalization.

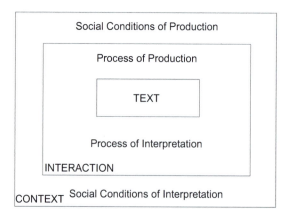

Figure 8.1 Discourse as Text, Interaction, and Context
Based on Fairclough, 1989

Naturalization refers to the process through which what is arbitrary is rendered *natural* and legitimate.

The fact that the police controls the discourse in witness interviews, for example, may be an entirely arbitrary matter. There is no inherent merit in having the police ask all the questions that allow only for short answers as opposed to having the witness volunteer their accounts in extended turns. Yet the discourse type of police interview where the act of filling out a form with short responses overtakes the sensitive nature of the situation is accepted as normal and treated as unproblematic by both parties. In Fairclough's words, one would say that the discourse type of police interview has been naturalized to favor the powerful. In a sense then, the goal of critical language studies is to unveil such naturalization.

Task 7: Think of one example of naturalization based on your knowledge and experience. Consider what evidence may exist in the discourse for such naturalization.

Ideological Analysis (van Dijk)

Like Fairclough, Dijk's (1995) ideological analysis begins with the assumption that "ideologies are typically, though not exclusively, expressed and reproduced in discourse and communication" (p. 17). His framework features a conceptual triangle that connects society, discourse, and social cognition.

Social cognition refers to "the system of mental representations and processes of group members" (Dijk, 1995, p. 18).

How does social cognition relate to ideology? According to van Dijk, ideologies are both cognitive and social: they are cognitive representations underlying situated individual interactions on the one hand and social representations of group characteristics and interests on the other. They are what van Dijk calls the crucial link between the micro (text and talk) and the macro (social and institutional structures). For Dijk (1995), ideologies and discourse are related at three levels of analysis: (1) social analysis addressed to social and institutional structures or group relations and structures (e.g., capitalism, racism, norms, and resources), (2) cognitive analysis addressed to sociocultural or personal knowledge, attitudes, values, and the like, and (3) discourse analysis addressed to structures of text and talk. The relationship among the three levels, according to van Dijk, is as follows: ideologies are "localized" between the social and the cognitive, allowing individuals to translate larger social structures into knowledge and beliefs of everyday experience, which in turn affects how discourse is produced and interpreted.

Task 8: Compare Fairclough's three-stage analysis with van Dijk's three levels of analysis. What are some of the similarities and differences?

It is not surprising then that for van Dijk, discourse analysis is essentially ideological analysis, where ideological work is done by highlighting the positives of self and the negatives of others while hiding the negatives of self and the positives of others. It is the prerogative of the analyst to uncover such ideological work by making evident how linguistic forms such as (1) phonological, graphical, and schematic representations, (2) lexicon and semantics, and (3) syntax can be manipulated to accomplish such highlighting and hiding.

Phonological, Graphical, and Schematic Representations

Phonological, graphical, and schematic structures are the surface features that can be engineered for implementing ideological work. Elongation, louder volume, and higher pitch, for example, can function subtly to highlight meanings that favor in-group ideologies and those that discredit out-group ones. In a news report entitled "British Invaded by an Army of Illegals," for example, the negatives of the immigrants are highlighted with such surface structures as capital and bolded letters: **DECEIVING, DISAPPEARING, FORGING**, and **RUNNING** (Dijk, 1995). By the same token, schematic structures can be manipulated to assign different levels of importance to different topics (e.g., a headline in a news story).

Lexicon and Semantics

Lexicon is also a rich area for manipulation when it comes to highlighting or hiding the positives of self or the negatives of others. The reference to abortion as pro-choice or pro-life each emphasizes the positive implications of in-group values. As shown in Table 8.1, the same idea may be represented in different wording to accentuate either its positive or negative aspects.

Table 8.1 Vocabulary and Ideology

Positive	Negative
whistle-blower	leaker
freedom fighter	terrorist
public diplomacy	cultural propaganda
charming	small
discerning	picky
frugal	stingy
defense of Vietnam	invasion of Vietnam
discovery of America	genocide of Native Americans
collateral damage	civilians killed

On a trip to Savannah, Georgia, years ago, I took a picture in an antique shop of an old hotel sign that says:

Ladies
Kindly Do Your
Soliciting Discreetly

I was amused by how the use of "ladies" and "soliciting" deftly hides the negatives of the identity (prostitute) and activity (prostitution) that are being referenced.

Task 9: What other pairs of vocabulary items can you think of that would do the ideological work of highlighting and hiding?

Further examples of the ideological work through highlighting and hiding are encapsulated in Bolinger's (1980) notion of the semantics of the powerful that involves euphemism, dysphemism, and mystification. **Euphemism** refers to substituting the inoffensive for the offensive: *involvement* for *invasion* or *pacification* for *bombing of civilians*. **Dysphemism** does the opposite: *terrorist* for *enemy soldier*. **Mystification** entails the use of jargon to conceal certain activities: *termination with prejudice* for *assassination* or *defoliate* for *bombing of countryside*.

Semantics as an ideological tool also works in the sense that meaning can be variously rendered along the continuum of implicit to explicit, general to specific, and incomplete to complete. **Disclaimers**, in particular, are powerful semantic resources for avoiding negative self-images (Dijk, 1995). Some examples of disclaimers are **apparent denial** (e.g., *I have nothing against X, but . . .*), **apparent concession** (e.g., *The French are not racist. But, facing the continuous increase of the foreign population in France . . .*), and **blame transfer** (e.g., *They are themselves to blame for discrimination . . .*). Information can be topicalized or detopicalized to highlight the positive self and the negative other. It should not be surprising, especially for those who follow the U.S. presidential elections, that rhetorical devices such as understatements, hyperbole, and metaphors can work effectively to glorify oneself and denigrate one's opponent.

Syntax

As linguistic resources marshaled to accomplish ideological work, lexicon and semantics or even surface structures such as font size and style seem to be obvious candidates, but how can grammatical structures be manipulated to promote certain ideologies? In fact, two grammatical structures have earned the well-established status as powerful ideological tools in the discourse literature: nominalization and passivization (Fairclough, 1992, 2003).

Nominalization refers to the conversion of a clause into a noun phrase.

Converting *Sam destructs things* into *destruction*, for example, achieves the purpose of generalizing, abstracting, and hiding agents. In a similar vein, representing the same sentence in its passive voice as in *Things are destructed* also downplays the agency. Not surprisingly, such resources for foregrounding and backgrounding responsible parties for positive or negative actions can be usefully engaged to promote the positive self and enhance the negative other.

Task 10: On the basis of what you have read so far, conduct an ideological analysis of the following excerpt taken from a campaign speech given by the 2016 U.S. Republican presidential nominee Donald Trump. Specifically, what linguistic features are deployed to highlight the positive self and the negative other?

01	Trump:	Our country is in serious trouble. We don't have
02		victories anymore. We used to have victories, but we
03		don't have them. When was the last time anybody
04		saw us beating, let's say, China in a trade deal? They
05		kill us. I beat China all the time. All the time.
06	Audience:	(*applause*) We want Trump. We want Trump.
07	Trump:	When did we beat Japan at anything? They send
08		their cars over by the millions, and what do we do?
09		When was the last time you saw a Chevrolet in
10		Tokyo? It doesn't exist, folks. They beat us all the
11		time. When do we beat Mexico at the border?
12		They're laughing at us, at our stupidity. And now
13		they are beating us economically. They are not our
14		friend, believe me. But they're killing us economi
15		cally. The U.S. has become a dumping ground for
16		everybody else's problems.
17	Audience:	(*applause*)

18	Trump:	Thank you. It's true, and these are the best and the
19		finest. When Mexico sends its people, they're not
20		sending their best. They're not sending you. They're
21		not sending you. They're sending people that have
22		lots of problems, and they're bringing those problems
23		to us. They're bringing drugs. They're bringing
24		crime. They're rapists. And some, I assume, are good
25		people. But I speak to border guards and they tell us
26		what we're getting. And it only makes common
27		sense. It makes common sense. They're sending us
28		not the right people. It's coming from more than
29		Mexico. It's coming from all over South and Latin
30		America, and it's coming probably—probably—
31		from the Middle East. But we don't know. Because
32		we have no protection and we have no competence,
33		we don't know what's happening. And it's got to stop
34		and it's got to stop fast.
35	Audience:	(*applause*)

Seven Building Tasks and Four Theoretical Tools (Gee)

To a great extent, the theoretical and analytical interests of James Paul Gee are very similar to those of Norman Fairclough and Teun van Dijk. Like Fairclough, who believed in the power of ideology in manufacturing inequality, Gee (2011) saw talk and text as inherently political, and it is the responsibility of discourse analysts to unveil "how talk and text function *politically* in social interactions" (p. 28). Like van Dijk, who sought to systematically locate evidence of ideology in actual talk and text, Gee also endeavored to systematically document the footprints of power in discourse. Without focusing on activities such as the highlighting or hiding of the positive or negative self or other, however, Gee drew attention to how discourse can be organized to build seven aspects of reality:

(1) Significance
(2) Activities
(3) Identities
(4) Relationships
(5) Politics
(6) Connections
(7) Sign systems and knowledge.

In other words, discourse is assembled to build significance, activities, identities, and the like, and as one might note, these seven building tasks encompass a wide range of issues that go beyond ideology. At the same time, at least for Gee, given his belief that all discourse is political, each of these issues may be saturated with ideology. While identities and relationships may be self-explanatory, the other items in the previous list are worthy of further explication. Language can be used to build significance in the sense that we use language to mark certain things as important. Gee made a distinction between action and activity, considering the former a component of the latter, which entails a larger course of action. Making a request such as *Will you be my advisor?* is an action, whereas seeking a new graduate advisor is an activity that might involve sharing one's background, knowledge and skills, and accomplishments for persuasive purposes. Politics is defined as the distribution of social goods—"anything a social group or society takes as a good worth having"—and language can be used to build or destroy such social goods (e.g., acceptance or respect) (p. 31). Language can also be used to forge connections regardless of whether they exist in the world (e.g., the connection made by politicians between Iraq and 9/11). Finally, sign systems and knowledge refer to any communication systems (e.g., world languages, images, equations, poetry) and different views of knowledge and belief represented in these systems. Language can be used, for example, to construct Spanish as superior or inferior or a controlled experiment as more or less scientific. These seven building tasks allow us to ask seven different questions of any piece of language (e.g., how is significance, activity, or identity being built in discourse?), and these seven questions can in turn be considered seven tools for discourse analysis.

Task 11: Consider the following extract from Gee (2011) that includes a teacher's responses to the interviewer's question of whether she discusses social issues in her classroom. How is language used to accomplish Gee's seven building tasks? That is, how is language used to build significance, activities, connections, and so forth?

01	Teacher:	Uh I talk about housing,
02		We talk about the [????] we talk about a lot of the low
03		income things,
04		I said "Hey wait a minute," I said, "Do you think the
05		city's gonna take care of an area that you don't take care
06		of yourself?"
07	Interviewer:	uh huh
08	Teacher:	I said, "How many of you have been up [Name] street?"
09		They raise their hands,

10		I say "How about [NAME] Ave.?"
11		That's where those gigantic houses are.
12		I said, "How many pieces of furniture are sitting in
13		the front yard?"
14	Interviewer:	mm hm
15	Teacher:	"Well, none."
16		I said "How much trash is lying around"?
17		"None."
18		I said, "How many houses are spray painted"?
19		"How many of them have kicked in, you know have
20		broken down cars."

Gee (2011) analyzed the previous exchange as such: The teacher marks the significance of neighborhood conditions that separate richer from poorer people without tapping into the social economic conditions that engender these conditions; she enacts the activity of advice giving on what to do or not to do to achieve success in society; she ascribes the "low income" identity to her kids and sets up a relationship where she is the wise middle-class advice giver that can help them change their lives; she connects the appearance of the neighborhood with the nature of people; she engages in the politics of blaming the victim, denying the kids the social good of being associated with things in the rich neighborhood and that of not being associated with "low income things"; finally, she privileges the way of knowing that involves observing behavior and appearances.

Aside from the seven building tasks to animate the kinds of questions to ask as one begins an analysis, Gee (2011) also proposed four theoretical tools of inquiry to facilitate the answering of those questions (see Chapter 7):

(1) Discourses
(2) Social languages
(3) Situated meanings
(4) Figured worlds

Discourse with a capital "D," as noted in Chapter 1, encompasses not just ways of speaking and listening, but also ways of being and behaving, where a particular social language embodies a particular identity.

Social language refers to a style or variety of language (or mixture of languages) that embodies a particular social identity.

For instance, one speaks the social language of medicine to embody the identity of a doctor, the social language of law to embody the identity of an attorney, or the social language of informal chat to embody the identity of a friend. Social language is one lens through which the analyst can get at the answer concerning how identities and relationships are built. The uncovering of situated meaning, on the other hand, would permeate the entire process of the analysis.

> **Situated meaning** refers to specific, as opposed to abstract and decontextualized, meaning in specific contexts of use.

In the previous interview excerpt, answering the seven building task questions would entail locating the situated meaning of, for example, *Do you think the city is going to take care of an area you don't take care of yourself?*, where the second-person pronoun is not a generic *you* but addressed specifically to the kids who are now positioned as irresponsible individuals not taking care of themselves. Finally, answering the teacher's question would also require finding her figured world in which poverty is a result of one's behavior.

> **Figured world** is "a picture of a simplified world that captures what is taken to be typical or normal" (Gee, 2011, p. 42).

Task 12: What are some other terms you might be aware of or you can think of that express the same or similar ideas of figured world? What kinds of figured worlds do you have?

Gee (2011) expressed the relationships between the four theoretical tools in these words:

> Situated meanings, social languages, figured worlds, and Discourses move us from the ground of specific uses of language in specific contexts (situated meanings) up to the world of identities and institutions in time and

space (Discourses) through varieties of language (social languages) and people's taken-for-granted theories of the world (figured worlds).

(p. 43)

Task 13: Returning to the interview excerpt in Task 11, consider how the four theoretical tools of inquiry may be utilized to answer the questions regarding the seven building tasks.

Importantly, Fairclough, van Dijk, and Gee have each made the case that aside from its structural elegance, its effectiveness in getting things done, and versatility in negotiating identities, discourse is also a critical resource for manufacturing ideology and managing the distribution of power that has far-reaching consequences in people's lives. Each has also offered us a specific lens through which to critically examine the issues of power and ideology in discourse. Fairclough does so by, for example, alerting us to how ideology is a result of naturalized assumptions; van Dijk draws our attention to the subtle traces of ideology in such specifics as lexicon, semantics, and syntax; and Gee directs us to the analysis of Discourse, situated meaning, social language, and figured world in considering how various aspects of reality are built.

Critical Discourse Analysis

The works of Norman Fairclough, Teun van Dijk, and James Paul Gee may be considered the canon of what has come to be called critical discourse analysis—an extension of (or used interchangeably with) critical linguistics developed in the 1970s. **Critical discourse analysis** is the study of language and ideology, where ideology, as it might have become clear by now, can be defined in two related ways: (1) a system of ideas and practices that operate to the advantage of a social group; (2) a system of ideas and practices that disguise or distort the social, economic, and political relations between dominant and dominated classes (Mesthrie, Swann, Deumert, & Leap, 2000, p. 320).

Task 14: What are some examples of ideology based on your own experience or what we have discussed so far according to definition (1) and (2) respectively?

The meaning of "critical" in critical discourse analysis is a technical one. Being critical is not the same as offering criticisms. Rather, it entails not being seduced or fooled by what you see. It requires maintaining distance from the data (Wodak & Meyer, 2009), understanding that reality is constructed (Cameron, 2001), uncovering nonobvious connections (Fairclough, 2001), and taking a stance toward changing the world (Fairclough, 2001). Put otherwise, critical discourse analysts are concerned about (1) the constructed nature of reality/thought, (2) how reality/thought is constructed to favor the powerful, and how (3) social changes are manifested in changing constructions of reality/thought. The Franz Boas quote placed at the beginning of Fairclough's (1989) introduction to his classic text says it best: "How do we recognize the shackles that tradition has placed upon us? For if we can recognize them, we are also able to break them" (p. 1). Critical discourse analysts recognize that those shackles are located in text and talk, and making evident the ideological workings of discourse is a path toward breaking the shackles. In short, as contributors to an extremely heterogeneous enterprise that encompasses a wide range of theoretical approaches, critical discourse analysts are united in their interest in the role of discourse in formulating power, dominance, ideology, hidden agenda and, in particular, in their belief in using critical discourse analysis as a tool for addressing social problems (Fairclough & Wodak, 1997). (For further discussions on critical discourse analysis as a methodology as well as the range of studies conducted in critical discourse analysis, see Wodak & Chilton, 2005; Wodak & Meyer, 2009).

Key Points

- The relationship between language and thought can be captured in such notions as linguistic relativity and cognitive metaphor, with the former emphasizing the influence of language on thought and the latter of thought on language.
- Fairclough's critical language studies emphasize the role of naturalized assumptions—ideologies—in manufacturing consent and exercising power, where the role of the discourse analyst is to uncover such nonobvious connections by considering the features of text and talk, how they are produced and interpreted, and how such productive and interpretive processes are influenced by the larger social context.
- Van Dijk situates ideology within the conceptual triangle of society, cognition, and discourse, where the analysis of discourse entails unveiling the ideological work of highlighting the positive self and the negative other located in aspects of language use such as phonological and graphical representations, schematic structures, lexicon and semantics, and syntax.

- For Gee, language can be used to construct reality through seven building tasks; and the four theoretical tools of Discourses, social languages, situated meanings, and figured worlds make up the lenses through which questions about the seven building tasks may be answered.
- Despite its inherent heterogeneity, critical discourse analysis can be described as an approach (although not the only one) broadly and exclusively devoted to the study of language and ideology.

References

Bolinger, D. (1980). *Language—The loaded weapon: The use and abuse of language today*. London and New York: Longman.

Brooks, D. (2011, April 11). Poetry for everyday life. *The New York Times*. Retrieved from www.nytimes.com/2011/04/12/opinion/12brooks.html

Cameron, D. (2001). *Working with spoken discourse*. London: Sage.

Chan, S. (2007, July 30). Council mulls symbolic ban on 2 slurs against women. *The New York Times*. Retrieved from http://cityroom.blogs.nytimes.com/2007/07/30/council-mulls-symbolic-ban-on-2-slurs-against-women/

Deutscher, G. (2010). *Through the language glass: Why the world looks different in other languages*. New York: Henry Holt and Company.

Dijk, T. van (1995). Discourse analysis as ideological analysis. In C. Schäffner & A. Wenden (Eds.), *Language and peace* (pp. 17–33). Aldershot: Dartmouth Publishing.

Dijk, T. van (1998). *Ideology: A multidisciplinary approach*. London: Sage Publications.

Ericson, M. (2011, April 17). The words they used. *The New York Times*. Retrieved from www.nytimes.com/interactive/2008/09/04/us/politics/20080905_WORDS_GRAPHIC.html

Fairclough, N. (1989). *Language and power*. London and New York: Longman.

Fairclough, N. (1992). *Discourse and social change*. Malden, MA: Polity Press.

Fairclough, N. (2001). Critical discourse analysis. In A. McHoul & M. Rapley (Eds.), *How to analyse talk in institutional settings: A casebook of methods* (pp. 25–38). London: Continuum.

Fairclough, N. (2003). *Analyzing discourse: Textual analysis for social research*. London: Routledge.

Fairclough, N., & Wodak, R. (1997). Critical discourse analysis. In T. van Dijk (Ed.), *Discourse studies: A multidisciplinary introduction* (Vol. 2) (pp. 258–284). London: Sage.

Gee, J. P. (2011). Discourse analysis: What makes it critical? In R. Rogers (Ed.), *An introduction to critical discourse analysis in education* (2nd ed.) (pp. 23–45). New York and London: Routledge.

Gramsci, A. (1971). *Selections from the prison notebooks of Antonio Gramsci* (Q. Hoare & G. N. Smith, Eds. & Trans.). New York: International Publishers.

Lakoff, G., & Johnson, M. (1980). *Metaphors we live by*. Chicago: University of Chicago Press.

Loftus, E. F., & Palmer, J. C. (1974). Reconstruction of auto-mobile destruction: An example of the interaction between language and memory. *Journal of Verbal Learning and Verbal Behavior, 13*, 585–589.

Mesthrie, R., Swann, J., Deumert, A., & Leap, W. L. (2000). *Introducing sociolinguistics.* Philadelphia, PA: John Benjamins.

Slobin, D. I. (2003). Language and thought online: Cognitive consequences of linguistic relativity. In D. Gentner & S. Goldin-Meadow (Eds.), *Language in mind: Advances in the study of language and thought* (pp. 157–192). Cambridge, MA: MIT Press.

Wodak, R., & Chilton, P. (Eds.) (2005). *A new agenda in (critical) discourse analysis: Theory, methodology, and interdisciplinarity.* Philadelphia, PA, and Amsterdam: John Benjamins.

Wodak, R., & Meyer, M. (2009). Critical discourse studies: History, agenda, theory and methodology. In R. Wodak & M. Meyer (Eds.), *Methods of critical discourse analysis* (2nd ed.) (pp. 1–22). London: Sage.

9 Empirical Endeavors in Discourse and Ideology

Introduction

In the previous chapter, we showed how the issue of discourse and ideology can be traced back to such influential theories as linguistic relativity and cognitive metaphor that encapsulate the deeply intertwined relationships between language and thought. More pertinent to the interests of discourse analysts were also the key frameworks proposed by Norman Fairclough, Teun van Dijk, and James Paul Gee that have powerfully shaped the study of discourse and ideology. These scholars have reminded us in no uncertain terms that it is in discourse that we can locate evidence of how naturalized assumptions are built to manufacture consent, how ideologies are produced to highlight the positive self and the negative other, and how realities are constructed to favor the powerful. In this chapter, we illustrate how precisely such evidence is located with a series of empirical exhibits. Although critical discourse analysis is the approach most distinctly and unapologetically associated with the study of discourse and ideology, such study, as will be demonstrated in this chapter, is not the exclusive territory of critical discourse analysis, but can be investigated with a variety of approaches. Given that issues of discourse and ideology are vast and varied, and the empirical landscape they occupy is impossible to do justice to within a single chapter, what we gather in the following is merely a brief snapshot of the kinds of analytical objects in discourse and ideology that have animated the interests of discourse analysts who approach their work with an assortment of analytical frameworks. To that end, we offer a sampling of works in (1) discourse and gender ideology and (2) discourse and race ideology. We draw upon portions of individual studies for illustrative purposes without presenting each in its totality. The discerning reader might be alarmed, and reasonably so, by the apparent overlap between identity and ideology. Issues of gender and race are indeed issues of identity as well. The works to be sampled in this chapter, however, are calibrated to unveil hidden ideologies in the discourses of gender and race rather than demonstrate the negotiation of such identities in discourse.

Discourse and Gender Ideology

In this section, we offer three exhibits of how gender ideology has been explored in discourse analysis, ranging from a corpus analysis of sexualization in media discourse, to an interactional sociolinguistic analysis of gender discrimination in a dissertation defense and, finally, to a conversation analysis of heteronormativity in after-hours calls to the doctor.

Sexualization in Media Discourse

Our first exhibit involves a corpus analysis that has become an increasingly popular research tool for critical discourse analysts (for the various aspects of doing corpus analysis, see Baker, 2006). Using data from the Bank of English corpus, Caldas-Coulthard and Moon (2010) were interested in how "gender is construed, and sexualization and discrimination performed through lexical labeling" (p. 124). In order to uncover the ideological underpinnings of how *man* and *woman* are categorized in the media, for example, the authors focused their analysis on what kinds of adjectives are used to premodify these nouns based on 45 million words of tabloid data (e.g., *The Sun*) and around 112 million words from broadsheets or quality newspapers (e.g., *The Guardian*). Part of their analysis involves identifying the pre-modifying adjectives, also referred to as collocates, that occur within three words to the left of *man* and *woman* in the original newspaper articles. In extract (1),where the focus is on *boy*, for example, we see three words before and after the key word (Caldas-Coulthard & Moon, 2010, p. 132).

(1) Collocates

> was a old BOY who his his
> 14 year new BOY was was was
> </dt> the little BOY and died has
> 15 my bad BOY band he is
> a month golden BOY s </hl> who

By collecting corpus data such as the previous, the authors were able to quickly gather a large amount of information to answer the question of which high-frequency adjectives are used to modify *man* and *woman*. To further understand the nature of these adjectives, they resorted to Leeuwen's (1996) three ways of categorizing people: functionalization, identification, and appraisement. While **functionalization** is a way of categorizing people by what they do, **identification** underscores who they are in terms of gender, ethnicity, relationships, and physical or personal features. **Appraisals**, on the other hand, involve general evaluative and affective terms.

Task 1: Consider the two sets of adjectives taken from Caldas-Coulthard and Moon (2010). Which set do you think is used to modify *man*, and which set *woman*? Explain your reasoning.

(1) beautiful, attractive, good-looking, real, sexy
(2) best, great, leading, working, ideal, lovely

By superimposing Leeuwen's (1996) categorization on the corpus data, the authors found that despite some differences, in both tabloids and broadsheets, *men* are mostly labeled in terms of age, status, and behavior, with positive evaluations outweighing the negative as evidenced in the proliferation of evaluative labeling such as *best, great, nice, lovely, perfect,* and *wonderful.* In the following lexical strings, for example, the functions of *man* in a team or group are highlighted (Caldas-Coulthard & Moon, 2010, p. 112).

(2) Man

    a. striker Stephen Baxter. The big man is automatically suspended after his

    b. off their best win of the season. Hard-man Brennan, who is the squad for

    c. at Old Trafford for being the quiet man at the club. The Salford man is the

    d. before halftime. <p> But forgotten man Michael Hughes cheered up the

Notably, while men are evaluated in terms of their function and status in society, women are evaluated *additionally* in terms of their appearance and sexuality. One telling example is that *professional* is the only premodifying adjective for *woman* that may be placed into van Leeuwen's functionalization category—categorizing by what one does.

Task 2: Consider the adjectives used to describe men and women's physical attributes respectively taken from Caldas-Coulthard and Moon's broadsheet data (2010). What would you consider to be the biggest differences between the two sets of adjectives?

(1) Premodifiers for *man*

    Size: big, little, fat, tall, small, stocky, tallest, burly, shriveled, emaciated, skinny
    Coloring: white/gray/dark/-haired, swarthy

> Appearance/Clothing: naked, bearded, balding, clean-shaven, muscular
> Attractiveness: good-looking, handsome, scruffy
>
> (2) Premodifiers for woman
>
> Size: fat, tall, tiny, small, petite, flat-chested, stout, voluptuous
> Coloring: blonde, dark/gray/haired
> Appearance/Clothing: naked, smartly/well/-dressed, bare-breasted, topless
> Attractiveness: beautiful, pretty, attractive, real, sexy, alluring, glamorous

One of Caldas-Coulthard and Moon's (2010) major findings is that although women are also categorized by age, status, and personality, their categorization by physical appearance and sexuality seems particularly distinct. Women are far more likely to be commented on for their appearance, and many of these comments are sexualized as evident in the previous lists. In the authors' words, this type of discourse analytic work is instrumental in raising awareness of "the discrimination in practice to which women are still exposed daily" (Caldas-Coulthard & Moon, 2010, p. 125).

Subtext of Gender Discrimination in Dissertation Defense

Looking at language as a means of illuminating social problems is also an interest of interactional sociolinguistics, one of its strengths being linking the macro and the micro (Gordon, 2011, p. 78). In their study on a dissertation defense, for example, Gumperz and Gumperz (1996) showed how a subtext of gender discrimination lies beneath the ritual of evaluation. The participants are Lee, a 40-year-old woman defending her dissertation; Adam, her advisor; Pat, the only woman on the committee; Sherm, the most senior of the group; and James, the examiner from outside the department. In the following extract, James conveys his evaluation of the dissertation as a *good job* (Gumperz & Gumperz, 1996, p. 178). (Key: / = the end of a minor tone group; // = end of a major tone group ending in falling intonation; dots = pauses of various lengths.)

(3) Good job

```
01   James:        Well I think .. my sense is that .. uh  .. she has done .. /
02        →        a good job/. . .and she certainly has .. uh. . ./I mean this
03                 project for her is being everything and more I think ..
```

04		that a dissertation. . ./should be ..// and at the state
05	→	of her professional development I think ... a ... *a good*
06		*job* /and she ought to be commended //

The authors observe that James's evaluation is delivered in the contour style that conveys the "on record" nature of his talk.

Contour style refers to the co-occurrence of frequent short tone groups, pausing and accenting that signals "on record" as opposed to "off-record" and informal delivery (Gumperz & Gumperz, 1996, p. 175).

Underneath the veneer of this on record evaluation, however, something else appears to be conveyed with the unique prosody in which *good job* is delivered (lines 02, 05): a rise on *good* and a fall on *job*. The prosody serves as a contextualization cue (see Chapter 4) that signals that more is meant than said. Exactly what is being signaled is then uncovered by considering other passages of talk in the defense and, most notably, the male committee members' joking observations of the length of Lee's dissertation (Gumperz & Gumperz, 1996, pp. 174, 179).

(4) Seven thousand pages

01	James:	Well uh /I. . .I mean she's quite clear/. . .uh ..
02	→	what she said /as she left/that she obviously enjoyed
03		this / and it came through/. . .I mean she could not
04		have written
05	→	seven thousand pages (laugh) .. if she didn't
06		thoroughly enjoy it / . . .and urm/. . .in urm terms
07		of what a dissertation should be / .. a. . .a a learning
08		experience in which y'know the student pulls
09		together /.. everything ((continues))

(5) Wished it was shorter

01	Sherm:	oh. . .it's a fine job //. . .by my/.. lights uh. . .
02	→	I would have wished it was shorter// (laughing) I have
03		some sympathy for the twenty five/. . .page psych .. /
04		dissertations//
05	Pat:	(laughing). . .Right! (clears throat)
06	Sherm:	Uh ,.. the uh. . .uh. . ./this/. . .the one comment I'd
07		have/. . .((continues))

Task 3: Consider previous extracts (4) and (5). Is it possible at all that the committee members' joking commentaries on the dissertation's length signal negative evaluation of any sort? Whether your answer is *yes* or *no*, try to find evidence in the data and explain your reasoning.

Elsewhere, as the authors pointed out, Adam also refers to a conversation he had with Lee regarding the length of the dissertation quoting himself as joking: *break it up with white space or something* (Gumperz & Gumperz, 1996, p. 185). It appears that Lee's involvement with the dissertation (e.g., finding it *thoroughly enjoyable* and producing a document of extraordinary length) is treated by these members of the committee as an indication of "lack of academic distance" and "professional judgment" (p. 185). The authors grounded their interpretation in the larger academic climate at the time that favors the impersonal perspective, which is considered by the feminist scholarship as a reflection of male dominance. As such, "a dominantly male committee is likely to have regarded expressions of enthusiasm and involvement as academically and 'scientifically' inappropriate" (Gumperz & Gumperz, 1996, p. 185). In other words, Lee's enthusiasm and involvement as evidenced in the length of her dissertation was negatively evaluated by the committee members given the academic climate at the time.

Heteronormativity in Medical Calls

Of all the approaches to discourse analysis, conversation analysis is undoubtedly considered the least capable of addressing larger social problems, often occupying the opposite end of the continuum from critical discourse analysis. In this section, we introduce a rare and exemplary conversation analysis study designed explicitly to address a larger social problem—that of heteronormativity.

Heteronormativity refers to "the mundane production of heterosexuality as the normal, natural, taken for granted sexuality" (Kitzinger, 2005, p. 477).

On the basis of recordings of 59 after-hours calls to the doctor in the UK, Kitzinger (2005) showed how family reference terms are used to construct a normative version of a heterosexual family with a married couple living with their biological children. In extract (6) , a woman is calling for a sick boyfriend (Kitzinger, 2005, pp. 483–484). (Key: Clr = caller; Doc = doctor; < = jump start; > < = quickened pace.)

(6) Family

```
01  Clr:       Um my boyfriend's uhm: really ill at the moment.
02             <'E's got really bad stomach pains. An' fever.
03             Em::symptoms.
04  Doc:       R:ight¿
05  Clr:       Can anyone: come out tuhnight to look at im?=
06  Doc:  →    =((sniff)) Welb- uh:m: u- >sorry< who's is doctor?
07             (0.4)
08  Clr:       'is doctor's ((deleted))
09  Doc:       R:ight. .hh Wull what's actually been happening
10             with'im
((32 lines of diagnostic questioning omitted))
43  Doc:  →    Anybody else in the fa- the house got a fu- o:-
44             [got ] hmm
45  Clr:       [No,]
```

In her analysis, Kitzinger highlighted the fact that in line 43, the doctor cuts off the delivery of *family* and proceeds to replace it with *house*, displaying his understanding of "family" as an inappropriate term for this unmarried couple. For him, then, marriage is integral to the definition of "family." We thus observe the taken-for-granted conceptualization of family as consisting of husband and wife.

Task 4: Without looking ahead, consider how heteronormativity is reproduced in the following call taken from Kitzinger (2005, p. 483). Point to the specific item(s) or line(s) as evidence, and spell out your reasoning.

```
01  Doc:  Hello:,
02  Clr:  Hello, can I speak to the doctor on call please,
03  Doc:  Yes, Doctor ((deleted)) speaking,
04  Clr:  Hello, ehm (0.5) I was wo nderin', I think my
05        son's got measles,an': (what I should give it to
06        'im) or anythin',
07  Doc:  Sor[ry?
08  Clr:     [(and that) whether I should give 'im anything
09        for measles,
10  Doc:  .hhh Oh right, ew: how old is your son?
11  Clr:  Ah he was one last week, .hh[h
```

```
12  Doc:                              [B:right, an' an'
13            what's actually been happening to 'im
((61 lines of diagnostic questioning omitted))
75  Doc:    .hh Fine, Any other children in your family?
76  Clr:    Yeah, I've got another boy,
77  Doc:    Ha- older or younger?
78  Clr:    Ah- [older,
79  Doc:          [Well, must be older, mustn't he?
80  Clr:    Olde[r, yeah]
81  Doc:        [ .hhhh] ehhehm! Well, unless you're very
82            quick, sorry .hh
83            ah:m yeah has he had measles?
```

Kitzinger (2005) called our attention to the doctor's talk in lines 79 and 81–82, which in her analysis, evidences the heteronormative understanding of family as a unit with all biological children of the same mother. In line 79, for example, the doctor ventures to guess with great certainty that the other child must be older given his knowledge of the patient being 12 months old (line 11) and of pregnancy lasting 9 months. He could only have arrived at this conclusion if the assumption is that the woman also gave birth to the other child. The same line of logic is maintained in the subsequent lines of 81–82, where the doctor continues to joke about the "quick" second conception.

The participants' inadvertent reproduction of heteronormativity also becomes manifest in the following call, where the assumption of co-residence is built into the definition of family (Kitzinger, 2005, p. 486).

(7) Where do you live

```
01  Doc:     Hel:lo:,
02  Clr:     Hel:lo, is tha' do- doctor¿
03  Doc:     Yes, Doctor ((deleted)) speaki:ng,
04  Clr:     i:i:Couldja's call an' see my wife please, .h[h
05  Doc:                                                   [Yes:.
06  Clr:     She's breathless. She can't .hh get 'er
07            breath.hh! .h[hhh  ]
08  Doc:                  [What]'s: her name?
09  Clr:     ((deleted))
10  Doc:  →  Ru-an' where do you live.
```

In response to the caller's request to see his wife, the doctor asks in line 10 *where do you live* instead of *where does she live*, thus assuming co-residence of the couple.

That none of these issues is oriented to by the participants themselves as troublesome constitutes powerful evidence, according to the author, for how taken-for-granted heterosexual privilege is reproduced at the mundane level of social interaction.

Task 5: All three studies referenced so far deal with gender ideologies. To the best of your abilities, specify the similarities and differences among the three.

In sum, as we have seen in this section, the issue of gender ideology may be examined with a variety of tools in a variety of contexts. Despite the heterogeneity of data types and investigative means, analysts have uncovered discursive evidence of gender ideology in its diverse manifestations: the frequency of adjectives that characterize women by appearance and sexuality in newspapers, the subtle cues that negatively evaluate a female academic's personal involvement with her writing, and the taken-for-granted treatment of family as a unity of a heterosexual couple with biological children. (For a recent review on gender and discourse, see Kendall & Tannen, 2015).

Discourse and Race Ideology

Race ideology has been of great interest to discourse analysts as well. In this section, we provide a sketch of what discourse analyses of racism look like, and we do so by sampling a critical discourse analysis of racism in media discourse, a sociocultural linguistics analysis of racial reversal among white teenage girls, and a discursive psychology analysis of racism among white New Zealanders (Päkehäs).

Racism in Media Discourse

Recall that one of the goals of critical discourse analysis is to uncover non-obvious connections of deep ideological underpinnings that often escape an otherwise uncritical reading. Hodges's (2015) study on race talk in the media about the Trayvon Martin shooting in the United States is a poignant example of how such nonobvious connections can be uncovered. Trayvon Martin is a 17-year-old African American young man shot to death by a 28-year-old mixed-race Hispanic neighborhood watch volunteer, George Zimmerman, in February 2012 during an encounter where Zimmerman claimed self-defense. Drawing upon the distinction between the folk theory of race and racism and critical race theory (Hill, 2008), the author asked: to what extent does the mainstream media discourse about race and racism reflect the

Table 9.1 Folk Theory of Race/Racism vs. Critical Race Theory

Folk Theory	Critical Race Theory
based on taken-for-granted assumptions	based on (social) scientific research
race as biologically evident	race as socially constructed
racism as located in the individual	racism as systemic and institutional
racism as intentional outward conduct	racism as unconscious biases and prejudices

folk theory or move beyond it? Put otherwise, what are the hidden assumptions about race and racism that can be uncovered from the mainstream media discourse surrounding this event? Table 9.1 highlights the distinction between the two types of race theory.

Thus, from the perspective of the folk theory, racism can be identified case-by-case in the individual who uses racial slurs and acts in overtly racist ways. Critical race theory, on the other hand, views racism as a larger societal problem of naturalizing biases and prejudices, which ultimately and implicitly supports the domination of one racial group over another.

Task 6: On the basis of your understanding of the distinction between the folk theory of race/racism and critical race theory, consider which framework dominates the discussion of racism in the following two extracts (Hodges, 2015, pp. 407–408. Courtesy CNN.). Ground your arguments in the specific lines of each extract and work through your reasoning.

a.   what do you think should happen

```
01   Malveaux:   ((after recounting the Trayvon Martin incident))
02                Which brings us to today's 'Talk Back' question,
03                what do you think should happen?
04                Nazim says, "Outragous [sic]. If I, a black man, had
05                done that to a white youth going home, just like
06                this young man did, I would be in jail.
07                Why did the block watch captain have a gun in
08                the first place?"
```

b.   listen for yourself

```
01   Cooper:   Up close tonight, what George Zimmerman said
02              or did not say in the 911 call that he made
03              moments before he shot Trayvon Martin. Did
04              he use a racist slur? There's a big debate raging over
```

05	two words Zimmerman used in the call or may have
06	used. Some hear an ugly racial insult and an expletive.
07	Others hear nothing of the sort. . . . Now, before we
08	tell you what the alleged slur is, we're going to
09	let you listen for yourself with fresh ears and make
10	up your own mind what you hear. For that, we
11	enlisted the help of one of CNN's top audio
12	engineers. We need to warn some of you, the
13	language you're going to hear is offensive, but
14	we're going to play it for you without bleeping
15	anything, because it's evidence, and if we bleep it,
16	you're going to have a harder time hearing what
17	some believe is a racial slur.

To answer his question of what the hidden assumptions of race and racism are in the contemporary mainstream discourse, Hodges (2015) collected transcripts from the LexisNexis database from three major cable channels with a range of ideological leanings in the United States: CNN, Fox News, and MSNBC. His major finding is that overwhelmingly, the media discourse perpetuates the folk theory of race and racism, and a Fox news interview with George Zimmerman's father, Robert Zimmerman, is just one such example. The interviewer sets up his question with the controversy surrounding the possible racial slur uttered by George Zimmerman and proceeds to seek confirmation of two stories of him acting kindly toward African American individuals (Hodges, 2015, p. 411).

As Hodges (2015) showed in his analysis, Zimmerman confirms the veracity of the stories and proceeds to furnish further details of his son's benevolent actions toward African American individuals. He also denies categorically that his son ever used a racial slur. A similar case may be found in extract (b) in Task 6, where Anderson Cooper, a CNN journalist, focuses the viewer's attention on *what George Zimmerman said or did not say in the 911 call* (lines 01–02) and whether a *racist slur* (line 4) is uttered. Despite the claim of wanting the viewers to decide for themselves (lines 09–10), Cooper warns the latter for the upcoming language as potentially *offensive* (lines 12–13) and as *what some believe is a racial slur* (line 17). As such, the discussion of racism is reduced to the presence or absence of a single utterance. The question of whether George Zimmerman is a racist or whether racism could have factored into his shooting of Trayvon Martin then is exclusively attributed to individual words and action. This direct line drawn from individual words and actions to the identification of racism is supported not only by the folk theory of race and racism but also by the language ideology of "personalism" (Rosaldo, 1982).

Personalism refers to the language ideology that what determines linguistic meaning is largely the speaker's beliefs and intentions.

In other words, according to personalism, whether George Zimmerman uttered a racial slur gives us evidence of whether he harbors racist beliefs and intentions, the presence or absence of which, according to the folk theory of race and racism, determines whether racism exists.

There are, however, rare occasions where the dominant race ideology in the media is resisted by an interviewee. In the following segment, Piers Morgan, a CNN interviewer, again foregrounds the question of whether a racial slur has been uttered (lines 01–07) and proceeds to specifically link the absence of a racial slur to George Zimmerman not being a racist (lines 06–09) (Hodges, 2015, p. 413. Courtesy CNN).

(8) Little evidence

```
01   Morgan:   Now, earlier on CNN, this was played repeatedly.
02             Enough times, and, you know, again, this is changing
03             every day. Yesterday, it appeared to be f-ing cold. Today,
04             it seems to be more likely and this is the view being put
05             forward by Zimmerman's attorneys that actually the
06             wording was 'F-ing punks'. Now, whether it's F-ing cold
07             or F-ing punks, what it isn't is a racist comment. I mean,
08             you know, there's very little evidence if you actually
09             study it. Very little evidence to suggest that he is racist.
10             There just isn't any . . . the allegation that he's racist and
11             acting from a racially motivated intent with Trayvon
12             Martin at the moment, I think, is unproven.
13   Blow:     Well, it's not proven, however, that—setting it up that
14             way, Piers, is a logical fallacy. You do not have to be a
15             raging, you know, white sheet wearing racist your entire
16             life to act in a moment on a racial prejudice. And so
17             I think we have to always separate those two things out.
18             I can be involved with all sorts of people my entire life,
19             treat them very nicely, and at the same time, at a point
20             here I find myself feeling threatened, I can act on racial
21             prejudice. Those things are not usually [mutually]
22             exclusive. People have to really stop setting those things
23             up to be opposites.
```

What Charles Blow, the *New York Times* columnist interviewee, offers in response may be viewed as an attempt to reject the assumptions of the folk theory, which he calls a *logical fallacy* (line 14) and to inject "a more nuanced understanding of racism per the critical theory" (Hodges, 2015, p. 414). As shown, he purports that one does not have to be *raging . . . white sheet wearing* to be a racist (line 15), but racist actions can be motivated by underlying racial prejudice by otherwise perfectly decent human beings (lines 18–21). Such a nuanced understanding of race and racism grounded in the critical theory (also evidenced in extract (a) in Task 6), unfortunately, is an exception rather than the norm in contemporary U.S. mainstream media, according to Hodges's (2015) case study.

In the final analysis, Hodges argued that the media's narrow focus on the racial slur and individual actions in the Trayvon Martin case fails to engage the viewers in seeing and understanding that it is "the biases that perpetuate a racialized system" that makes the killing of Trayvon Martin and others possible (p. 421).

Racial Reversal Among White Teenagers

Rather than focus on the official platforms of media discourse by way of examining race talk, Bucholtz (2011) turned her attention to casual conversations among white teenagers in a large, urban, and racially tense high school, where African American and European American make up the two largest groups with neither being the majority. Without formulating a specific research question from the outset, Bucholtz was broadly interested in race talk among white teenagers. She collected data for this inquiry through ethnographic fieldwork (1995–1996), which in part involved interviewing the white teenagers on their youth styles and friendships groups, from which race talk emerged without any overt prompting. On the basis of these recorded and transcribed interviews along with ethnographic field notes, the author identified a discourse of racial reversal among these white teenagers (Bucholtz, 2011, p. 387).

Racial reversal is an ideology that asserts the racially dominant group's disadvantage *vis-à-vis* a racially subordinated group despite empirically observable racial asymmetries.

Task 7: Consider the following narrative of a white teenager taken from Bucholtz (2011, p. 396). Identify any evidence of the discourse of racial reversal. Locate the specific lines and explain how the talk manifests racial reversal. (Key: < > = transcriber comment/nonvocal noise; . . . = omitted material; number in parentheses = length of silence in seconds.)

```
01  Brand One:  two months ago this du:de,
02              um,
03              (1.5)
04              <tongue click>
05              I was walking up to u:h,
06              to:,
07              the bus stop,
08              and he—
09              and he was in my backpack right?
10              This,
11              this black dude was like s:ix,
12              maybe like,
13              fi:ve ten,
14              he was big,
15              he was a lot bigger than me,. . .
```

To locate evidence of racial reversal, you might have pointed to the description of the *black dude's* (line 11) attempt to steal from the narrator's backpack (line 09) and the description of the former of being tall (lines 11–13), *big* (line 14), and *a lot bigger than me* (line 15). Indeed, by juxtaposing putative physical threat with an explicit racial label while highlighting the size advantage of the *black dude*, the white narrator has effectively painted a scene of white disadvantage—in this specific incident. Bucholtz (2011), however, went a step further, on the basis of her ethnographic research, by pointing out that narratives like this "disregard the actual conditions of physical danger at the school and in the larger community, where black boys rarely posed a threat to white boys but were often victims of violence themselves" (p. 399). She also pointed out that the connection between black males and physical threat is not just specific to this particular narrative but indicative of white racial discourse that features the "Big Black Man Syndrome" (Vogelman, 1993) in the larger society, thus offering further evidence of racial reversal in Brand One's fight story.

While racial differences are highlighted in white boys' narratives, racial reversal manifests itself with greater subtlety or what Bucholtz (2011) called "racial vagueness" (p. 385) in the white girls' narratives. In the following extract, the girls express resentment of "reversed discrimination" as they complain about the school's controversial multiculturalism class designed to celebrate multicultural diversity (Bucholtz, 2011, p. 388). (Key: @ = laughter with each token marking one pulse; { } = stretch of talk to which transcriber comment applies; ' ' = reported speech or thought.)

(9)   Multiculturalism

```
01   Claire:      It's so like,
02   Christine:   <sniff>
03   Claire:      'We a:ll got to show each other respect.'
04                It's like,
05                'Yeah well,
06                you should be doing that [anyway.]
07   Christine:                          [<sniff>]
08   Claire:      We don't need to,
09                make a big,
10                deal: out of it.
11                We shouldn't make [people go and,]
12   Christine:                     [A big politi    ]cal campai:gn,
13                a[bout giving people re]spect,
14   Claire:      [ I kno::w.            ]
15   Christine:   it's [like,    ]
16   Claire:           [It's like,]
17                <whisper> {Multi[culturalism,}
18                                 oh my] go:d,
19   Christine:                   ['Why don't you just,
20                                 do it.']
21   Claire:      Teach people how to hate white kids.
22   Mary:        Oh yeah?
23   Claire:      I'm really bitter about [that class.]
24   Mary:                                [@@@       ]
```

Bucholtz (2011) highlighted two observations in her analysis of the previous extract. First, instead of producing specific incidents of reversed discrimination, the story of the girls' experience with the multiculturalism class is framed as a series of typifications (Agha, 2007) through general characterizations such as *it's (so) like* (lines 01, 04). Second, the girls then launch into a series of negative assessments of the class: first explicitly by claiming that showing respect is a given that doesn't warrant *A big political campaign* (lines 04–06, 08–13), then implicitly through a whispering voice in which *Multiculturalism* is delivered and the ensuing *oh my god* gasp and, finally, with the accusation that suggests the hypocrisy of the class with the real purpose to *Teach people how to hate white kids* (lines 19–21). Bucholtz (2011) went on to note that Claire and Christine's expression of resentment was not idiosyncratic but representative of "many other White students at Bay City High," who viewed the multiculturalism class as "overblown," "more talk than action," and "coercive" (p. 389).

Bucholtz (2011) termed her approach **sociocultural linguistics**—one that incorporates both interactional analysis and ethnography, attending to the details of social interaction, the ethnographic situation of such interaction, and the larger social, cultural, and political context that informs and is shaped by the interaction (p. 400).

Language of Racism Among White New Zealanders

Our final exhibit comes from the earlier work of the discursive psychologists Wetherell and Potter (1992), who mapped the language of racism in New Zealand, where the white majority of European descendants (Päkehäs) co-exist with the indigenous Maoris. Using a form of discourse analysis influenced by the intellectual traditions of Speech Act Theory, poststructuralism as well as ethnomethodology and conversation analysis, Wetherell and Potter (1988) were able to challenge the view in traditional social psychology that talk simply represents certain stable, coherent, and consistent mental structures that either capture or distort an external reality. Instead, talk is seen as action-oriented (Speech Act Theory, ethnomethodology, and conversation analysis): it is assembled to achieve particular purposes. In addition, talk can have unintended consequences beyond the speaker's control (poststructuralism). As such, Wetherell and Potter (1992) treated interviews as social interaction in their own right and sought, for example, to document how the Päkehäs construct versions of reality in ways that discredit, blame, and denigrate the Maoris in ways that protect the racially stratified status quo. A key term in Wetherell and Potter's approach to discourse analysis is interpretative repertoire.

Interpretative repertoire refers to a range of discursive resources—"discernible clusters of terms, descriptions, and figures of speech often assembled around metaphors or vivid images"—employed to build versions of reality (Wetherell & Potter, 1988, 1992, p. 90).

One example of an interpretative repertoire is what Wetherell and Potter (1988) called, in their investigation of racism among white New Zealanders' talk, **pragmatic realism**, which is a collection of terms and ideas that emphasize modernity and relevance. This interpretative repertoire can be used to build a version of Maori cultural practices as outdated and impractical for coping in the modern society. Another interpretative repertoire is **togetherness**, which embodies a position that people should simply be treated as people without any barriers and divisions. This interpretative repertoire can be used to represent any challenge of the racial status quo as unproductive and divisive. In the following segment, the Päkehä interviewee

Wood is sharing her views when asked about Maori protests as a result of disputes between Maori and Päkehä (Wetherell & Potter, 1988, pp. 76–77).

(10) The other way around

```
01   Wood:   Um (.) they're making New Zealand a racist country.
02            Um but you know you usually feel, think, that racism is
03            um (.) putting the, putting the darker people down but
04            really they're doing it the other way around, I feel. Um,
05            everything seems to be to help the Maori people, um,
06            you know. I think at the moment sort of the Europeans
07            sort of they're just sort of watching and putting up with it,
08            but they'll only go so far. Um you know we've got Maori
09            friends out here, uh who we have into the house, you
10            know they're friends, um but when things happen when
12            they suddenly say oh they're going to make Maori lan
13            guage compulsory, um it is, it's antagonising and the
14            Maori friends that we've got, they don't agree with it.
15            OK you've got your extremists there too, the ones who
16            feel, you know, that everyone should learn it but um I
17            think the average Maori sort of perhaps is worried too.
```

Wood is able to discredit Maori activists in a number of ways. First, in Wood's version of reality, the *extremists* (line 15) are not representative of the *average* Maori people she is friends with (lines 08–10, 12), who seem to be included paternalistically as *worried* (line 17) and "antagonised" (line 13). Second, the Maori activists are positioned as powerful and threatening "racists" who act unfavorably to the Päkehäs by attending only to the interests of the Maoris (lines 03–08). Third, the Maori protest is described as "sudden" and disruptive to the normal harmony that features friendship between the Päkehäs and the Maoris (lines 10–13). In various ways, then, Wood's account uses the **togetherness** repertoire to protect the status quo existing between Päkehäs and the Maoris by building a version of reality where the Maori activists who seek to challenge the status quo are depicted as irrational, disturbing, and abnormal.

Task 8: Consider the following extract taken from Wetherell and Potter (1992). Do you observe any language of racism in Shell's talk? If yes, what precisely makes you think so? What, if any, interpretative repertoire is engaged in Shell's talk?

```
01   Shell:   There's too big a demand (mmhm) being made on
02            New Zealand society from Maoris which (.) who
03            have, I guess they've been feeling deprived (yeah) in
```

04		the past and now they're suddenly (yes) finding
05		their feet and making themselves very vocal. It is
06		starting to build a resent ment (mmhm), there's no
07		doubt about that,
08	Wetherell:	among the Päkehä majority?
09	Shell:	within the Päkehä majority. There's no doubt about
10		that. And I think that people feel that we're getting
11		almost a reverse apartheid situation.

In sum, the three exhibits are testimony to the power of discourse analysis in unveiling the subtle, nuanced, and complicated ways in which racism can be traced in a variety of contexts among a variety of groups (also see Alim & Reyes, 2011; Reyes, 2011). Because of such close analyses of discourse, we become privy to how media discourse fails to engage discussions of racism as a systemic and institutional phenomenon, how racial reversal among white teenagers lacks any substantial grounding, and how racism becomes rationalized under the veneer of **togetherness** (For a recent review on discourse and racism, see Wodak & Reisigl, 2015.)

Task 9: Consider the three studies on race ideology discussed so far. To what extent are they similar, and to what extent are they different?

Approaches to Discourse and Ideology

As we have shown earlier, the question of discourse and ideology can be addressed using a variety of approaches such as corpus analysis, conversation analysis, interactional sociolinguistics, sociocultural linguistics, and discursive psychology. These approaches vary in terms of the focus of the inquiry, the kinds of data collected, the analytical concepts marshaled, and how the arguments are made. Objects of inquiry range from specific linguistic items such as premodifying adjectives and reference terms, to the presence of a subtext and, finally, to the various (rhetorical) moves such as hunting for the racist, expressing white resentment, and constructing the other as menacing and disruptive. The data range from types of corpora to audiorecordings or videorecordings as well as ethnographic field notes. With the exception of the sociocultural linguistics study that combines audiorecordings with ethnography, others tend to engage a single source of data. While a well-bounded and narrowly defined item such as pre-modifying adjectives appears to work well with massive amounts of data that corpus analysis affords, more elusive objects such as subtexts seem to be more effectively tackled within a single speech event like the dissertation defense. When it comes to building the analytical argument, aside from the critical discourse analysis study that begins with the theoretical distinction between the folk theory of race and critical race theory, others tend to begin with the data from which arguments regarding gender or race ideologies are worked up. Some ground their argument within the text and talk themselves (e.g., conversation analysis), and others resort to the ethnographic context of the situation and/or the broader social and cultural climate relevant to the discourse (e.g., sociocultural linguistics). Finally, some approaches are easily recognizable by the specific analytical concepts they engage (e.g., contextualization cue for interactional sociolinguistics, interpretative repertoire for discursive psychology).

Despite the various approaches they take, analysts strive to locate evidence of ideology in the text and talk they examine. In reading a discourse analytic study on ideology then, it would be useful to ask the following questions:

a. What is the ideology that is being conveyed through the discourse?
b. Where exactly in the discourse is such an ideology located?
c. What kinds of analytical resources does the author draw upon to make the argument that this particular piece of discourse manifests this particular kind of ideology? In other words, what types of reasoning are engaged in the argument building?
d. Are the analyses convincing?

Task 10: Read Subtirelu (2015) (see References) or any study on discourse and ideology that is of interest to you and answer the previous questions.

Key Points

- The question of how ideology is constructed in discourse is not an exclusive territory of critical discourse analysis and can be approached from a variety of methodological perspectives.
- A majority of discourse analytic works in discourse and ideology has been devoted to issues of gender and race.
- The types of premodifying adjectives for *women* found in British newspapers provide evidence of ideologies that discriminate against women.
- Comments on a woman candidate's work by male committee members during a dissertation defense offer subtle clues of a gender bias that treats a woman's scholarship as of less academic rigor.

- Unproblematized and taken-for-granted family reference terms during after-hours calls to the doctor reveals the participants' naturalized heteronormative assumptions of family as comprising a married, heterosexual couple who live together with their biological children.
- U.S. media discourse surrounding the Trayvon Martin case largely enacts the folk theory of race and racism, where racism is located in the speech and behavior of the individual rather than seen as a systemic problem at the level of society.
- The ideology of racial reversal is observed in talk among white teenagers in an urban high school, where their black peers are constructed as menacing and the multicultural curriculum as implicitly discriminating against the white students.
- The language of racism among white New Zealanders can be traced in their ways of building a reality in which the harmonious co-existence between the Päkehäs and the Maoris is threatened by the powerful and sudden disruption of the Maori activists.
- Empirical work on discourse and ideology involves specifying what ideology is at issue and in what precise ways such ideological work is done in and through discourse.

References

Agha, A. (2007). *Language and social relations.* New York: Cambridge University Press.

Alim, H. S., & Reyes, A. (2011). Complicating race: Articulating race across multiple social dimensions. *Discourse & Society, 22*(4), 379–384.

Baker, P. (2006). *Using corpora in discourse analysis.* London: Continuum.

Bucholtz, M. (2011). 'It's different for guys': Gendered narratives of racial conflict among white California youth. *Discourse & Society, 22*(4), 385–402.

Caldas-Coulthard, C. R., & Moon, R. (2010). 'Curvy, hunky, kinky': Using corpora as tools for critical analysis. *Discourse & Society, 21*(2), 99–133.

Gordon, C. (2011). Gumperz and interactional sociolinguistics. In R. Wodak, B. Johnstone, & P. E. Kerswill (Eds.), *The Sage handbook of sociolinguistics* (pp. 67–84). London: Sage.

Gumperz, J. C., & Gumperz, J. J. (1996). Treacherous words: Gender and power in academic assessment. *Folia Linguistica, 30*(3–4), 167–188.

Hill, J. H. (2008). *The everyday language of white racism.* Chichester, UK: Wiley-Blackwell.

Hodges, A. (2015). Ideologies of language and race in US media discourse about the Trayvon Martin shooting. *Language in Society, 44*, 401–423.

Kendall, S., & Tannen, D. (2015). Discourse and gender. In D. Tannen, H. Hamilton, & D. Schiffrin (Eds.), *The handbook of discourse analysis* (2nd ed.) (pp. 639–660). Malden, MA: Wiley Blackwell.

Kitzinger, C. (2005). Heteronormativity in action: Reproducing normative heterosexuality in 'after hours' calls to the doctor. *Social Problems, 52*(4), 477–498.

Leeuwen, T. van (1996). The representation of social actors. In C. R. Caldas-Coulthard & M. Coulthard (Eds.), *Texts and practices: Readings in critical discourse analysis* (pp. 32–70). London: Routledge.

Reyes, A. (2011). 'Racist!': Metapragmatic regimentation of racist discourse by Asian American youth. *Discourse & Society, 22*(4), 458–473.

Rosaldo, M. Z. (1982). The things we do with words: Ilongot speech acts and speech act theory in philosophy. *Language in Society, 11*(2), 203–237.

Subtirelu, N. C. (2015). 'She does have an accent but . . .': Race and language ideology in students' evaluations of mathematics instructors on RateMyProfessors.com. *Language in Society, 44,* 35–62.

Vogelman, L. (1993). Big black man syndrome: The Rodney King trial and the use of racial stereotypes in the courtroom. *Fordham Urban Law Journal, 20*(3), 571–578.

Wetherell, M., & Potter, J. (1988). Discourse analysis and the identification of interpretative repertoires. In C. Antaki (Ed.), *Analysing everyday explanation: A casebook of methods* (pp. 168–183). London: Sage Publications.

Wetherell, M., & Potter, J. (1992). *Mapping the language of racism: Discourse and the legitimation of exploitation.* New York: Cambridge University Press.

Wodak, R., & Reisigl, M. (2015). Discourse and racism. In D. Tannen, H. Hamilton, & D. Schiffrin (Eds.), *The handbook of discourse analysis* (2nd ed.) (pp. 576–596). Malden, MA: Wiley Blackwell.

Index